PARLIAMENTS AND LEGISLATURES
Janet M. Box-Steffensmeier and David T. Canon, Series Editors

101 CHAMBERS

*Congress, State Legislatures, and the
Future of Legislative Studies*

PEVERILL SQUIRE | KEITH E. HAMM

The Ohio State University Press
Columbus

Copyright © 2005 by The Ohio State University.
All rights reserved.

Library of Congress Cataloging-in-Publication Data

Squire, Peverill.
101 chambers : Congress, state legislatures, and the future of legislative studies / Peverill Squire, Keith E. Hamm.—1st ed.
  p. cm.—(Parliaments and legislatures)
Includes bibliographical references and index.
ISBN 0-8142-0938-6 (cloth : alk. paper)—ISBN 0-8142-9063-9 (cd) 1. Legislative bodies—United States—States. 2. Representative government and representation—United States—States. 3. United States. Congress. I. Title: One hundred and one chambers. II. Hamm, Keith E. III. Title. IV. Parliaments and legislatures series.

JK2488.S69 2005
328.73—dc22
            2004023577

Paper (ISBN: 978-0-8142-5688-6)
Cover design by Jason Moore
Type set in Times New Roman

For the pioneers of comparative legislative research,
Mac Jewell, Jerry Loewenberg, and Pat Patterson

CONTENTS

List of Illustrations	ix
Introduction	1
1. The Lineage of American Legislatures	5
2. Fundamental Structures	35
3. Institutional Characteristics	67
4. Organizational Characteristics	99
5. Legislators and Legislative Careers	128
6. Concluding Thoughts on American Legislatures in Comparison	146
Notes	153
References	169
Index	193

ILLUSTRATIONS

Figures

Figure 3–1	Range and Mean of State Legislative Salaries Compared to Congress, 1910–99	82
Figure 3–2	Salaries in Most Professional States Compared to Congress, 1910–99	83
Figure 3–3	Salaries in Professionalizing States Compared to Congress, 1910–99	84
Figure 3–4	Range and Mean of State Legislative Days in Session Compared to Congress, 1909–99	85
Figure 5–1	Career Movement between State Office and Congress, 1789–1960	130
Figure 5–2	Occupations of Massachusetts Legislators, 1780–1950	133
Figure 5–3	Women Serving in American Legislatures, 1895–2003	137
Figure 5–4	Mean Turnover Rate in Early New York and Georgia Legislatures by Decade, 1777–1867	141
Figure 5–5	Turnover Rate in Connecticut House of Representatives, 1790–1919	141

Tables

Table 1–1	American Colonial Assemblies	7
Table 1–2	The Rise of the Institutionalized Speakership in Colonial Assemblies	15
Table 1–3	The Importance of Seniority in the Leadership of Four Colonial Assemblies, 1688–1775	16
Table 1–4	Constitutional Features of Original American Legislatures—Lower Houses	22
Table 1–5	Constitutional Features of Original American Legislatures—Upper Houses	24
Table 1–6	Early American Constitutional Provisions on Legislative Leadership and Procedures (in Order of Adoption)	31
Table 1–7	Early American Constitutional Provisions on Origination of Revenue Bills (in Order of Adoption)	32
Table 1–8	Early American Constitutional Provisions on Executive Veto Power (in Order of Adoption)	33
Table 2–1	Ratio of Upper House to Lower House Members in American Legislatures, 2003	41
Table 2–2	Change in Membership Size by State and Legislative Chamber, 1960 and 2000	47

ILLUSTRATIONS

Table 2–3	Membership Size and State Population Correlations, 1960 to 2000	48
Table 2–4	Age Qualifications for Election to American Legislative Office, 2003	51
Table 2–5a	Residency Requirements for Election to American Lower Houses, 2003	52
Table 2–5b	Residency Requirements for Election to American Upper Houses, 2003	52
Table 2–6a	Constituency Size by American Lower House Chamber, 2003	56
Table 2–6b	Constituency Size by American Upper House Chamber, 2003	57
Table 2–7	States Using Multi-Member Legislative Districts in the 2001–2003 Elections	59
Table 2–8	American Legislative Terms, 2003	62
Table 2–9	Term Limits in 2004 and Year of Adoption	65
Table 3–1	Annual and Biennial Legislative Sessions in the States, 1960 and 2004	68
Table 3–2	American Legislative Pay on Annual Basis in 1910	72
Table 3–3	American Legislative Pay on Annual Basis in 2003	73
Table 3–4	State Legislative Staff Compared to Congressional Staff in the 1990s	77
Table 3–5	Legislative Professionalization in the American States Compared to Congress in the Late 1990s	80
Table 3–6	Explaining State Legislative Pay Compared to Congress, 1910–99	89
Table 3–7	Explaining Change in State Legislative Pay Compared to Congress, 1910–99	91
Table 3–8	Explaining State Legislative Days in Session Compared to Congress, 1910–99	93
Table 3–9	Explaining Change in State Legislative Days in Session Compared to Congress, 1910–99	94
Table 4–1	Institutional Power Index of Lower House Speakers	102
Table 4–2	The Importance of Committees in State Legislative Decision Making	109
Table 4–3	Work Productivity in American Legislatures, 1997–98	117
Table 4–4	The Extent of Supermajoritarian Requirements in American Legislatures	119
Table 4–5	Discharge Procedures in Several Lower Houses	125
Table 5–1	Selected Occupations of State Legislators, 1909, 1949, and 1999, in Percent	134
Table 5–2	Turnover in U.S. House and State Legislatures by Chamber and Decade, 1930–2000, with Highest- and Lowest-Turnover Chambers, in Percent	143

INTRODUCTION

The legislative studies subfield of political science is thriving. More than 650 articles dealing with legislatures appeared in ten leading political science journals between 1995 and 2000 (Hamm 2001).[1] Much of this work is among the most methodologically advanced and theoretically sophisticated in the discipline. In our view, however, the study of legislative politics suffers from one glaring weakness: a lack of truly comparative, cross-institutional research. This is surprising because comparative research is central to the scientific enterprise. Those who study state legislatures typically conduct comparative analyses in their research, with almost 90 percent of the 70 or so state legislative articles published between 1995 and 2000 focusing on more than one institution. The remainder of the subfield, however, tends to focus on a single institution.[2] Research on the U.S. Congress is the obvious example. In approximately 95 percent of the more than 280 published articles in which Congress was a case, it was the only case. Indeed, typically only one of its two houses was examined. Only very occasionally was Congress compared with another national legislature such as the British Parliament or Japanese Diet. Direct comparison between Congress and state legislatures was even less frequent (Hamm 2001).

What accounts for the typically exclusive nature of legislative research? One explanation can be traced to the apparently widely held belief that both houses of Congress are unique, and therefore cannot be easily compared to each other, much less to other legislative institutions. This notion of institutional exceptionalism is unfortunate because it limits the way researchers approach testing many interesting and compelling theories of legislative organization and behavior. But even if we accept the idea that the Congress differs so much from most legislative bodies found outside the United States that comparison is futile, this singular concentration ignores the research possibilities that comparison with the other 99 American legislative chambers offers.[3] State legislatures provide enormous variation along almost every dimension of interest to scholars. As Price (1975, 20) observed over a quarter of a century ago, "For anyone interested in the variety of historical patterns of organization presented by the House and Senate in the nineteenth century, the current range of state legislative practices have quite a familiar look. One does not need to go, like Darwin, to the Galapagos Islands to rediscover long missing species of legislative operation." Indeed, as Price intimates, legislatures operating along the lines of the long vanished House of speakers Reed and Cannon can still be found today in some states. State legislatures, however, do not simply mimic the structures and rules employed at some point by Congress; they have in many cases developed completely different ones as well. Thus, to promote more legislative research of a truly comparative nature, we offer this primer on comparing and contrasting Congress with the American state legislatures.

We think this is an important undertaking because state legislatures are suitably compared with Congress for many reasons. In at least three fundamental ways the two sorts of institutions are remarkably similar. First, they arise out of the same culture, the same political history, and the same republican ideals. This sameness allows legislative scholars to sidestep the thorny problems faced by those comparing legislative systems arising out of very different cultures and histories. Second, the electoral context of the two sorts of legislatures is the same. Most state legislatures elect their members using single-member plurality districts, as do the U.S. House and Senate. Indeed, members of both institutions face some of the same voters at the same elections. And, although there are some differences across the states, the basic political party system is the same. Finally, and perhaps most importantly, at a macro level the functions and roles that the two sorts of legislative institutions play are the same. In Polsby's (1975) terms, state legislatures, like both houses of the U.S. Congress, are "transformative" bodies, fully capable of initiating, debating, and passing legislation. Moreover, with the exception of trade and defense issues, state legislatures and Congress consider the same sorts of legislation regarding taxation, spending, and the like. And, in addition, legislators in both sorts of institutions engage in oversight of the executive and bureaucracy and provide services for their constituents. Thus, none of the methodological problems found when comparing a presidential system legislature with parliamentary system legislatures arise when comparing Congress and the state legislatures.

But while there are great similarities there are, of course, important differences between the two sorts of institutions. These differences provide legislative scholars leverage for rigorously testing important theories. We intend to compare and contrast Congress with state legislatures to identify organizational structures and rules that do and do not lend themselves to comparative analysis. Specifically, we compare and contrast Congress and the state legislatures on their histories, fundamental structures, institutional characteristics, organizational characteristics, and members. One of our goals is to highlight the viability of using state legislatures to better test many of the theories currently confined to the congressional realm, while occasionally raising a caution flag where difficulties may be encountered.

The methodological advantages of testing theories on multiple bodies rather than on just one body are obvious. It is hard to argue against providing more cases and more variation on variables of interest. Indeed, it is important to note that state legislatures provide impressive variation both cross-sectionally *and* longitudinally. More significantly, as Price implies, looking at state legislatures often provides scholars counterfactuals for studying Congress (e.g., what if Congress was unicameral, or nonpartisan, or larger, or smaller, or more centralized or more decentralized, etc.). It seems profitable, then, to explore the differences and similarities among state legislatures and the U.S. House and Senate.

Thus, we would like to help build bridges between the study of Congress and the study of state legislatures by identifying the points of comparison and contrast between the two sorts of institutions. As suggested earlier, one of our goals is to highlight possible opportunities to liberate the development and testing of theories of legislative organization and behavior from shackles imposed by a singular fixation on Congress, and on the U.S. House in particular. Truly generalizable theories should be portable from one American legislature to another. If theories prove not to be portable, at least their limitations will be illuminated in the effort. Another compatible and not so subtle objective of our effort is to encourage the study of state legislatures by introducing legislative scholars to (or, more likely, reminding them of) the vast array of organizational schemes and behavioral patterns evidenced in state legislatures. The potential for the combined study of American legislatures, as opposed to the separate efforts of Congressional and state legislative scholars, is too great to leave unexplored.

We start in chapter 1 by examining the historical evolution of American legislatures, establishing their common roots in colonial assemblies and the original state legislatures. By pointing out the fact that Congress and the state legislatures started out with great similarities, we raise important and interesting questions about how and why their evolutionary processes differed over the next two centuries.

In the second chapter we examine the fundamental structures of American legislatures to begin to suggest how and why different evolutionary processes arose. We explore issues of organizational design by looking at constitutional dictates and the choices made about the number of houses, membership size, membership qualifications, constituency size, terms of office, and term limits. More than just making a series of cross-sectional comparisons, we emphasize how legislative characteristics change over time.

Chapter 3 offers an analysis of legislative professionalization over time and in comparison across American legislatures. In particular, we assess limitations on sessions and session lengths, member pay and pensions, and staff and facilities. We propose and test a theory that links professionalization with state wealth, demonstrating that legislative evolution is in part driven by the resources available to the institution to exploit. And we explore why the notion of professionalization is central to the study of the evolution of legislative organizations.

The focus in chapter 4 is on organizational characteristics of American legislatures. We offer a comparative analysis of organization and rules, including leadership, political parties, legislative committees, and legislative procedures. We give particular attention to the use of filibusters and discharge petitions across chambers. We argue that, given the current centrality of rules and procedures in the field of legislative studies, many of our most compelling theories need to be tested outside the confines of the U.S. House, something that is achievable because of the rich variation provided by state legislatures.

We shift attention away from institutional characteristics in favor of an examination of members and legislative careers in chapter 5. Here we provide both cross-sectional and temporal comparisons between state legislatures and Congress in terms of who serves and for how long. The relationship between member careers and organizational characteristics of legislatures is explored.

We conclude by offering a summary of the advantages and problems in trying to expand the pool of legislative institutions being examined. We think the payoff for expanding the scope of legislative studies is stronger theories. There is no doubt of the importance and central place of the U.S. Congress, and it is not surprising that the study of it has dominated legislative studies. But the U.S. House and Senate each represent just one configuration of organizational rules and structures. Additional configurations are found in the other 99 chambers in the United States, and we think that theories that can explain features or behaviors across all 101 chambers ought to be our collective goal.

· 1 ·

The Lineage of American Legislatures

When we look at American legislatures today, we usually emphasize their differences. Congress is seen as contrasting greatly with state legislatures. And, in turn, the considerable differences among state legislatures are noted. These divergencies across legislative institutions are real, yet our focus on them often obscures their substantial similarities. In this chapter we explore the common heritage shared by American legislatures, highlighting their evolution from the same ancestral colonial assemblies.

The evolutionary line is actually quite straightforward. All of the 13 colonies that became the original states had colonial legislatures, and almost all of these assemblies provided their citizenries with extensive backgrounds in representative government. The assemblies produced substantial familiarity with legislative structures and processes in the colonies, at both the elite and popular levels. These experiences proved invaluable in the institutional designs of the legislative branches in the emerging American democracies. As Donald Lutz (1999, 49) observed,

> The relationship between Congress and its Anglo-American ancestors is a profound one for the simple reason that the U.S. Congress more or less smoothly evolved from these earlier institutions. Those who sat down to organize the First Congress did not start de novo, but drew on their collective experience in the Continental Congresses and early state legislatures. Those who sat down in the First Continental Congress and newly independent state legislatures drew on their collective experience in colonial legislatures.

Thus, in a very real sense, understanding today's American legislatures requires an understanding of their direct evolution from earlier representative assemblies.

We begin our investigation of the American legislative development by examining the rise of representative assemblies in the colonies. We then document how almost all of these rudimentary assemblies became bicameral bodies, and came to share other characteristics as well. Indeed, we show that colonial assemblies evolved along the same lines the U.S. House would later follow (Polsby 1968) by adopting more complex and sophisticated rules of procedure, creating standing committee systems, and coming to experience stable memberships and leadership structures.

The second part of the evolutionary story is structured by the events of 1776. By the time of the Revolution, the colonists had enjoyed anywhere from 21 years to 157 years of experience with governance by representative assemblies. With the move for independence, each of the colonies was given the opportunity to rethink its government structure as it adopted new rules for governing itself. We examine the original state constitutional provisions regarding the legislature and show the substantial continuity between the colonial assemblies and the state legislatures that replaced them. More important, perhaps, we then demonstrate the robust lineage between the original state legislatures and the Congress later created by the Constitution. Thus, from our perspective, the Congress under the Articles of Confederation was something of an evolutionary mutant, one that had remarkably little influence on the later development of American legislatures. Legislatures of the sort we see in the United States today are rooted in the colonial assemblies and the original state legislatures.

The Rise of Representative Assemblies in America

Historians have long examined the rise of legislatures in the American colonies.[1] These representative assemblies were notable in part because they developed in all British colonies in North America (except for Quebec, which was under French control for most of its history prior to the American Revolution) despite the fact that the colonies were settled and populated by different people at different points in time for different reasons. Yet, within a decade or two of coming under English control, representative assemblies emerged in each of the future American states (Kammen 1969, 11–12). Legislatures arose for different reasons in different colonies. In Virginia, for example, a representative assembly first met in 1619 because the commercial directors of the colony in London saw it as a mechanism that would promote economic stability (Bosher 1907, 734–35; Kammen 1969, 13–15; Kukla 1985, 284.) Assemblies in Maryland, Massachusetts, and Connecticut were rooted in their early charters, but the initiative for their development came from the colonists themselves (Kammen 1969, 19). The establishment of colonial assemblies during the 1660s later came at the behest of external proprietary boards that saw them as essential structures for the development of successful societies (Kammen 1969, 32).

A chronology of the emergence of representative assemblies in the American colonies is provided in table 1–1. It is important to note that assemblies were established throughout the seventeenth century and into the eighteenth century. Thus, they were not, in some simple sense, modeled on the English governmental system, because English government itself, particularly in regard to Parliament's role in the system, evolved dramatically over this time period (Kammen 1969, 54–55). Indeed, the legislative systems that arose in America bore more in common with the English system of the Tudor period than with that of the time after the Glorious Revolution (Huntington 1968, 109–21). Yet, despite the fact that the colonial assemblies emerged at different times for different reasons, and

TABLE 1–1 American Colonial Assemblies

Colony	Year of First Meeting of Assembly	Number of Representatives at Initial Meeting	Year Assembly Became Bicameral	How Upper House Filled
Virginia	1619	22	Pre-1660[a]	Appointed
Massachusetts Bay	1634	24	1644	Elected by Lower House[b]
Connecticut	1637	12	1698	Elected
Maryland[c]	1638	24	1650	Appointed
Rhode Island	1647	24	1696	Elected
North Carolina	1665	12	1691	Appointed
South Carolina	1671	20	1691	Appointed
East Jersey[d]	1668	10	1672	Appointed
West Jersey	1681	34	1696	Appointed
New Hampshire	1680	11	1692	Appointed
Pennsylvania[e]	1682	42		
New York	1683	18	1691	Appointed
Delaware	1704	18		
Georgia	1755	18	1755	Appointed

Sources: For Delaware, Bushman, Hancock, and Homsey (1986); Conrad (1908, 78–79), Greene (1981, 461), and Munroe (1979, 72); for Georgia, Jones, Jr. (1883, 463–65) and Gosnell and Anderson (1956, 14); for New Jersey, Moran (1895, 33–34); on the colonies in general, see Kammen (1969, 11–12) and Frothingham (1886, 18–21); on colonial upper houses specifically, see Main (1967).
[a]Kukla (1981, 10; 1985, 289) holds that Virginia's legislature became bicameral in 1643; Walthoe (1910, 1) a bit earlier; Bailey (1979, 28) in the 1650s; Billings (1974, 234), Frothingham (1886, 19), and Miller (1907) not until the 1680s.
[b]After 1691, members of the upper house were elected by the lower house.
[c]Maryland might have had an assembly as early as 1635.
[d]New Jersey was separated into East Jersey and West Jersey in 1676. The two parts were reunited as New Jersey in 1702, and the first assembly met in 1703 with twelve representatives from each part.
[e]Pennsylvania was bicameral from its first assembly in 1682 until a new charter in 1701 instituted a unicameral system.

that their distant parent government was at best a moving target in its capacity as a model, they relatively quickly came to resemble one another in important ways (Andrews 1944, 40; Greene 1961, 453–54; Kammen 1969, 58, 69). In their almost universal struggles to assert their independent power from the governor, the assemblies took on most of the same responsibilities across the colonies. As Kammen (1969, 58) observed of the power assumed by the evolving assemblies, "In all of them . . . the time-honored clichés about counsel and consent, advice and assent, taxation and representation have astonishing validity." By the end of the seventeenth century the assemblies were permanent components of existing colonial governmental structures, and had become recognizable legislative organizations (Kammen 1969, 57).[2]

Beyond their similar powers and duties, the colonial assemblies also came to look alike structurally. As table 1–1 shows, over time almost all of them, save for Pennsylvania and its offspring, Delaware, became bicameral bodies. In simple terms the original governmental form for the early colonies consisted of a governor, a council, and a general assembly (Morey 1893–1894, 204). The Crown in all but two cases—Connecticut and Rhode Island—appointed the governor and councilors, while the general assembly consisted of the colony's freemen. Each of these governing units—the governor, the councilors, and the assembly—was a distinct entity. But they were for all intent and purposes undifferentiated in terms of power. The units, in what was usually referred to as the "General Court," collectively made most important decisions. The general assemblies, however, rapidly evolved into representative bodies as it became geographically impracticable for all freemen to participate in their regular sessions (Haynes 1894, 22–23; Morey 1893–1894, 206–9; Young 1968, 154). Thus each of the towns came to elect one, two, or occasionally three representatives to speak on their behalf in the general court.

In general, bicameral legislatures emerged from what looked like unicameral bodies in the colonies because of the original distinctions inherent in their colonial systems between councilors as agents of the Crown or proprietors, and representatives as agents of the freemen of the colonies.[3] The council and the general assembly first became unmistakably separate chambers in Massachusetts (Kammen 1969, 22–23; Morey 1893–1894, 212).[4] Their process of becoming bicameral was to some extent inchoate. Through the early 1630s, the councilors and the members of the assembly developed different interests and concerns, and these differences led to conflict between them. The most prominent policy dispute between the two groups involved the legal disposition of a case involving a wandering sow.[5] Their disagreement was so great that it led directly to a split. In 1636 a working arrangement was reached between the two groups, the language of which strongly suggests the glimmerings of separate chambers and a bicameral legislature (Morey 1893–1894, 212–13):

Whereas it may fall out that in some of these General Courts to be holden by the magistrates [councilors] and deputies [representatives], there may arise some difference of judgment in doubtful cases, it is therefore ordered, that no law, order, or sentence shall pass as an act of the court without the consent of the greater part of the magistrates on the one part and the greater part of the deputies on the other part; and for want of such accord the cause or order shall be suspended; and if either party think it so material, then there shall be forthwith a committee chosen the one half by the magistrates and the other half by the deputies, and the committee so chosen to elect an umpire, who together shall have the power to hear and determine the cause in question.

The division between the councilors and the representatives became permanent by law in 1644. At that point it was agreed that the two bodies would sit apart and that laws proposed and passed by one body would be sent to the other body, and both bodies would have to agree for a bill to become law (Kammen 1969, 22–23; Morey 1893–1894, 213).

The movement toward bicameralism in the other colonies did not follow the same course of events as in Massachusetts. In Rhode Island, for example, it took almost 50 years of agitation on the part of the colony's freemen to gain a bicameral legislature (Moran 1895, 22). The first intimations of bicameralism came when representatives asked for and were given permission to meet separately for 30 minutes during sessions to discuss important issues (Moran 1895, 25). As late as 1672 attempts were made to keep the councilors and representatives meeting together. In that year, for example, the colonial treasurer was authorized to spend public funds for a dinner (Moran 1895, 25), "ffor the keepinge of the Magistrates and Deputies in love together, for the ripeninge of their consultation, and husbandinge of their time." There is evidence that by then the two chambers already thought of themselves as being separate. Their partition, however, was not formalized until 1696 (Moran 1895, 26).

In Connecticut few substantial conflicts arose between the councilors and the representatives, but a process of separate consideration of legislation evolved over the last quarter of the seventeenth century. In 1698 a law was passed designating the council as the "upper house" and the assembly as the "lower house" and requiring that all laws have the approval of both chambers (Morey 1893–1894, 213–14). Similar processes unfolded in North Carolina and Maryland. The legislature in North Carolina was created as a unicameral body in 1665, but over time councilors and assemblymen began to consider legislation separately and they were formally recognized as distinct chambers in 1691 (Bassett 1894, 55–58). In Maryland, by 1642, after only a few years of the legislature's existence, representatives already sensed a critical difference in perspective from the councilors. In that year one representative said publicly that he (Jordan 1987,

26–28), "in the name of the rest desired that the house might be Seperated & the Burgesses [representatives] to be by themselves and to have a negative." The governor refused to grant the request at that time and it took until 1650 for a formal separation of the two bodies to occur. Even then unicameralism returned briefly in the mid-1650s and only from 1660 on was Maryland's assembly permanently bicameral (Falb 1986, 46–59; Jordan 1987, 26–33). A weak commitment to bicameralism also surfaced in South Carolina, but with a different twist. In the mid-1740s—a half-century after the advent of two houses in that colony—the lower house changed its name to General Assembly from House of Commons and attempted unsuccessfully to deny the upper house any part in the legislative process (Sirmans 1961, 384–85; Weir 1969, 490–91). Overall, then, the evolution to a bicameral system varied across the colonies, and it some cases the process was murky and tentative.[6]

Once the freemen successfully asserted the right for their representatives to initiate legislation, a bicameral system was virtually inescapable (Kammen 1969, 54–55; Morey 1893–1894, 214–15). It must be noted, however, that Pennsylvania went against the tide, starting with a bicameral legislature in 1682 and switching to a unicameral system with the institution of a new charter in 1701. (The Delaware Assembly, which spun out from the Pennsylvania Assembly shortly thereafter, was unicameral throughout its colonial period.)

It is critical to emphasize that the emergence of bicameral legislatures in the colonies was not the result of colonists or the Crown consciously choosing to imitate the British system, although colonial representatives often cited Parliament's two houses to justify their desire for a similar system (Moran 1895, 13, 26; Johnson 1938, 21), and colonists saw the obvious parallels between the two systems (Lokken 1959, 574). American bicameralism was fundamentally different from the British version in two ways. First, the historical reasons behind the split between the House of Commons and the House of Lords were not the same reasons that drove the colonies to develop separate legislative chambers. Bicameralism arose in England over questions of representation of different classes in society (Taswell-Langmead 1946, 169–71; see also Loewenberg 1995, 737). In a real sense, the movement toward bicameralism in America was triggered by policy disagreements between differently appointed groups, initially one over a wayward pig. The policy differences between the colonial councils and assemblies were not class based in the same way. Second, the House of Lords was in the main a hereditary body, and thus politically independent of both the Crown and the people. In contrast, the upper houses in most of the colonies consisted of political appointees of the Crown or in the case of Maryland the proprietor and thus politically dependent on them (Luce 1924, 47–50; Main 1967, 3, 199–200; Pole 1969, 68; Sirmans 1961 387).[7] As Weir (1969, 492) notes of colonial South Carolinians, "Everyone recognized that the composition of the upper house did not reflect a separate stratum of society comparable to that of the British Lords."

And, of course, as table 1–1 reveals, upper house members in Connecticut and Rhode Island were elected by the freemen of the colony, while in Massachusetts they were elected by members of the lower house. Thus bicameral systems in the colonies developed in response to local conditions and problems.[8]

As the colonial assemblies became discrete chambers, they moved from being subordinate to the governor and council to eventually becoming dominant. Greene (1961, 454) identified three phases of legislative development in the colonies. In the first phase during the seventeenth century, the assemblies asserted their autonomy from the councils and established their right to initiate money bills and other legislation. Early in the eighteenth century, the assemblies moved to the second phase, assuming political power equal to that of the governor and council. By 1763, most of the colonial assemblies achieved the final phase, one of political supremacy, setting the stage for their ultimate challenges to the parent British government.

The rise of legislative power was not, however, uniform across the colonies. The assemblies in Connecticut and Rhode Island were always dominant in their government systems because of the favored position granted to them by their charters. Among the other assemblies, those in Massachusetts and Pennsylvania were the most powerful, followed closely by their counterparts in New York and South Carolina (Greene 1961, 454–55). Assemblies in New Jersey, North Carolina, and Virginia lagged behind. Among the older assemblies, only those in Maryland and New Hampshire failed to become the dominant political institution in their colony by the time of the revolution (Greene 1961, 456–57).

Beyond their generally successful challenge of the governor and council for political preeminence, during the eighteenth century the colonial assemblies developed into institutions organized to respond to the demands of their constituents (Olson 1992; Rainbolt 1970, 422). Arguably, the colonial assemblies had closer ties to their constituents than did the British Parliament because the assemblies in New Hampshire, New Jersey, New York, North Carolina, Rhode Island, and South Carolina, for example, had approximately one member for every 1,187 constituents while the House of Commons had one member for every 14,362 constituents (Clarke 1943, 268; Pole 1962, 638; see also Greene 1981, 461).[9] Much of the assemblies' time was consumed dealing with petitions, which had become vehicles for individuals and groups to call for legislative action on problems of interest.[10] Petitions also functioned as an import source of information for legislators about the problems and concerns of their constituents (Higginson 1986, 153–55). Through the 1700s the number of petitions in most assemblies climbed significantly (Bailey 1979, 62; Leonard 1948b, 376–80; Olson 1992, 556–58; Purvis 1986, 179). Their importance increased as well. Olson (1992, 556) estimates that approximately half of all laws passed by the colonial assemblies during the eighteenth century originated as petitions, a conclusion supported by data on New Jersey (Purvis 1986, 178), Pennsylvania (Tully

1977, 99), and Virginia (Bailey 1979, 64). And legislators clearly responded to local concerns through the introduction of legislation. Richard Bland, a mid-seventeenth century member of the Virginia House of Burgesses, for example, introduced (Rossiter 1953, 41), "a Bill, To prevent Hogs running at Large in the Town of Port Royal," and "a Bill for destroying Crows and Squirrels in the County of Accomack."

In many respects the colonial assemblies in the eighteenth century institutionalized along the same lines Polsby (1968) observed in the U.S. House in the nineteenth century. Increased demands on the assemblies forced them over time to become more efficient organizations, essentially through increasing their internal complexity.

Legislative sessions generally became longer over time. In Virginia, for example, the first House of Burgesses in 1619 met for only five days in July—the burgesses adjourned earlier than anticipated because they were too hot and too sick to continue (Bosher 1907, 737). Over time the House came to meet in longer sessions. According to Pargellis (1927b, 156) the burgesses met for an average of 89 days prior to 1728, 157 days from 1728 to 1749, and 176 days in the final period. Similar numbers are found in New York. There the Assembly met for an average of 76 days annually from 1691 to 1727, and 108 days from 1728 to 1775.[11]

Standing committees were established in most colonial assemblies as a means to handle recurring matters of importance (Bushman, Hancock, and Homsey 1986; Cook 1931, 266; Corey 1929, 123; Frakes 1970; Greene 1959; Harlow 1917, 1–23; Jameson 1894, 261–67; Jillson and Wilson 1994, 24–38; Leonard 1948a, 237–38; Pargellis 1927a, 84–86; 1927b, 143–45; Ryerson 1986, 114). Indeed, assemblies in Pennsylvania and Virginia even employed subcommittees (Olson 1992, 560). The committee system in Virginia was particularly well developed and functioned much like committee systems in American legislatures today. Harlow (1917, 14) observed of standing committees in Virginia's House of Burgesses, "they were vigorous, hard-working groups, actively engaged in legislative work." These committees were even empowered to frame and amend legislation before it was sent to the chamber's floor (Harlow 1917, 16–17). Referral procedures were so well established that by 1750 petitions presented to the House of Burgesses were quickly sent to the appropriate standing committees (Bailey 1979, 29; Harlow 1917, 14–15). And the House added standing committees to respond to societal problems. The Committee on Religion, for example, was established in 1769 at the height of mounting tensions over religious issues (Longmore 1996, 780).

Virginia's standing committee system surpassed the others in terms of its development, although South Carolina's also reached an impressive level of institutionalization, becoming the primary centers of legislative power by the middle of the eighteenth century (Frakes 1970, 84). And both standing and ad hoc committees in almost all of the colonial assemblies came to engage in serious efforts to gather and analyze information, through, among other devices, holding hearings and traveling to conduct investigations (Olson 1992, 562; Miller 1907, 109; Zemsky 1971, 14).

Colonial assemblies evolved in other important ways as well. More complex and sophisticated rules and procedures were adopted. Olson (1992, 559) observes, "The loose organization, informal procedure, and lax approach to law making that had characterized legislatures at the beginning of the [eighteenth] century gradually gave way to tighter organization, better managed debates, more professional drafting of laws, more substantive laws, and more publicity for the laws." In Maryland, for example, Jordan (1987, 173) notes "the general development of a more effective internal organization within the lower house" leading to "the slow but sure establishment of influential precedents contributing to achievement of the delegates' objectives." Precedents also accumulated slowly over time in Virginia (Kukla 1981, 13–15). But although they built up slowly, rules and procedures accrued in considerable numbers. Examining legislative procedures in the Virginia House of Burgesses, Pargellis (1927a, 83) marvels at the "contrast between the few quaint orders of 1663 and the long complete list of 1769." In substantively important ways legislative procedure became more detailed. The House of Burgesses, for example, followed British parliamentary tradition by requiring all bills to be read three times. The initial reading was in essence preliminary. Serious consideration of the measure followed the second reading (Pargellis 1927b, 148–49):

> A bill might then be referred to a committee of the whole house, to a standing committee, to the committee that prepared it, or to a special group varying in size from four to twelve. . . . After the committee report, it might be re-committed, amended, engrossed or rejected. Debate and amendment could follow the third reading, and the ample opportunity for thorough understanding of the amendments was ensured by the practise of reading them as many times as the bill itself had been read. The house of burgesses used more sparingly than certain other colonial assemblies that principal of coercion embodied in the modern "rider" . . . though in the closing years of the period several references to "riders" occur. Another late development, to which the house did not often resort until the 1760's, was the use of the power to amend to reverse entirely the meaning of the original bill or question, and thus evade an expression of opinion upon the main subject.

Legislative procedures in Virginia evolved to the point that by 1750 at least four different devices existed by which a legislator could strategically delay consideration of a measure: a motion to adjourn during a debate, moving that the orders of the day be read, moving the previous question, and offering amendments (Pargellis 1927b, 152–53). Indeed, rules developed in colonial assemblies to govern debate. The Virginia burgesses had "almost limitless opportunities for debate," but members could speak only once during the same debate (Pargellis 1927b, 151). The other assemblies also limited members to speaking only once during a debate, save for Delaware which allowed members to speak three times. Pennsylvania even devised a cloture rule to cut off limitless debate: If four members stood and requested that a speaker conclude his speech, he had to do so (Clarke 1943, 177–78).

Institutional assistance increased over time. Colonial assemblies acquired clerks who, in turn, were later allowed to hire assistants, all of which contributed to better record keeping (Cook 1931, 264; Falb 1986, 127–130; Leonard 1948a, 235; Olson 1992, 561–62). At the beginning of the eighteenth century, legislative records were remarkably poorly kept. They were stored in (Olson 1992, 547), "taverns, homes, and college rooms and in Pennsylvania, in one small trunk that seems to have been carried from place to place." Fifty years later the situation was much improved. The assemblies were sufficiently staffed so that clerks could notify the public about the legislative schedule in advance and keep much more detailed minutes of assembly business. Over the course of the eighteenth century colonial assemblies started publishing their journals and codifications of the laws they passed (Cook 1931, 264; Leonard 1948b, 394; Olson 1992, 562–64).

The assemblies also became more bounded. When the assemblies were to meet and their terms of office became regularized over time. Initially, the assemblies were open ended, but the strong trend over time was for definite session lengths. Consequently, terms of office were established, typically one-year in the New England colonies and Pennsylvania, and two- or three-years in the others (Luce 1924, 103–8). Membership turnover in the colonial assemblies declined from 1696 to 1775. Most assemblies experienced very high turnover rates at the end of the seventeenth century, but these figures were dramatically lower in most chambers by the time of the Revolution (Greene 1981). Indeed, there is evidence that the memberships of colonial assemblies were as politically experienced as their counterparts in the British Parliament (Kukla 1985, 296–97). Leadership patterns also stabilized over time. As table 1–2 reveals, over time colonial speakers came to serve longer apprenticeships within the chamber before achieving the highest post. In Massachusetts, for example, every speaker held numerous important committee assignments before gaining the top job (Zemsky 1969, 504). And once in the speakership they came to serve longer tenures (Wendel 1986, 175).

Finally, there is evidence that universalistic standards evolved in at least some assemblies. Initially, colonial assemblies were highly status-conscious organizations. The men who served in them were from their colony's social and economic elite (Main 1966). Moreover, within lower house chambers, an elite of the elite dominated. In Georgia (Corey 1929, 124), Maryland (Jordan 1987, 175), Massachusetts (Zemsky 1969), New Jersey (Purvis 1986, 106), Pennsylvania (Tully 1977, 96), and Virginia (Greene 1959), for example, committee assignments

TABLE 1-2 The Rise of the Institutionalized Speakership in Colonial Assemblies

Year	Average Years in Assembly Prior to Becoming Speaker	Average Years Serving in Speakership
1700	2.3	5.5
1725	6.6	7.6
1750	8.5	11.3

Source: Adapted from Wendel (1986, 175).

were doled out unequally, with just a handful of assembly members getting most of the posts, and consequently making most of the important decisions. But, at least in Virginia, which came to rely heavily on standing committees, power became more decentralized over time. Committee membership sizes grew throughout the eighteenth century, allowing more members to be given positions (Bailey 1979, 33–34; Pargellis 1927a, 84–85), a trend also witnessed in Pennsylvania (Ryerson 1986, 116). According to Greene (1959, 486), in 1736:

> twelve burgesses—one-sixth of the total membership—occupied more than half of the committee seats. Until 1742 it was not uncommon for as many as one-third to one-half of the burgesses to serve on no committee at all. . . . Beginning in 1748, the speaker adopted the practice of giving each member at least one post on a standing committee . . .

Moreover, the House of Burgesses developed a custom of adding members to standing committees over the course of a session. In 1774, for example, the Committee on Propositions and Grievances started with 37 members but had 73 members by the end of the session (Harlow 1917, 13). Expanding committee sizes, of course, gave more members the opportunity to exercise influence within the chamber.

The use of seniority in allocating positions of power was rare. Seniority came to play a significant role in the committee assignment process in South Carolina (Frakes 1970, 21–27). But committee assignments in Massachusetts (Zemsky 1969, 506), Pennsylvania (Ryerson 1986, 130) and Virginia (Pargellis 1927a, 86) appear to have been made without much, if any, reference to how long a member had served in the assembly.[12]

But even without the existence of an explicit seniority rule of the sort found in the modern U.S. House, there is evidence to suggest that seniority mattered in colonial assemblies and that its importance increased over time. Greene (1963, 463–92) devised a measurement scheme based on committee assignments and leadership positions to determine first-rank and second-rank leaders in the southern colonies from 1688 to 1776, a measure subsequently used by Purvis (1986, 255–58) for New Jersey. Using their rankings we looked to see if

TABLE 1-3 The Importance of Seniority in the Leadership of Four Colonial Assemblies, 1688–1775

Colonial Assembly	Years Leaders First Elected to Assembly	Number of Leaders	Mean Years to First Reach Second Leadership Ranks	Mean Years to First Reach First Leadership Ranks
Virginia	1668–1699	44	2.5	5.2
	1700–1730	35	2.7	5.9
	1731–1772	90	4.3	6.3
South Carolina	1692–1698	22	2.1	2.5
	1700–1728	80	1.5	2.3
	1731–1772	95	1.7	3.3
North Carolina	1697–1730	16	1.6	1.6
	1731–1775	53	2.4	4.6
New Jersey	1703–1730[a]	36	2.5	4.1
	1731–1772	31	5.0	4.6

Source: Calculated by authors from data on Virginia, South Carolina, and North Carolina presented in Greene (1963, 463–92), and on New Jersey presented in Purvis (1986, 255–58).
[a] If previous experience in the East Jersey and West Jersey assemblies is included in the calculations, the mean number of years to reach the second leadership rank is 2.9 and the mean number of years to the first leadership rank is 4.8.

seniority mattered in determining which legislators made it into the leadership ranks, and if the importance of seniority changed over time. The results of this analysis are presented in table 1–3. In each time period save for two, first-rank leaders were, on average, more senior than second-rank leaders. More interestingly, the importance of seniority in both leadership ranks increased over time, except for the second time period in South Carolina. By the 1730s, leaders, particularly those in the first rank, had acquired significant seniority before first gaining a position of prominence. These data are clearly suggestive of institutionalization.

Colonial assemblies also came to control decisions over contested elections for their seats, and the existing evidence suggests that they developed mechanisms and rules pushing them toward deciding such disputes on their merits (Clarke 1943, 132–50; Greene 1963, 189–99). Once a dispute was brought to an assembly, most assigned a committee to investigate it. Virginia was the first to use a committee for such a purpose, starting in 1663.[13] Most other assemblies followed suit: Maryland in 1678, Pennsylvania in 1682 (the assembly's first meeting), South Carolina in 1692, New York in 1699, New Jersey in 1710, North Carolina in 1739, and Georgia in 1755 (the assembly's first meeting) (Clarke

1943, 145–46). Only the New England assemblies failed to employ committees; instead, they used other mechanisms to investigate elections disputes. In Massachusetts, for example, a joint committee composed of lower and upper house members met to make an inquiry (Clarke 1943, 144–45).

The available evidence suggests that investigations of disputed elections by colonial assemblies were thorough. By 1760, for example, the elections committee in North Carolina was empowered to call for persons, papers, and records in order to gather information for their decisions (Cook 1931, 277). More generally, across the colonial assemblies (Clarke 1943, 146–47),

> The committee on elections frequently investigated such petitions at length, heard witnesses, and listened to arguments by the legal advisors. . . . Sometimes a petition was declared frivolous and vexatious, and was dismissed without ceremony. But if evidence upheld the petitioner's contention, the decision would be in his favor.

The observation that outcomes could be changed based on the evidence is an important one that Kolp (1992, 656) also makes.

Over time, legislative life in colonial America became more routinized. Colonial assemblies acquired improved facilities. The seventeenth century Virginia House of Burgesses, for example, initially met in churches, taverns, and private homes (Pargellis 1927a, 74). Later in that century they met in several successive statehouses in Jamestown (Daniel and Daniel, 1969, 135). The burgesses moved into the more famous "Capitoll" in Williamsburg in the early 1700s. As Pargellis (1927a, 74–75) describes the building, "The west wing was set apart for the use of the general court and the council, the east wing was for the hall of the burgesses and their committee rooms, while the room over the porch was used for conferences between the council and the burgesses."[14] A similar story unfolded in Pennsylvania. The Assembly moved into a new capitol in the 1730s (Olson 1992, 562).[15] Prior to that they met in various places, among them the Bank Meeting House, Thomas Makin's schoolhouse, and the Widow Whitpain's house, the last being a particular favorite because it had a "great ffront Room" (Leonard 1948a, 221). Assemblies in several other colonies also enjoyed statehouses. New York moved into one in the first decade of the eighteenth century, Massachusetts in the second, Delaware in the third, and Rhode Island in the fourth (Daniel and Daniel 1969; Hitchcock and Seale 1976). South Carolina moved into its first capitol in 1753 (Lounsbury 2001). Maryland was in the midst of constructing its capitol when the Revolution started. Ultimately, most legislative business came to be conducted in official settings. Committees in Massachusetts' lower house, for example, initially met over a meal at a tavern on the colony's tab.[16] In 1741 members of the House questioned the ethics of such arrangements. By the early 1750s most committees were convening in special meeting rooms in the Court House attic (Zemsky 1971, 13). Along the same lines, a wing was later added to the Pennsylvania statehouse to accommodate committee meetings; prior to that they met in courthouses and the Coffee Shop (Leonard 1948b, 386).[17] Olson (1992, 562) notes that in Virginia during the 1740s, "all the committees began shifting their meeting sites from taverns and homes to accommodations in the capitol buildings."

More broadly, the assemblies (Andrews 1926, 227–28), "regulated membership, conduct, and procedure; ruled against drinking, smoking, and profanity, against unseemly, unnecessary, and tedious debate, against absence, tardiness, and other forms of evasion." Rules typically adopted across the colonies required a member to stand with his head uncovered when he spoke and to address his remarks to the speaker. In Georgia, Maryland, Pennsylvania, and Virginia members were expressly prohibited from naming other members when speaking in opposition to their proposals. Speaking without first being recognized by the speaker brought a shilling fine in Connecticut; similar rules were adopted in Georgia, Maryland, New Hampshire, Pennsylvania, and Virginia. Members of the Maryland Assembly were not allowed to bring swords or guns onto the floor starting in 1648. Being drunk on the floor brought a stiff fine of 100 pounds of tobacco in Virginia; ironically, smoking or chewing tobacco on the floor was against the rules (Clarke 1943, 177–81). Ultimately, the colonial assemblies controlled legislative behavior to a greater degree than did the British Parliament (Andrews 1926, 227).

Structurally, what did the colonial legislatures look like on the eve of the Revolution? The popularly elected assemblies varied in size, from small chambers of 18 to 36 members in Delaware, Georgia, New Hampshire, New Jersey, New York, and Pennsylvania, to much larger chambers with 118 to 138 members in Connecticut, Massachusetts, and Virginia (Corey 1929, 112; Greene 1981, 461; Harlow 1917, 63; Main 1966; Lutz 1999, 65–66).[18] The councils were much smaller. Typically, they had twelve members (Main 1967, 3). Although the councils' importance declined as the assemblies' power ascended, they still contributed to colonial governance in significant ways (Main 1967, 96):

> The council in most colonies was an extremely active legislative body, in many cases originating bills, passing resolutions, considering and acting upon petitions. In others, it served primarily in a revisory capacity, reviewing and improving legislation. Since the councillors were men of better education, wider experience, and, as a rule, greater intelligence than the representatives, they proved to be exceedingly valuable.

Thus, by the time the break with Great Britain became irreparable, the colonists had considerable experience with and faith in legislatures, particularly those with two chambers. And the legislatures had themselves evolved into efficient lawmaking and representative institutions.

The Original American State Legislatures

As the movement toward independence caused the colonies to assume the standing of states, each new polity was afforded the opportunity to consider anew its form of government. In a sense, the writing of constitutions—an activity in which all but Connecticut and Rhode Island engaged—presented the new states with the possibility of starting with clean slates in terms of governmental structures.[19] That they chose not to wipe them clean and instead preserved many of their existing forms and structures is not surprising. After all, as colonies the states had enjoyed considerable experience with self-government, and many of their institutions had evolved in response to local conditions and demands, making them American in nature rather than simple imitations of British government. Particularly in regard to legislatures, the states had existing institutions with which they were comfortable. Moreover, many of the leading political lights in the age of independence had served in colonial assemblies. As Greene (1961, 470) notes,

> In the decades before Independence there appeared in the colonial statehouses John and Samuel Adams and James Otis in Massachusetts Bay; William Livingston in New York; Benjamin Franklin and John Dickinson in Pennsylvania; Daniel Dulany the younger in Maryland; Richard Bland, Richard Henry Lee, Thomas Jefferson, and Patrick Henry in Virginia; and Christopher Gadsden and John Rutledge in South Carolina.

Indeed, of the 39 men who signed the U.S. Constitution in 1787, 18 had served in colonial legislatures. One of them—John Dickinson—had been a member of both the Delaware and Pennsylvania assemblies. Even more impressive is the fact that 32 of the signers had served in the new state legislatures, among them James Madison, Alexander Hamilton, and Gouverneur Morris.[20] Thus many of the men who helped write and who governed under the Articles of Confederation and the new state constitutions, and who were to write the federal Constitution, were intimately familiar with existing American legislative structures and practices. Not surprisingly, many of the features of the new state legislatures later appeared in the Congress created in 1787.[21]

Following the recommendation of the Continental Congress, between 1776 and 1777, ten of the thirteen new states adopted constitutions asserting their independent standing. These documents were, in many ways, quick and dirty efforts (Nevin 1924, 125–26). Colvin (1913, 30–31) notes of the effort to write New York's first constitution,

> It was not a group of wise men who, after research and deliberation were trying to utilize the accumulated experience of the centuries in framing their new form of government. Rather, it was a group composed of mostly young men surrounded by

the activities of war, in frequent fear of capture, compelled to change their meeting place half a dozen times, who were setting up a government to meet the needs of the immediate situation.

Thus Selsam's (1936, 183) observation about the Pennsylvania constitution of 1776 holds true for the other nine early ones: "The constitution was the hurried and necessarily imperfect work of actual revolution . . ."

The first two constitutions to be adopted, New Hampshire's and South Carolina's, were intended to be provisional (Nevin 1924, 126; Wright 1933, 176–77). South Carolina's was replaced with a permanent constitution in 1778 (Adams 1980, 71–72). New Hampshire's proposed replacement in 1778 failed to be adopted. A new constitution was finally ratified in 1784. The other early constitutions were written to be permanent, but eventually all of them were replaced as well, some relatively quickly (Georgia in 1789, Pennsylvania and South Carolina in 1790, and Delaware in 1792), the others more slowly (New York in 1822, Virginia in 1830, New Jersey in 1844, Maryland in 1851, and North Carolina in 1868). Among the eleven states writing constitutions during the revolution, only Massachusetts was truly deliberative, taking until 1780 to adopt one. Not surprisingly, perhaps, it is the only original state constitution still in effect among the initial 13 states, albeit having been subsequently amended over 100 times.[22]

The main features of the new constitutions as they pertained to legislative design are given in tables 1–4 and 1–5 (see pages 22–25). The relevant provisions from the Articles of Confederation and the federal Constitution also are included, for the purpose of comparison and to allow us to discern patterns of constitutional evolution. The first thing to note is that nine of the eleven states writing new constitutions opted for bicameral legislatures. (In addition, both Connecticut and Rhode Island maintained their bicameral systems.) In most states, there was relatively little serious discussion given to the number of houses since they were simply maintaining the current bicameral system. Moreover, bicameralism was the prevailing legislative theory of the time (Selsam 1936, 184). The topic was, however, given considerable debate in several places. Notably, the question of the proper number of houses was raised in two important revolutionary publications. In *Common Sense,* Thomas Paine wrote in favor of unicameral legislatures in the states. In response, John Adams penned *Thoughts on Government,* arguing in favor of bicameral legislatures. Adams (quoted in Main 1967, 206; see also Luce 1924, 25) made the case that unicameral bodies tended to be

> productive of hasty results and absurd judgments. And all these errors ought to be corrected and defects supplied by some controlling power. . . . A single assembly is apt to be avaricious, and in time will not scruple to exempt itself from burdens, which it will lay, without compunction, on its constituents.

In essence, supporters of bicameral systems argued that unicameral legislatures were to be feared because they would be unchecked and therefore too powerful and they would act too quickly without sufficient deliberation (Adams 1980, 264–65). John Adams' argument was persuasive in Massachusetts, but in Pennsylvania, Benjamin Franklin's position in favor of maintaining that state's unicameral system carried the day (Fisher 1897, 80; Selsam 1936, 185–86; Stourzh 1953, 1108–9).[23] Franklin asserted that a bicameral legislature was like putting one horse in front of a cart and another horse behind it, with the end result being that each horse pulls the cart in the opposite direction (Selsam 1936, 186). Pennsylvania's constitution was particularly influential on those subsequently adopted in Georgia and Vermont (which adopted a constitution in 1777, but was not admitted as a state until 1791), both of which also created unicameral legislatures (Moran 1895, 53). In each unicameral system, however, an executive council performing some of the functions associated with upper houses also was created (Webster 1897, 74).[24] The other colony with a unicameral legislature, Delaware, switched to a bicameral system in its 1776 constitution.

The lower house was given different names in different states. The original constitutions referred to houses of assemblies in four states (although New Jersey's was the General Assembly), houses of representatives in two states, houses of delegates in two states, and a house of commons in North Carolina.[25] South Carolina originally called its lower house the General Assembly in its 1776 constitution but changed its name to the House of Representatives in its permanent constitution two years later. New Hampshire's 1776 constitution makes an initial reference to "a house of Representatives or Assembly" and the two labels were used interchangeably throughout the rest of the document.

The new constitutions made relatively few structural changes to the lower houses, in large part because their earlier colonial manifestations were already republican in nature (Morey 1893–1894, 220).[26] Perhaps the most noticeable change in almost all lower houses was a substantial increase in the number of seats compared to their colonial predecessors (Harlow 1917, 63; Main 1966; Lutz 1999, 65–66). Increased membership sizes were an effort to make the chambers more representative of the electorate, and most of the new seats came from previously unrepresented towns and inland areas (Main 1966, 404; Zagarii 1987, 42–43). Seats were generally apportioned on the basis of counties and cities as they had been in each colonial assembly. Thus, membership sizes increased as states added new counties and cities. But a few states, notably the largest population states, began to experiment with representation based not on geographic unit, but rather on equal population (Zagarii 1987, 36–46). The smallest chamber was Delaware's with 21 members. The largest lower house was South Carolina's with around 200 members.[27]

Changes in the upper houses, were, of course, more dramatic because almost all of them had to be converted to elected bodies from appointed ones. In

TABLE 1-4 Constitutional Features of Original American Legislatures—Lower Houses[a]

	Lower House Name	Initial Membership Size and Apportionment	Member Qualifications	Term of Office
DE 1776	House of Assembly	21 members, 7 from each county	Freeholder, county resident, no current minister or persons having military contracts may serve	1 year
GA 1777	House of Assembly	90 members, 10 from each of 7 counties; 14 from Liberty County, 4 from Savannah, and 2 from Sunbury	Protestant, state resident 1 year and county resident for 3 months, 21 years old, own 250 acres or property worth £250, no clergy allowed	1 year
MD 1776	House of Delegates	80 members, 4 members from each of 19 counties and 2 from Annapolis and 2 from Baltimore	County resident for one year, 21 years old, worth £500, no minister may serve, no current supplier to military may serve	1 year
MA 1780	House of Representatives	Variable, based on number of towns and their populations	Town resident for 1 year, freehold of £100 in town	1 year
NH 1776	House of Representatives or Assembly	Variable, based on number of towns and their populations	None	1 year
NJ 1776	General Assembly	39 members, 3 members from each of 13 counties, subject to change by the legislature but never less than 39 members	County resident 1 year, worth £500 in county	1 year
NY 1777	Assembly	70 members, 70 member minimum, apportioned by county, revised after census in 7 years to be proportional to voters, never more than 300 members	No minister of any denomination may serve	1 year
NC 1776	House of Commons	70 members, 2 members from each of 32 counties and 1 from each of six designated towns	County resident 1 year, possess 100 acres, Protestant, no military officer, no current supplier to military, or clergy may serve.	1 year
PA 1776	House of Representatives	78 members, initially 6 from each of 12 counties and Philadelphia, subsequently to be made proportional to number of taxpayers	Live in county or city for 2 years	1 year, may serve only 4 terms in 7 years

(Continued)

THE LINEAGE OF AMERICAN LEGISLATURES

TABLE 1-4 Constitutional Features of Original American Legislatures—Lower Houses[a] *(Continued)*

	Lower House Name	Initial Membership Size and Apportionment	Member Qualifications	Term of Office
SC 1776	General Assembly	202 members, apportioned by parish and district with 4 to 30 members from each	Clear of debt. Other qualifications in Election Act (freeman, 100 acres or house worth £60) no military commission except in militia	2 years
SC 1778	House of Representatives	199 members, apportioned by parishes and districts with 3 to 30 members from each, made proportional to number of white inhabitants and taxable property in 7 years and every 14 years thereafter	Protestant, state resident 3 years, live and own property in district and be clear of debt, or non-resident with estate worth £3,500, no minister within last 2 years may serve	2 years
VA 1776	House of Delegates	126 members, 2 members from each of 62 counties and from the district of West-Augusta and 1 from Williamsburg and Norfolk and such other cities as legislature designates	Live in city, county, or district as freeholders, no minister may serve	1 year
U.S. 1777	Congress	Variable, 2 to 7 members per state, elected by state legislature, recallable by state legislature	None	1 year, may serve only 3 terms in 6 years
U.S. 1787	House of Representatives	65 members, then proportional by population, at least 1 per state	25 years old, 7 years citizen of United States, resident of state	2 years

Sources: See Constitution of Delaware, 1776; Constitution of Georgia, February 5, 1777; Constitution of Maryland, November 11, 1776; Constitution of the Commonwealth of Massachusetts, 1780; Constitution of New Hampshire, 1776; Constitution of New Jersey, 1776; Constitution of New York, April 20, 1777; Constitution of North Carolina, December 18, 1776; Constitution of Pennsylvania, September 18, 1776; Constitution of South Carolina, March 26, 1776; Constitution of South Carolina, March 19, 1778; Constitution of Virginia, June 29, 1776; The Articles of Confederation and Perpetual Union; The Constitution of the United States. Additional information was gleaned from Adams (1980); Bolles (1890, 462); Leonard (1978); Lutz (1980, 87–92); McCormick (1964); Morey (1893–94); Scharf (1879, 282) and *The Book of the States 2000–2001*.

[a]CT continued to operate under the colonial charter of 1662 until 1818. RI continued to operate under the colonial charter of 1663 until 1842.

CHAPTER 1

TABLE 1-5 Constitutional Features of Original American Legislatures— Upper Houses[a]

	Upper House Name	Initial Membership Size and Apportionment	Member Qualifications	Term of Office
DE 1776	The (Legislative) Council	9 members, 3 from each county	Freeholder, resident in county, no current minister or persons having military contracts may serve	3 years— staggered annually, 1 seat from each county
GA	*Unicameral*			
MD 1776	Senate	15 members, 9 from western and 6 from eastern shore, elected by 2 electors from each county and 1 elector each from Baltimore and Annapolis	25 years old, live in state 3 years, worth £1,000, no minister may serve, no current supplier to military may serve	5 years
MA 1780	Senate	40 members, elected by districts (district number proportionate to taxes paid)[b]	Live in state 5 years, live in district, worth £300 freehold, live in district	1 year
NH 1776	Council	12 members, apportioned by county, elected by House of Representatives	Freeholders and state residents	1 year
NJ 1776	Legislative Council	13 members, 1 member from each of the 13 counties	Live in county and be freeholder for 1 year, worth £1,000 in county	1 year
NY 1777	Senate	24 members, elected in 4 electoral districts, revised after census in 7 years to be proportionate to voters, never more than 100 members	Freeholder worth £100 clear of debt, no minister of any denomination may serve	4 years— staggered annually
NC 1776	Senate	32 members, 1 from each county	Live in county 1 year, possess 300 acres, Protestant, no military officer, no current supplier to military, or clergymen may serve	1 year
PA	*Unicameral*			

(Continued)

TABLE 1–5 Constitutional Features of Original American Legislatures—
Upper Houses[a] *(Continued)*

	Upper House Name	Initial Membership Size and Apportionment	Member Qualifications	Term of Office
SC 1776	Legislative Council	13 members, elected from and by membership of General Assembly	Clear of debt and other qualifications in Election Act (freeman, 100 acres or house worth £60), no military commission except in militia	2 years
SC 1778	Senate	30 members, 1 from each parish and district, except 2 each from District of Saint Philip and Saint Michael's Parish, and Charleston, made proportional to number of white inhabitants and taxable property in 7 years and every 14 years thereafter	Protestant, 30 years old, live in state 5 years, and own freehold estate in parish or district worth £2000, or non-resident with freehold estate worth £7,000 in district, no minister or public preacher within last 2 years may serve	2 years
VA 1776	Senate	24 members, 1 from each electoral district	Live in district and be freeholder, 25 years old, no minister may serve	4 years— staggered annually
U.S. 1777	*Unicameral*			
U.S. 1787	Senate	26 members, 2 per state, elected by state legislatures	30 years old, 9 years citizen of United States, resident of state	6 years— staggered biennially

Sources: See Constitution of Delaware, 1776; Constitution of Georgia, February 5, 1777; Constitution of Maryland, November 11, 1776; Constitution of the Commonwealth of Massachusetts, 1780; Constitution of New Hampshire, 1776; Constitution of New Jersey, 1776; Constitution of New York, April 20, 1777; Constitution of North Carolina, December 18, 1776; Constitution of Pennsylvania, September 18, 1776; Constitution of South Carolina, March 26, 1776; Constitution of South Carolina, March 19, 1778; Constitution of Virginia, June 29, 1776; The Articles of Confederation and Perpetual Union; The Constitution of the United States. Additional information was gleaned from Adams (1980); Bolles (1890, 462); Leonard (1978); Lutz (1980, 87–92); Main (1967); McCormick (1964); Morey (1893–94); Scharf (1879, 282); and *The Book of the States 2000–2001*.

[a]CT continued to operate under the colonial charter of 1662 until 1818. RI continued to operate under the colonial charter of 1663 until 1842.

[b]In Massachusetts, senators could be elected only with a majority of the vote. If there was no majority winner in a district, the members of the House and those senators who won election would select a senator from among the candidates who ran.

Delaware, New Hampshire, New Jersey, and initially in South Carolina, the upper house kept its designation as the council. The other states, following Virginia's lead, chose to call their upper house the senate. Thomas Jefferson first suggested the name in his proposed draft of Virginia's constitution (Luce 1924, 21). Eventually the states referring to their upper houses as councils switched to calling it the senate as well.[28]

The upper house in each state had fewer seats than its lower house counterpart. Their sizes ranged from 9 members in Delaware to 40 members in Massachusetts. Most of the upper houses were apportioned on the bases of counties, regardless of populations. Upper house members in Massachusetts, New York, and Virginia were to be elected from newly designed electoral districts.

Unlike all of the lower houses, and most of the upper houses in the other states, upper houses in New Hampshire and South Carolina in its 1776 constitution were elected by the members of the lower house. In South Carolina, lower house members elected upper house members from their own ranks. The vacancies created in the lower house were then, in turn, refilled through special elections (Green 1930, 87). Massachusetts instituted a variation on that system. In senate districts where no candidate secured a majority, the members of the House and those senators who won election selected the senator from among the top candidates who had run. Maryland created a unique system. Upper house members in that state were elected using an electoral college. Voters elected electors—two from each county and one each from Annapolis and Baltimore—who then elected the 15 members of the senate.

The smaller membership sizes and occasionally different election systems suggest that the new upper houses were intended to retain some of the aristocratic qualities of their council predecessors. Further evidence of this is the difference between the two houses in membership qualifications in most states. By and large, the upper houses were not intended to be democratic institutions (Main 1967, 188). Imposing qualifications, however, was not new; colonial assemblies established standards for residency, age, and religion among other characteristics (Greene 1963, 186–89; Phillips 1921). In Georgia, for example, colonial assembly members had to be (Corey 1929, 110), "free white men twenty-one or more years old . . . [with] a belief in Jesus Christ, a year's residence in the province, and free hold estate of 500 acres." Potential assemblymen in Pennsylvania had to be qualified voters and subscribe to the anti-Catholic English Tolerance Act (Young 1968, 157).[29] Some of the qualifications were more focused. In Maryland, for example, between 1704 and 1716 tavern keepers were disqualified from legislative service (Clarke 1943, 161).

In the new constitutions, qualifications were almost always set higher for the upper house than for the lower house. The qualification most likely to discriminate among the population at large was one for property or wealth. Such a standard was found in most, but not all, constitutions. Where they did appear they were higher for the upper house than for the lower house (Lutz 1980, 88–89). The most stringent requirement was in South Carolina's 1778 constitution: a district resident would only have to own property and be free of debt to run for the lower house, but to run for the senate he would have to own a freehold estate worth £2,000. (Non-district residents could get elected in South Carolina, but for each house they had to meet even higher qualification standards.) Overall, however, property qualifications may not have exerted the discriminatory effect intended. According to Main (1967, 189), "Probably no person who lacked a freehold, and exceedingly few who possessed less than the average amount of property, would have been a serious contender for a seat in an upper house." This may have been because the new upper houses were conceived to represent landed members of society, while lower houses were to be the province of the commoners.[30] Moreover, there was likely a carryover of the colonial norm of deference, a feeling among the masses that officeholding was best left to a disinterested economic elite (Kirby 1970; Tully 1977).

Age was explicitly included as a qualification in only a few constitutions, but it was to be inferred from the standards set for being a qualified voter in the others. Thus, unless otherwise specified, the minimum age for service was 21 years (Webster 1897, 76), the standard for service in each lower house. But in several states upper house members had to be older than their lower house counterparts: at least 25 years old in Maryland and Virginia, and 30 years old in South Carolina. State and county or electoral district residency requirements typically were established for both houses. Again, South Carolina set the most stringent standards in its 1778 constitution: three years state residency for election to the house and five years state residency for election to the senate.

A few states set other notable qualifications. Military suppliers were disqualified from service in Delaware, Maryland, and North Carolina. Given that the constitutions were written at a time of war, the desire was clearly to prevent the appearance or reality of impropriety in the awarding of contracts for supplying army units raised in these states. Indeed, all of the constitutions written in 1776 save for South Carolina's generally excluded holders of other governmental positions from serving in the state legislature, in part to keep the taint of corruption from impairing the ability of the new governments to govern with legitimacy, but also to prevent the concentration of power in the hands of relatively few people (Wood 1969, 158–59).

Religious qualifications also appeared in many state constitutions. Legislators were required to be Protestants in Georgia, North Carolina, and South Carolina. But ministers were explicitly disqualified from service in seven states: Delaware, Georgia, Maryland, New York, North Carolina, South Carolina, and Virginia. The prohibition against ministers was rooted in both British parliamentary and American colonial experience, where from time to time they were prevented from serving (Clarke 1943, 161–63; Swem 1917, 74–75, 77–79). Ministers were banned from serving because there was a desire to keep them from getting too involved in politics and, concomitantly, to also keep them focused on religious matters (Stokes 1950, 622).[31] Although the exclusion of ministers from legislative service under the Articles of Confederation was debated but rejected, disqualification did subsequently appear in a number of later state constitutions (Stokes 1950, 622).[32] Over the nineteenth century most states dropped these provisions, but they lasted almost to the end of the twentieth century in Maryland and Tennessee before the federal courts declared them unconstitutional.[33]

The new constitutions also set term lengths. Almost all of the lower houses followed the New England colonial tradition of one-year terms. There were a few deviations. Connecticut and Rhode Island maintained their six-month terms (Bryce 1906, 147; Webster 1897, 75), while South Carolina granted its lower house members two-year terms in both of its revolutionary constitutions. According to Bryce (1906, 147), a one-year term was maintained because it was, "So essential to republicanism . . . that the maxim 'where annual elections end tyranny begins' had passed into a proverb."[34] One-year terms would allow voters to keep elected officials close to home and if needed to replace them quickly (Adams 1980, 243–44; Luce 1924, 109–110). Indeed, so powerful was the pull of the traditional one-year term that Madison had to devote two *Federalist* papers (numbers 52 and 53) to arguments in support of the two-year term given members of the U.S House. The only term limits imposed in any state legislature by the first constitutions were in Pennsylvania, where members of its unicameral legislature could serve only four one-year terms in any seven-year period.[35] The Congress under the Articles operated with a similar term limit; members could serve only three one-year terms in any six-year period.

Terms in upper houses were more variable. One-year terms were found in four states, giving both upper and lower house members in those states the same term. South Carolina gave its upper house members two-year terms matching those granted to members of the lower house. In four states, upper house members were given longer tenures. Senators in Maryland were given the longest terms, five years, all on the same electoral cycle. Upper house members in New York and Virginia had four-year terms, and those in Delaware three-year terms. In each of these cases, the terms were staggered, so that seats of one-quarter of the senators in New York and Virginia, and one-third of the council seats in Delaware, were up for election each year.

The National Legislature

The new American states adopted a number of different legislative structures between 1776 and 1780. Many of their features later appeared in the two national legislatures created by the Articles of Confederation and the Constitution.

Indeed, examination of the structures of the national legislatures presented in tables 1–4 and 1–5 reveals that the design of the constitutional Congress owes more to the state legislatures that preceded it than it does to the Congress under the Articles. Most obviously, the constitutional Congress is bicameral, as were 11 of the original 13 state legislatures.[36] In contrast, the Congress under the Articles was, of course, unicameral. And the two houses created by the Constitution were given the names most commonly found in the states. The great similarity between the two sorts of institutions is actually somewhat ironic because many of the men who wrote the Constitution, most notably James Madison and George Mason, held the state legislatures in very low regard because they thought the legislatures held too much power within state governmental structures (Riker 1984, 2–4).

The initial size of the new House of Representatives was roughly in line with many of the state lower houses. The method of apportionment was very similar to that employed in New York, Pennsylvania, and South Carolina. Like the senates in the states, the new U.S. Senate was considerably smaller than the House of Representatives. And, of course, equal representation by state as used in the Senate was equivalent to the equal representation by county used in state senates in Delaware, New Jersey, and North Carolina. The men who wrote the Constitution explicitly designed the House to be elected by the same people allowed to vote for the lower house of the state legislature. In contrast, the senate was to be elected by the state legislature. Similar indirect elections for the upper house were part of the state legislative systems in Maryland, New Hampshire, and South Carolina under its first constitution.[37]

The qualifications imposed for service in the U.S. Congress were grounded in those found in the original state legislatures—there were no qualifications set for membership in the Congress under the Articles. Age and residency requirements were similar between the constitutional Congress and the original state legislatures, even to the extent of having higher requirements for the upper house than for the lower house. Religious and property standards were, of course, debated but not incorporated into the U.S. Constitution, although they appear in many state constitutions. The Senate was given longer terms than the House, as were the upper houses in four states. U.S. senators were given six-year terms, longer than any upper house in the states. The Senate's terms, however, were three times longer than those for the lower house, as were those for Delaware's councilors compared to members of the Assembly. And, although all but one state legislature had only one-year terms for the members of their lower houses—as the Congress under the Articles did—South Carolina gave its representatives the same two-year terms that members of the U.S. House were later granted.

Beyond structures, other significant provisions of the U.S. Constitution appear in earlier manifestations in the original state constitutions. One notable example is the provisions allowing each house to adopt its own rules and to select its own leaders. This particular power is of considerable importance in current explanations of how the modern Congress came to be. Stewart (2001, 67–68), for example, notes,

> One matter that entered the Constitution has rarely rated much comment in the histories of the convention but should interest students of Congress greatly: the question of the internal organization of Congress. The Articles of Confederation were largely silent about the internal organization of the Confederate Congress . . . By giving both chambers of Congress the unambiguous power to govern themselves without regard to the special rights of states or minorities within the legislature, the groundwork was laid for a much more independently powerful and coherent legislature in the future.

Rosenthal (1996, 190) also sees legislative control over leaders and procedures as a crucial aspect of institutional independence.

It is significant to note that the Constitutional powers governing the internal organization of Congress were completely grounded in the colonial and early state legislative experiences. Colonial assemblies asserted the right to establish their own rules of procedure and to select their own leaders. Generally, the Crown allowed assemblies to develop their own rules and procedures without much interference (Greene 1963, 216–19). Gaining control over selection of their leaders was more difficult. The Crown never contested appointment of minor officials, such as the sergeant at arms or messengers, but control over the selection of the speaker was occasionally a source of conflict with the executive branch and the Crown. Assemblies usually, but not always, succeeded in getting their own candidates into the speakership without interference from the executive (Greene 1963, 206–07, 429–31; Wendel 1986, 173).

More directly, as table 1–6 shows, ten of the original state constitutions (including South Carolina's second constitution) explicitly granted the legislature extensive authority to select its own leaders and five to devise its own rules. The latter rulemaking power was first adopted in the Virginia constitution, although there is no record of why it was included (Castello 1986, 529). All of the rulemaking clauses are unicameral in that they apply to both houses. The Massachusetts constitution, however, uses slightly different rulemaking clauses for its two houses, although nothing has ever been made of the difference (Castello 1986, 528). The leadership selection and rulemaking provisions found in the U.S. Constitution are very similar to those found in several of the earlier state constitutions.[38] Indeed, Hines (1909, 156) observed, "There was no debate whatever over the clause of the Constitution which provides that the house shall choose its speaker and other officers. There was very good reason for this. That clause was taken from the State constitutions adopted in 1776 . . ."

A second important provision involves the power to originate tax legislation. The idea that "money bills," as they were originally called, originate in the lower

THE LINEAGE OF AMERICAN LEGISLATURES

TABLE 1-6 Early American Constitutional Provisions on Legislative Leadership and Procedures (in Order of Adoption)

South Carolina Constitution 1776: "That the general assembly and legislative council shall each choose their respective speakers and their own officers without control."

Virginia Constitution 1776: "each House shall choose its own Speaker, appoint its own officers, settle its own rules of proceeding"

New Jersey Constitution 1776: "That the Assembly, when met, shall have power to choose a Speaker"

Delaware Constitution 1776: "each house shall choose its own speaker, appoint its own officers, judge of the qualifications and elections of its own members, settle its own rules of proceedings"

Maryland Constitution 1776: House, "their Speaker (to be chosen by them, by ballot)" . . . Senate, "their President (to be chosen by them, by ballot)"

North Carolina Constitution 1776: "That the Senate and House of Commons, when met, shall each have power to choose a speaker and other their officers"

Georgia Constitution 1777: "and the house shall choose its own speaker, appoint its own officers, settle its own rules of proceeding"

New York Constitution 1777: "That the assembly, thus constituted, shall choose their own speaker, be judges of their own members, and enjoy the same privileges, and proceed in doing business in like manner as the assemblies of the colony of New York of right formerly did"

South Carolina Constitution 1778: "That the senate and house of representatives shall each choose their respective officers by ballot, without control"

Massachusetts Constitution 1780: "The Senate shall choose its own President, appoint its own officers, and determine its own rules of proceeding" [. . .] "The House of Representatives . . . shall choose their own Speaker; appoint their own officers, and settle the rules and orders of proceeding in their own house"

U.S. Constitution 1787: "The House of Representatives shall choose their Speaker and other officers" [. . .] "The Vice-President of the United States shall be President of the Senate, but shall have no vote, unless they be equally divided. The Senate shall choose their other officers, and also a President pro tempore" [. . .] "Each House may determine the rules of its proceedings"

---

house was well rooted in English parliamentary history, with the first assertion of such exclusive authority occurring around 1407 (Taswell-Langmead 1946, 208–09).[39] Colonial assemblies made similar claims for exclusive origination privileges very early in their histories. Most achieved origination rights without much resistance from the governor or the council (Corey 1929, 121; Greene 1963, 51–71; Miller 1907, 157–59).

The majority of the new state constitutions continued the tradition by granting the lower house exclusive rights to initiate tax legislation, with New Hampshire's being the first to provide that authority in a formal document in America (Fisher 1897, 73). Most, but not all, states followed New Hampshire's lead, as table 1–7 shows. During the national Constitutional Convention, there was considerable debate over the origination powers (Galloway 1961, 3). As part of the

TABLE 1-7 Early American Constitutional Provisions on Origination of Revenue Bills (in Order of Adoption)

New Hampshire Constitution 1776: "That all bills, resolves, or votes for raising, levying and collecting money originate in the house of Representatives."

South Carolina Constitution 1776: "All money-bills for the support of government shall originate in the general assembly, and shall not be altered or amended by the legislative council, but may be rejected by them. All other bills and ordinances may take rise in the general assembly or legislative council, and may be altered, amended, or rejected by either."

Virginia Constitution 1776: "All laws shall originate in the House of Delegates, to be approved of or rejected by the Senate, or to be amended, with consent of the House of Delegates; except money-bills, which in no instance shall be altered by the Senate, but wholly approved or rejected."

New Jersey Constitution 1776: "That the Council shall also have power to prepare bills to pass into laws, and have other like powers as the Assembly, and in all respects be a free and independent branch of the Legislature of this Colony; save only, that they shall not prepare or alter any money-bill which shall be the privilege of the Assembly"

Delaware Constitution 1776: "All money-bills for the support of government shall originate in the house of assembly, and may be altered, amended, or rejected by the legislative council."

Maryland Constitution 1776: "That the House of Delegates may originate all money bills, propose bills to the Senate, or receive those offered by that body; and assent, dissent, or propose amendments" [. . .] "That the Senate may originate any other, except money bills, to which their assent or dissent only shall be given; and may receive any other bills from the House of Delegates, and assent, dissent, or propose amendments."

South Carolina Constitution 1778: "That all money bills for the support of government shall originate in the house of representatives, and shall not be altered or amended by the senate, but may be rejected by them. . . . All other bills and ordinances may take rise in the senate or house of representatives, and be altered, amended, or rejected by either.

Massachusetts Constitution 1780: "All money-bills shall originate in the House of Representatives; but the Senate may propose or concur with amendments, as on other bills."

U.S. Constitution 1787: "All bills for raising revenue shall originate in the House of Representatives; but the Senate may propose or concur with amendments as on other bills."

Great (or Connecticut) Compromise, exclusive origination powers were granted to the House of Representatives. The next question concerned the ability of the Senate to amend tax bills passed by the House. Most state constitutions forbade the upper house from amending tax bills. The Constitutional Convention, however, opted for the process established in Delaware and Massachusetts, where tax bills originated in the lower house, but the upper house could amend them. Indeed, the language in the U.S. Constitution is virtually identical to that contained in the Massachusetts constitution.

Another important similarity between the Massachusetts constitution and the federal Constitution is the executive veto power. As shown in table 1–8, both gave the executive the right to reject legislation and the legislature the right to override

THE LINEAGE OF AMERICAN LEGISLATURES

TABLE 1-8 Early American Constitutional Provisions on Executive Veto Power (in Order of Adoption)

South Carolina Constitution 1776: "Bills having passed the general assembly and legislative council may be assented to or rejected by the president and commander-in-chief. Having received his assent, they shall have all the force and validity of an act of general assembly of this colony."

New York Constitution 1777: "Be it ordained, that the governor for the time being, the chancellor, and the judges of the supreme court, or any two of them, together with the governor, shall be, and hereby are, constituted a council to revise all bills about to be passed into laws by the legislature; and for that purpose shall assemble themselves from time to time, when the legislature shall be convened; for which, nevertheless they shall not receive any salary or consideration, under any presence whatever. And that all bills which have passed the senate and assembly shall, before they become laws, be presented to the said council for their revisal and consideration; and if, upon such revision and consideration, it should appear improper to the said council, or a majority of them, that the said bill should become a law of this State, that they return the same, together with their objections thereto in writing, to the senate or house of assembly (in which soever the same shall have originated) who shall enter the objection sent down by the council at large in their minutes, and proceed to reconsider the said bill. But if, after such reconsideration, two-thirds of the said senate or house of assembly shall, notwithstanding the said objections, agree to pass the same, it shall together with the objections, be sent to the other branch of the legislature, where it shall also be reconsidered, and, if approved by two-thirds of the members present, shall be a law.

And in order to prevent any unnecessary delays, be it further ordained, that if any bill shall not be returned by the council within ten days after it shall have been presented, the same shall be a law, unless the legislature shall, by their adjournment, render a return of the said bill within ten days impracticable; in which case the bill shall be returned on the first day of the meeting of the legislature after the expiration of the said ten days."

Massachusetts Constitution 1780: "No bill or resolve of the Senate or House of Representatives shall become a law, and have force as such, until it shall have been laid before the Governor for his revisal: And if he, upon such revision, approve thereof, he shall signify his approbation by signing the same. But if he have any objection to the passing of such bill or resolve, he shall return the same, together with his objections thereto, in writing, to the Senate or House of Representatives, in which soever the same shall have originated; who shall enter the objections sent down by the Governor, at large, on their records, and proceed to reconsider the said bill or resolve: But if, after such reconsideration, two thirds of the said Senate or House of Representatives, shall, notwithstanding the said objections, agree to pass the same, it shall, together with the objections, be sent to the other branch of the legislature, where it shall also be reconsidered, and if approved by two thirds of the members present, shall have the force of a law: But in all such cases the votes of both houses shall be determined by yeas and nays; and the names of the persons voting for, or against, the said bill or resolve, shall be entered upon the public records of the Commonwealth.

And in order to prevent unnecessary delays, if any bill or resolve shall not be returned by the Governor within five days after it shall have been presented, the same shall have the force of a law."

U.S. Constitution 1787: "Every Bill which shall have passed the House of Representatives and the Senate, shall, before it become a Law, be presented to the President of the United States: If he approve he shall sign it, but if not he shall return it, with his Objections to that House in which it shall have originated, who shall enter the Objections at large on their Journal, and proceed to reconsider it. If after such Reconsideration two thirds of that House shall agree to pass the Bill, it shall be sent,

(Continued)

TABLE 1-8 Early American Constitutional Provisions on Executive Veto Power (in Order of Adoption) *(Continued)*

together with the Objections, to the other House, by which it shall likewise be reconsidered, and if approved by two thirds of that House, it shall become a Law. But in all such Cases the Votes of both Houses shall be determined by yeas and Nays, and the Names of the Persons voting for and against the Bill shall be entered on the Journal of each House respectively. If any Bill shall not be returned by the President within ten Days (Sundays excepted) after it shall have been presented to him, the Same shall be a Law, in like Manner as if he had signed it, unless the Congress by their Adjournment prevent its Return, in which Case it shall not be a Law."

---

the veto with a super-majority vote of two-thirds. This resemblance is of particular interest because only two other constitutions of the original states granted the executive a veto, but in both cases they were of a very different sort (Fairlie 1917, 474–75). The provisional South Carolina constitution of 1776 continued the colonial tradition of an absolute executive veto, one that the legislature could not override. But, when South Carolina adopted a permanent constitution two years later, the executive was not granted any veto power. The veto provided for in the 1777 New York constitution was not the governor's alone to exercise. Instead, a council of revision composed of the governor, the chancellor, and the judges on the state supreme court was entitled to reject legislation passed by the state legislature. But the legislature could override the council of revision's veto with a two-thirds vote of all members.[40]

Conclusion

By 1789, Americans had enjoyed 170 years of experience with legislative institutions. The evolution of colonial assemblies leads directly to the structures and rules adopted by new state legislatures. In turn, the original state legislatures greatly influenced the design of the new Congress under the Constitution. Thus, in most fundamental ways, the Congress under the Constitution was very similar to the legislatures in the original states. The evolution of American legislatures starts from common ancestors.

· 2 ·

Fundamental Structures

Questions about institutional design occupy a central place in the study of the evolution of legislative organizations (Shepsle and Weingast 1994). Before looking at structures or rules and procedures in American legislatures, however, we must first examine what Buchanan and Tullock (1962, 210) referred to as "the fundamental organization of activity." From our perspective, fundamental organization involves matters of constitutional design, including separation of powers, number of houses, membership size, constituency size, term of office, and qualifications for membership. How does the fundamental organization of activities vary across American legislatures?

In the preceding chapter we established that current American legislatures share common roots: that colonial legislatures morphed into state legislatures, which in turn were the models for the Congress created by the Constitution. But, since the late eighteenth century, American legislatures have evolved in many different ways. In this chapter we begin to examine those differences by looking at the fundamental organization of activities across legislatures and over time.

Constitutional Dictates

As shown in chapter 1, Congress and state legislatures are all constitutionally created and grounded institutions. That is, their basic forms and rules—relationships among branches, number of houses, number of members, terms of office, and qualifications for office—are established in constitutions. But there are significant differences between Congress and the state legislatures in the instructions their constitutions impart. As congressional scholars well know, the U.S. Constitution provides remarkably few structural directives to Congress. In contrast, state constitutions usually provide much more direction to their legislatures, thereby giving the institutions much less flexibility. Moreover, in those states that allow for direct constitutional initiatives, voters influence legislative organization and behavior in ways they cannot influence Congress.

There are, of course, significant similarities between the U.S. Constitution and state constitutions in regard to the structures and rules imposed on their legislatures. Compare, for example, the following provisions from the U.S Constitution and the most recent state constitutions, those adopted since 1950:

> "Each House may determine the Rules of its Proceedings." (1787 U.S. Constitution, Article 1, section 5)

> "Each house shall choose its own officers, determine the rules of its proceedings and keep a journal." (1950 Hawaii Constitution, Article 3, Section 12)

> "The houses of each legislature shall adopt uniform rules of procedure." (1956 Alaska Constitution, Article 2, section 12)

> "Each house, except as otherwise provided in this constitution, shall choose its own officers and determine the rules of its proceedings." (1963 Michigan Constitution, Article 4, section 16)

> "Each house shall determine the rules of its own proceedings." (1965 Connecticut Constitution, Article Third, section 13)

> "Each house shall determine its rules of procedure." (1968 Florida Constitution, Article 3, section 4(a))

> "Each house shall determine the rules of its proceedings." (1970 Illinois Constitution, Article 4, section 6(d))

> "Each house shall select its officers and settle its rules of procedure." (1970 Virginia Constitution, Article 4, section 7)

> "Each house shall choose its officers from among its members, keep a journal, and make rules for its proceedings." (1972 Montana Constitution, Article 5, section 10(1))

> "Each house shall be the judge of the qualifications and elections of its members; shall determine its rules of procedure, not inconsistent with the provisions of this constitution." (1974 Louisiana Constitution, Article 3, section 7(a))

A phrase granting the legislature the right to establish its own rules and procedures appears in every state constitution, save for North Carolina's (Erickson

2001). Such similarities are unsurprising because, of course, as tables 1–4 and 1–5 demonstrated, early state constitutions influenced the federal constitution. And, of course, later state constitutions often lifted concepts and language from both the federal constitution and other state constitutions.[1] But, while there are similarities between the U.S. Constitution and state constitutions, there also are stark differences.

The U.S. Congress has operated under the same constitution since 1789, with only the Seventeenth Amendment substantially changing the initial set of rules governing it. In contrast, most states have had more than one constitution—Louisiana is on its eleventh—and most states have amended their constitutions more often—Alabama has amended its 1901 constitution more than 700 times. Thus, at the state level, there have been many more opportunities to change legislative rules, chances taken up by generations of reformers. Particularly in the second half of the nineteenth century, state constitutions came to place significant limitations on state legislatures, in response to perceived and real abuses of legislative power (Barnett 1915, 457; Bryce 1906, 319; Friedman 1973, 303–314).[2] According to one study (Abernathy 1959, 15), "Between 1864 and 1880, thirty-five new constitutions were adopted in nineteen states. Distrust of the legislature was the predominant characteristic of all of them." The writers of Mississippi's 1890 constitution included 24 sections that placed limitations on the lawmaking powers of the legislature; 15 of those limits had not appeared in earlier constitutions (Fortenberry and Hobbs 1967, 83–84). Writing at the end of the era when significant restrictions were regularly imposed, Ostrogorski (1910, 359) observed of state legislatures more generally,

> Their improvement being considered hopeless, attempts were made . . . to limit their powers, to leave them as few opportunities of legislating as possible. With this object the reformers tried to insert in the constitutions—which the ordinary legislatures have not the right to touch—as many general provisions as possible, so much so that the most recent constitutions, made very voluminous, contain many clauses which do not fall within the scope of constitutional law, properly so called, at all, but relate to private, to administrative law.

It is important to note that, even though the intense period of constraints being placed on state legislatures ended around the beginning of the twentieth century, anti-legislative feelings permeated state constitution-making over a much longer period. In the middle of the twentieth century, for example, one constitutional scholar observed (Powell 1948, 370),

> each of Louisiana's nine conventions since 1812, except that of 1861, imposed new policy mandates and additional restrictions upon the legislature. Distrust of legislative discretion has been traditional. The political majority dominant in each

convention, whether composed of Whigs, Democrats, or Republicans, has sought to fix permanently in the Constitution its own notions of needful public policies, hoping in this way to make them secure against both legislative inertia and the changing tides of political sentiment that wash up periodically in the legislature.

In general, the rules placed on state legislatures by state constitutions are far more detailed and restrictive than those placed on the U.S. Congress by the federal Constitution. Bryce (1906, 340–41) identified ten different sorts of constitutional restrictions on state legislative procedures at the beginning of the twentieth century.[3] Take, for example, Article 4, section 62 of the 1901 (and still current) Alabama constitution, which states, "No bill shall become a law until it shall have been referred to a standing committee of each house, acted upon by such committee in session, and returned therefrom, which facts shall affirmatively appear upon the journal of each house." The same steps are required of the Mississippi state legislature by Article 4, section 74 of that state's constitution: "No bill shall become a law until it shall have been referred to a committee of each house and returned therefrom with a recommendation in writing." Thus, unlike the U.S. House and Senate, where committees and referral procedures are the creations of rules promulgated by their own memberships, in Alabama and Mississippi the existence of committees and the procedures involving them are given constitutional status.

This highlights a fundamental difference between the rules under which the U.S. House and Senate operate and the rules under which most state legislatures operate. Almost all congressional rules are endogenously generated. They represent choices made over time by members of each house. In contrast, many state legislative rules are exogenous because they are imposed from outside, either by those who wrote the constitution or by voters who passed amendments to the constitution. The latter, a force that cannot directly dictate congressional rules and structures, can have a dramatic impact on state legislative rules and structures (Rosenthal 1996, 191–92). In 1988, for example, Colorado voters passed the GAVEL (Give a Vote to Every Legislator) amendment. GAVEL required every bill referred to a committee to be brought up for a committee vote, thereby negating a chair's traditional prerogative to kill legislation by failing to put it on the agenda, that all bills reported by committee go to the floor, thereby removing the Rules Committee's source of power (and leading to its abolition), and prohibited party caucuses from taking binding votes, thereby reducing the power of parties and party leaders (Rosenthal 1996, 191; Straayer 2000, 88, 109, 231).[4]

What difference does all of this make to the study of legislative institutions? It matters because who writes the rules shapes the evolution of legislative procedures and organizational structures in important ways. According to Cox (2000, 170–71), exogenously generated rules are stable. They are unlikely to change much over time because to alter them is difficult and requires the consent of actors outside the legislative chamber. In contrast, a legislative majority can manipulate endogenously generated chamber rules to suit their own purposes. Constitutionally stipulated rules may be stable even though they result in the adoption of nonmedian policy outcomes, a situation that would likely be avoided where legislative rules can be determined by a majority of the legislature. This raises the possibility that differences between legislative bodies in policy outcomes may be rooted not just in different distributions of partisan or policy preferences, but also in who gets to write the basic set of rules under which decisions are made.

Separation of Powers

One of the enduring precepts of American government is the separation of powers, most notably as manifested in the U.S. Constitution. The existence of three distinct branches of government, each with its own sphere of influence, is accepted as a common feature of both the national and state governments. But in many crucial regards, the separation of powers is not a dichotomous variable, with a political system either having it or not. Instead, separation of powers is a complex concept, with different governments enjoying different degrees of separation. Neustadt (1990, 29) even talks of American government as having "separate institutions *sharing* power."

The notion of discrete executive, legislative, and judicial entities surfaced during the initial round of American constitution writing in 1776 and 1777. Explicit references to separation of powers were given in half of the new state constitutions (Holcombe 1931, 51). In most of the states, however, separation of powers existed more in fancy than in fact (Chambers 1928, 32–33; Wright 1933, 177). Only in New York and Massachusetts was the concept defined with much specificity (Holcombe 1931, 54–56; Wright 1933, 177–78). But even in those two states clear distinctions between the branches were not well drawn. Indeed, in the *Federalist 47,* Madison noted (Madison, Hamilton, and Jay 1961, 303–4), "If we look into the constitutions of the several States we find that, not withstanding the emphatical and, in some instances, the unqualified terms in which this axiom has been laid down, there is not a single instance in which the several departments of power have been kept absolutely separate and distinct."

Instead of creating a separation of powers, the revolutionary constitutions established legislative supremacy (Chambers 1928, 34; Kersh, Mettler, Reeher, and Stonecash 1998, 14–19). In particular, the fact that legislators elected governors and judges clearly gave legislatures the institutional upper hand. Take, for example the situation in Rhode Island, where (Holcombe 1931, 63), the supreme court, in the celebrated case of *Trevett v. Weeden,* decided in 1786, refused to enforce a legal tender law devised to compel the circulation of paper money. The legislature, however, being determined to have its will executed, declined to reelect those judges the following year, and filled their places with others more subservient.

The fact of legislative supremacy in the states was the reason many of the men who wrote the Constitution distrusted the state legislatures (Riker 1984, 4–5).

Perhaps not surprisingly, in most states, the era of legislative supremacy did not last long. As early as the 1780s states began to rein in their legislatures, by taking appointment powers away from them and giving greater independence to the judiciary (Dippel 1996, 34–35; Wood 1969, 446–53). This movement against legislative supremacy gained considerable steam during the first half of the nineteenth century (Kersh, Mettler, Reeher, and Stonecash 1998, 21–25). Since the end of the 1800s separation of powers in the American states appear to be much like that at the federal level. But, such similarities may be somewhat superficial, because as Kersh, Mettler, Reeher, and Stonecash (1998, 28) note, "states have developed a dizzying variety of approaches to the doctrine." A cursory glance across the states at gubernatorial veto powers and the means for gaining the bench is all it takes to substantiate the view that separation of powers comes in many different forms and in many different degrees.

Indeed, legislative supremacy can still arguably be found in Rhode Island.[5] Rhode Island's Royal Charter of 1663 placed almost all governmental powers in the hands of the legislature, including the ability to appoint its own members to executive and judicial bodies. When the state finally adopted a constitution in 1842, the framers inserted Article VI, section 10, which holds that "The general assembly shall continue to exercise the powers it has heretofore exercised, unless prohibited in this Constitution." Nothing in the constitution forbids the legislature from appointing members of executive bodies, including appointing themselves. Thus, by recent estimate, the legislature makes more than 300 appointments to 75 executive boards. And of the 300 or so appointees, over 200 are state legislators (Hogarty 1998, 138). Legislators holding these positions can, of course, intimately involve themselves in the affairs of the executive branch.

Separation of powers in the American governmental context is a complex concept. Because of the superficial similarities in governmental structures between the national and state governments it would be easy to assume that governors, state judges, and state legislators interact in the exact same ways that the president, federal judges, and members of Congress do. Given the substantial differences in constitutionally mandated relationships, such assumptions may not be warranted.

FUNDAMENTAL STRUCTURES

Number of Houses

Perhaps the most fundamental question of constitutional design is how many houses a legislature will have. As noted in chapter 1, bicameral legislatures have long been a fixture in the American political system. Bicameral systems are not, in and of themselves, particularly unusual, although they constitute a minority of legislative systems across the democratic world. What is distinctive about American bicameralism from a comparative perspective is the fact that both legislative

TABLE 2-1 Ratio of Upper House to Lower House Members in American Legislatures, 2003

Legislature	Lower House Members per Senator
NM	1.67
CO	1.86
DE	1.95
RI	1.97
AK, AZ, CA, ID, IL, IN, IA, MN, MT, NV, NJ, ND, OR, SD, WA, WY	2.00
HI	2.04
OK	2.10
MS	2.35
NC	2.40
NY	2.42
VA	2.50
UT	2.59
KY	2.63
LA	2.69
SC	2.70
AR	2.86
MI	2.89
WV	2.94
AL, FL, MD, OH, TN, WI	3.00
KS	3.13
GA	3.21
MA	4.00
PA	4.06
CT	4.19
ME	4.31
U.S. Congress	4.35
MO	4.79
TX	4.84
VT	5.00
NH	16.67

houses are powerful. This is true not just of the Congress, but also of the 49 bicameral state legislatures. It is possible then, to use American legislatures to generate hypotheses about the relationship between two powerful houses in a bicameral system that can be tested across a range of different dyads. These dyads differ in several critical respects. One difference is in the rules that dictate sequencing of bill consideration and voting, such as the constitutional provision currently found at the national level and in 20 states that require the lower house to originate all revenue legislation (Medina 1987, 166).[6] And, as discussed in more depth in chapter 4, there are differences in the rules governing how conflicts between two houses are to be resolved, with, for example, several states making little or no use of conference committees (Jewell and Patterson 1986, 170; Rogers 2001).

Another typical contrast between the two chambers in a bicameral system is the difference in membership sizes. This difference in size may affect their relationship, particularly in regard to information differentials. A chamber with far more members than its companion chamber enjoys considerably lower information acquisition costs, thereby conferring advantages on it (Rogers 1998). There also is evidence that disparities in membership size affect legislative productivity, with upper houses that are small in comparison to their lower houses creating substantial legislative bottlenecks (Leibowitz and Tollison 1980, 273).

As shown in table 2–1, the modal ratio between upper and lower house memberships in the states is 1:2, which is found in 16 states. But the ratios range from a low of 1:1.67 in New Mexico to a high of 1:16.7 in New Hampshire. Indeed, four state legislatures have higher ratios than the U.S. Congress. Thus, there is substantial variation of ratios with which to investigate bicameral relationships.

Data on state legislatures could be usefully employed, for example, in testing hypotheses generated by Diermeier and Myerson's (1999) theory on the consequences of bicameralism for the internal organization of legislatures. Diermeier and Myerson theorize that the number of internal veto players—committees and the like with gatekeeping powers—increases with the number of chambers or institutions with a veto power (including the executive) in a political system. Groseclose and King (2001, 195–96) label this the "bicameral rivalry theory," and discern several of its implications. They (Groseclose and King 2001, 196) observe that the theory, "sheds light on the multiple veto points in Congress," pointing to the gatekeeping roles played by committees, committee chairs, individual senators, and the House Rules committee. In contrast, they note that parliamentary systems with few constitutional veto points generally create very few internal veto players (committees and the like). The same argument is extended to unicameral legislatures because they also often have weak committee systems.

From our perspective, comparisons between parliamentary and presidential systems, as Diermeier and Myerson (1999) and Groseclose and King (2001) offer, provide a weak test of the bicameral rivalry theory. Given the fundamental differences in the two sorts of systems, finding different numbers of veto points is not terribly surprising. A much stiffer test would be comparisons across the 50 bicameral American legislatures, because, of course, they are all presidential systems, thus controlling for an important source of potential cross-national variation. And, importantly for studying the bicameral rivalry theory, the number of potential veto points varies significantly across American legislatures, both cross-sectionally and over time. Take, for example, the executive veto. As noted in chapter 1, governors in most of the original states were not granted any veto power. But, virtually every state admitted to the union from 1812 on granted the governor a veto. Many of the older states, however, did not follow suit for many years (Fairlie 1917, 476–77). Indeed, several waited until the second half of the nineteenth century. And others waited even longer: Ohio until 1902, Rhode Island until 1909, and North Carolina until 1996. Moreover, the actual veto power exercised by the governor varies over time and across states from very powerful to very weak. Currently, for example, most but not all governors enjoy a line-item veto. Even among those with the line-item veto, however, power varies, with 14 governors being allowed to veto selected words in addition to appropriations, and three governors even being allowed to change word meanings (National Association of State Budget Officers 2002, 30–32). Besides gubernatorial veto powers, the powers of committee systems also vary across the states, as do the powers of party caucuses and party leaders (Francis 1985; 1989). Thus the number of gatekeepers varies substantially across state legislatures. The question then is whether they vary in the way that Diermeier and Myerson predict.[7]

State legislatures also provide an opportunity to examine the consequences of unicameralism.[8] As mentioned earlier, among the world's national legislatures more than twice as many are unicameral as bicameral (Tsebelis and Money 1997, 45). But because almost all unicameral legislatures exist in unitary and parliamentary governmental systems, comparison with American legislatures is difficult. But we can easily compare the Nebraska Unicameral to American bicameral legislatures on any of a number of dimensions. And, of course, the earlier American unicameral legislatures in Georgia, Pennsylvania, and Vermont offer similar opportunities for comparison.

Perhaps even more interestingly, we can examine the organizational, behavioral, and policy effects of changing from a bicameral legislature to a unicameral legislature by looking at Nebraska in the 1930s when it made the change. The study of state legislatures also provides examples of the reverse change: unicameral bodies converted into bicameral bodies. The Georgia legislature became bicameral when the state adopted its second constitution in 1789. By and large, the change was motivated by a desire to bring the state into harmony with the bicameral design in the new federal Constitution (Johnson 1938, 32–33). Pennsylvania moved to a two-house system in its 1790 constitution because of considerable unhappiness with the performance of its unicameral legislature (Johnson 1938, 33–37; Main 1967, 210–11; Watts 1936). Support for the unicameral legislature in Vermont, however, continued well into the nineteenth century. Indeed, the unicameral system was maintained in both the state's 1786 and 1793 constitutions (Moran 1895, 54). A bicameral legislature was not adopted until 1836, a change driven in large part by public unhappiness with the unicameral legislature's handling of a disputed gubernatorial election (Moschos and Katsky 1965, 262–63; Johnson 1938, 38–39). Vermont was the last unicameral holdout; during the numerous constitutional conventions in the states in the first half of the nineteenth century there was virtually no support for unicameralism. Bicameralism was strongly supported because it was thought a second house prevented, or at least slowed down, the passage of legislation pressured by the political passions of the moment (Scalia 1999, 107).

Examination of the reasons for and consequences of the switch from one system to the other has been done using case studies of national legislatures that have undergone such a change (Longley and Olson 1991). Almost no work has been done using state legislatures, missing a rich source of data on the most fundamental question of institutional design.[9] Recently, however, Rogers (2003) has examined bill production before and after the shift in cameralism in the American states that have undergone such a change and found that, contrary to theoretical predictions, the switch to bicameralism does not reduce the production of legislation.

Finally, it is worth noting that the American legislative experience raises the possibility that unicameral and bicameral legislatures are not necessarily discrete categories. In Alaska, for example, although delegates to the state constitutional convention backed away from creating a one-house legislature, they incorporated some unicameral features into their bicameral system. Thus, the Alaska constitution requires the two chambers to meet and vote in joint session to consider gubernatorial appointments and gubernatorial veto overrides (McBeath and Morehouse 1994, 121). And three state legislatures—Connecticut, Maine, and Massachusetts—rely almost exclusively on joint committees, a mechanism inducing joint decision making. In practice, joint committees greatly reduce the need for conference committees to reconcile legislative differences between the two chambers (Zeller 1954, 260). With joint sessions and joint committees, the distinction between separate chambers is to some extent blurred.[10]

Membership Size

The importance of membership size as an explanatory variable in legislative studies is often taken for granted, and therefore little explored. Congressional scholars frequently cite the differences in membership size between the U.S. House and Senate to explain differences in their rules and procedures.[11] Davidson and Oleszek (2002, 28), for example, observe:

Size profoundly affects an organization's work. Growth compelled the House to develop strong leaders, to rely heavily on its committees, to impose strict limits on floor debate, and to devise elaborate ways of channeling the flow of floor business.

Baker (2001, 72) advances a similar perspective in comparing the two houses of Congress: "Senate rules differ from House rules largely because the Senate is a quarter the size of the House."

The focus on the difference in size between the two houses of Congress is intuitively plausible. But looking at membership size from a comparative perspective raises some doubts about its power to account for differences between the U.S. House and Senate rules. First, is the important difference in Congress the original difference between a Senate of 26 members and a House of 65 members, or the current difference between 100 senators and 435 representatives? It would appear that the initial difference in size did not matter organizationally or procedurally, because the first sets of rules adopted by the two houses were very similar (Binder and Smith 1998, 403). Differences between the two chambers in rules and procedures only appeared over time. Woodrow Wilson (1908, 88) suggests that the House changed its procedures dramatically over the years as it added more seats:

> Perhaps the contrast between [the House and Senate] is in certain respects even sharper and clearer now than in the earlier days of our history, when the House was smaller and its functions simpler. The House once debated; now it does not debate. It has not the time. There would be too many debaters, and there are too many subjects of debate. It is a business body, and it must get its business done.

But if the House tightened rules and procedures as it grew, why did the Senate fail to change in similar ways as it almost quadrupled in size?

Second, it is important to fully understand the consequences of legislative membership size because although we talk about the Senate as being a small body, it is only small in comparison with the U.S. House. Looking at state legislatures gives us a very different way to think about membership size.[12] Currently, state legislative chambers range from very small (20 members in the Alaska state Senate) to very large (400 members in the New Hampshire House of Representatives, down from 443 as recently as 1942).[13] None of the 50 state senates is as large as the U.S. Senate—the largest is Minnesota with 67 members. Indeed, only 22 of the *lower* houses in the states are larger than the U.S. Senate. Thus, if size alone matters in explaining the evolution of legislature rules and procedures, then most state legislatures ought to operate like the U.S. Senate, and only a handful ought to be regimented like the U.S. House. In fact, more state legislative chambers organize and proceed like the U.S. House than like the U.S. Senate, regardless of size.

Legislative membership sizes are not static. They change over time.[14] The U.S. House and Senate regularly grew in size during the nineteenth century. Their numbers of members, however, have changed very little since 1913. The House has stayed at 435 members except for a brief increase to 437 when Alaska and Hawaii were first admitted to the union in 1959.[15] The admission of those two states permanently increased the size of the Senate from 96 members to 100 members.

The over-time change in the size of state legislatures has, in many cases, been much more dramatic than that experienced by Congress. The lower house in Massachusetts in the early nineteenth century, for example (Luce 1924, 89; see also Banner 1969, 280–81, 362–63), "varied in size according as the towns cared or not to bear the cost of representation, in exciting times running up to six or seven hundred members, but often getting down to between two and three hundred, occasionally even below two hundred."[16] The speaker of the Massachusetts House in 1820, when the chamber membership was its largest, commented (quoted in Luce 1924, 89), "I am sorry to say it, but such is my opinion, that in no proper sense could it be considered a deliberative body. From the excess of numbers deliberation became about impossible."[17] The problem of a greatly fluctuating membership was not resolved until 1857 when the membership size of the Massachusetts House was set at 240 (Luce 1924, 90), a figure the chamber kept for the next 122 years.[18]

The membership size of many legislatures is still in flux. While the number of members of both the U.S. House and Senate stayed stable from 1960 to 2000 (except in the House for the brief period after Alaska and Hawaii were admitted to the union), as table 2–2 shows, 34 states changed the size of at least one of their legislative chambers. Some, but not all, of these changes were triggered by the Supreme Court's 1964 decision, *Reynolds v. Sims,* which forced many state legislatures to alter the way they apportioned one or both houses. But others were done to make the legislature more efficient or more representative. Over these four decades, only one state senate was cut in size (Idaho), while 20 others increased their number of seats. Just over half of the lower houses that changed in size, however, suffered a reduction. The cuts in several lower houses were dramatic. In 1979, for example, the number of seats in the Massachusetts House of Representatives was reduced to 160 from 240, and in 1983, the Illinois House of Representatives experienced a one-third cut in the number of seats, to 118 from 177. Changes in membership size continue to occur. The Rhode Island legislature downsized both chambers of its legislature by 25 percent in 2003 as mandated by the voters several years earlier.[19] A handful of states (Nevada, North Dakota, and Wyoming) often change the number of members in their legislatures following each Census. North Dakota, for example, downsized both chambers of its legislature in 2003 as a result of its redistricting process, going to 47 senate districts and 94 house districts from 49 senate districts and 98 house districts the decade before.[20] Redistricting also prompted New York to add a seat to its upper

FUNDAMENTAL STRUCTURES

TABLE 2-2 Change in Membership Size by State and Legislative Chamber, 1960 and 2000[a]

State	Senate 1960	Senate 2000	House 1960	House 2000
AL			*106*[b]	*105*
AZ	28	30	*80*	*60*
CT			*279*	*151*
DE	17	21	35	41
FL	38	40	95	120
GA	54	56	*205*	*180*
ID	*44*	*35*	59	70
IL	58	59	*177*	*118*
LA			101	105
ME	33	35		
MD	29	47	124	141
MA			*240*	*180*
MI	34	38		
MN			131	134
MS	49	52	*140*	*122*
MO			157	163
MT	56	60	94	100
NE	43	49		
NV	17	21	*47*	*42*
NJ	21	40	60	80
NM	32	42	66	70
NY	58	61		
ND			*113*	*98*
OH			*139*	*99*
OK	44	48	*121*	*101*
PA			*210*	*203*
RI	44	50		
SD			*75*	*70*
UT	25	29	64	75
VT			*246*	*150*
WA			*99*	*98*
WV	32	34		
WI			*100*	*99*
WY	27	30	56	60

Sources: *The Book of the States 1960–61*, page 37, and *The Book of the States 2000–2001*, page 70.
[a] The following states did not change in size between 1960 and 2000: AK, AR, CA, CO, HI, IN, IA, KS, KY, NH, NC, OR, SC, TN, TX, and VA.
[b] Italics indicate a reduction in the size of a chamber's membership.

TABLE 2-3 Membership Size and State Population Correlations, 1960 to 2000

	Number of Members of Upper Chamber	Number of Members of Lower Chambers	Total Number of State Legislators
All States (N = 50)	0.239	0.131	0.168
States with No Change in Size, 1960 to 2000 (N = 16)	0.164	-0.074	-0.056
States That Changed in Size, 1960 to 2000 (N = 34)	0.383*	0.440**	0.478**

*$p < 0.05$, two-tailed test; **$p < 0.01$, two-tailed test.

house in 2003, bringing the total number to 62.[21]

Generally speaking, there is no relationship between state population and legislative membership size. This has always been the case, as Madison (Madison, Hamilton, and Jay 1961, 341–42) observed at some length in the *Federalist 55*. Correlations between state population and legislative chamber membership size in 2000 are given in table 2–3. Among all state legislative chambers, there are small positive correlations between chamber membership sizes and state population, but the relationships are not statistically significant. Perhaps the most interesting finding is that the relationship between upper house size and state population is stronger than that for the lower house—usually deemed the more representative chamber—and state population. But we find some evidence that among the 34 states that changed the size of at least one of their legislative chambers from 1960 to 2000 there is a strong positive correlation between chamber size and state population. No such relationship obtains among the 16 states that failed to change their number of state legislators.

Why focus on membership size? Size raises a number of different issues. One simple problem driven by membership size is how to accommodate members in the legislative chamber. Here, of course, large chambers face different problems than do small chambers. And, of course, how seating is arranged is a matter of considerable interest because it can influence how members interact and how the legislative process flows (Wheare 1963, 7–19). Maintaining decorum is also more of a problem in larger chambers than in smaller ones. In 1842, for example, disorder in the 233 member U.S. House helped prompt a vote to decrease the number of seats, because, as one representative observed, having too many members created (Shields 1985, 373), "mob government, by confusion, crowing like cocks, braying like asses, shuffling with feet, coughing, and other similar expedients now pursued in the House of Commons."[22]

Perhaps even more important, as suggested in regard to the differences between the U.S. House and Senate, it seems reasonable to hypothesize that size influences organizational structures and rules. Francis (1985, 249), for example, in a study of decision making in 99 state legislative chambers, found that party caucuses are more important in smaller chambers while in larger chambers party leaders are more important. More generally, Rosenthal (1981, 132–34; see also Davidson and Oleszek 2002, 28; and Jewell and Patterson 1986, 85–86) observed:

> Size has its effects on the following: the atmosphere, with more confusion and impersonality in larger bodies and friendlier relationships in smaller ones; hierarchy, with more elaborate and orderly rules and procedures and greater leadership authority in larger bodies and informality and collegial authority in smaller ones; the conduct of business, with a more efficient flow and less debate in larger bodies and more leisurely deliberation and greater fluidity in smaller ones; the internal distribution of power, with more concentrated pockets possible in larger bodies and greater dispersion of power in smaller ones.

Thus, we would expect that as legislatures add and subtract seats organizational structures and rules and member behavior would be affected. Drawing on the congressional literature we might, for example, expect power to become more centralized as a legislature increases in size, and more decentralized as a legislature decreases in size. Or, we might anticipate that shirking is more apt to occur in larger chambers than in smaller chambers because of higher monitoring costs (Parker 1992, 75–76). Larger chambers may also experience greater problems with free riders as more legislators pursue constituency services and the like, leaving the legislative work to a few colleagues (Crain and Tollison 1982; Rogers 2002). And it may be that effective representation hinges on the size of the legislature, with smaller legislatures actually being more representative than larger ones (Stigler 1976). There also appears to be a link between size and fiscal policy; larger upper houses have been found to spend more money than smaller upper houses (Gilligan and Matsusaka 1995; 2001). The problem is, however, that without examining such questions across a number of chambers over time we cannot be sure what the effects of membership increases or decreases, or large or small chambers, might be. Much more systematic work on the importance of membership size needs to be conducted.

Membership Qualifications

Who is allowed to serve in a legislature is a fundamental question of institutional design. As noted in chapter 1, membership qualifications for legislative office were part of the colonial experience and were incorporated into both the original state and federal constitutions. At the national level, the three constitutional qualifications for service in Congress—age, state inhabitancy, and years of citizenship—have remained unchanged.[23] Qualifications for office at the state legislative level have changed over time, but only a little.

Perhaps the most obvious qualification to impose is a minimum age for service, something found in all legislatures around the world (Loewenberg and Patterson 1979, 79). As noted in chapter 1, colonial assemblies and the original state legislatures set age requirements—sometimes explicitly, sometimes implicitly—requiring members to be at least 21 years old. Several of the original state senates were to be populated with more mature members through the establishment of older age minimums. The federal Constitution followed that general pattern, although members of the House with a minimum age of 25 years were to be a bit older than their state counterparts, and senators were required to be older still at a minimum of 30 years old.

Age qualifications in the states have changed only infrequently over time. Delaware, for example, set the minimum age for membership in its lower house at 24 (a number chosen for unknown reasons) in 1792 and has not changed it since. Kentucky and Missouri also adopted a 24-year-old age minimum when they became states, and they too have kept it (Luce 1924, 209–10). A few states, such as Illinois, South Carolina, and Virginia, experimented with different ages during the nineteenth century (Luce 1924, 210). The period of greatest change in age requirements, however, occurred during the 1970s, as the minimum age for service was lowered to 18 years old in a number of states in response to the Twenty-sixth Amendment giving people that age the right to vote in federal elections. Overall, however, age requirements have been reasonably stable across the states and over time.

Current age qualifications for American legislatures are given in table 2–4. In lower houses, minimum age requirements range from 18 years old in 13 states, to 25 years old in three states as well as in the U.S. House. The range in upper houses is even greater, from 18 years old in 13 states, to 30 years old in the U.S. Senate and five state senates. The age requirement is the same for both chambers in 27 states. In the other 22 bicameral states and the U.S. Congress, different age qualifications are imposed on the two houses, but always with the older qualification being put on the upper house. The greatest gap in age minimums is in New Hampshire, where a member of the lower house may be only 18 years old, but an upper house member is required to be at least 30 years old. No state mimics the exact age requirements for the U.S. Congress in both houses.

The courts have upheld challenges to minimum age qualifications. In a 1990 case, a federal appeals court held that Missouri's minimum age of 24 years for service in the lower house was constitutional because it, "serves Missouri's interest in insuring that its legislators have some degree of maturity and life experience

FUNDAMENTAL STRUCTURES

TABLE 2-4 Age Qualifications for Election to American Legislative Office, 2003

		Minimum Age in Lower House			
		18 years	21 years	24 years	25 years
Minimum Age in Upper House	18 years	CA, HI, KS, LA, MA, MT, NY, ND, OH, RI, VT, WA, WI			
	21 years		CT, FL, ID, IL, MI, MN, NE, NV, OR, SD, VA		
	25 years	WV	AL, AK, AR, GA, IN, IA, ME, MD, MS, NC[a], NM, OK, PA, SC, WY		AZ, CO, UT
	26 years		TX		
	27 years			DE	
	30 years	NH	NJ, TN	KY, MO	**U.S.**

Source: *The Book of the States, 2003 Edition,* pages 118–19.
[a]The minimum age in North Carolina is unclear because of a conflict between two clauses of the state constitution, one which suggests age 18, the other specifying age 21.

before taking office."[24] Missouri college students, who regularly lobby to have the minimum age of service lowered, counter that because younger adults are not allowed to serve, the legislature tends to ignore their interests (*Jefferson City News Tribune* 2002). Voters, however, may not agree with the students' position. In 2002, Oregon voters were asked to amend the state constitution to lower the minimum age to serve in the legislature to 18 from 21. The amendment was placed on the ballot by overwhelming votes in both houses of the state legislature after the Oregon secretary of state was asked by a Portland Community College student why 18 year olds could run for offices such as secretary of state and attorney general, but not for the legislature. Unexpected organized opposition to the measure surfaced in the form of fundamentalist Christian groups that interpreted the Bible as holding that ruling positions should be held only by those age 30 or older. In the end, the constitutional amendment to lower the minimum age for legislative service failed, getting only 27 percent of the vote.[25]

Legislative chambers that allow younger people to serve do occasionally have younger people elected to them. In 2000, for example, an 18-year-old high school senior won election to the Ohio House of Representatives. Where nontrivial numbers of younger people serve, they can influence the legislative agenda. In Maine a sufficient number of young legislators sat in the lower house in the late 1990s

TABLE 2–5a Residency Requirements for Election to American Lower Houses, 2003

State Residency Requirement	District Residency Requirement	Lower House
	Resident	CT, KS, MI, NM, SC, WA
	1 year	CO, MA, OR
Resident	None	**U.S.**
Resident	6 months	OK
Resident	1 year	ID, NC, OH, WY
Resident	2 years	IL
30 days		RI
1 year	Resident	ND, VA, WI
1 year	30 days	NV
1 year	60 days	IA
1 year	3 months	ME
1 year	6 months	MD, MN, MT
2 years	Resident	FL, NH, SD,
2 years	1 year	AR, GA, IN, KY, LA, MO, NJ, TX, VT
3 years	Resident	HI
3 years	6 months	UT
3 years	1 year	AL, AK, AZ, CA, DE, TN
4 years	1 year	PA
4 years	2 years	MS
5 years	1 year	NY, WV

Source: Adapted from data in *The Book of the States, 2003 Edition*, pages 118–19.

TABLE 2–5b Residency Requirements for Election to American Upper Houses, 2003

State Residency Requirement	District Residency Requirement	Upper House
	Resident	CT, KS, MI, NM, SC, WA
	1 year	CO, OR
Resident	NA	**U.S.**
Resident	6 months	OK
Resident	1 year	ID, NE, OH, WY
Resident	2 years	IL
30 days		RI
1 year	Resident	ND, VA, WI
1 year	30 days	NV
1 year	60 days	IA
1 year	3 months	ME
1 year	6 months	MD, MN, MT
2 years	Resident	FL, SD,
2 years	1 year	AR, GA, IN, LA, *NC*, VT
3 years	Resident	HI
3 years	6 months	UT
3 years	1 year	AL, AK, AZ, CA, DE, *MO*, TN
4 years	1 year	*NJ*, PA
4 years	2 years	MS
5 years	Resident	*MA*
5 years	1 year	NY, WV, *TX*
6 years	1 year	*KY*
7 years	Resident	*NH*

Source: Adapted from data in *The Book of the States, 2003 Edition*, pages 118–19.
Note: States in italics have different requirements for the upper house than for the lower house.

to form what its members called the Kids Caucus. Caucus members pursued favored policies on campaign finance reform, higher education, and women's issues among other issues, and played an active role in House decision making (Teicher 1999).

In addition to age minimums, state constitutions also impose state and district residency requirements for legislative service. The federal Constitution is relatively relaxed on this score; members of the House and Senate are only required to be inhabitants of the state from which they are elected. (It is only by tradition that representatives are expected to reside in the district they represent.) Moreover, residency standards for federal office are remarkably loose; one only has to live in a state at the time of the election to qualify. In contrast, state residency requirements are much stricter.

A comparison of the residency requirements incorporated in the original state constitutions (tables 1–4 and 1–5) with the current requirements presented in tables 2–5a and 2–5b reveals some changes over time. Every state now has some residency standards in place. To serve in six state lower houses, a candidate need only be a resident of the district at the time of the election. Most states, however, use more stringent standards, requiring district residency anywhere from 30 days in Nevada, to two years in Illinois and Mississippi. And state residency of anywhere from a single year to five years is required in addition to district residency in over half the states.

Residency standards are even higher for service in several state senates. Every state requires residency in the senate district, although the time needed to establish that fact varies from a loose day-of-the-election standard to, again, two years in Illinois and Mississippi. State residency requirements also are stringent. At the most extreme, the state residency standard to qualify for service in the New Hampshire state Senate is seven years.

Why worry about residency qualifications? There are, of course, questions raised from time to time about whether a candidate or member has met the residency requirements in his or her state.[26] But residency standards raise more interesting questions than simply whether they are met in a specific case. Parliamentary systems generally do not require residency in an electoral unit as a condition to represent it.[27] By mandating residency, the American system places great value on local ties and knowledge of district residents and their opinions and interests. Not surprisingly, most state legislative candidates are long-time district residents when they run for office (Moncrief, Squire, and Jewell 2001, 35). But residency qualifications limit the pool of potential candidates, perhaps leaving some districts with too few capable candidates and other districts with too many. And, it can be argued that they force legislators to become too parochial in their activities and voting behavior as they cater to their constituents (Luce 1924, 225–28). Comparative study of legislatures with and without residency requirements, or between those with weak requirements and those with stringent ones, may help us understand the real positive and negative consequences of such qualification standards.

Prominent among the qualifications imposed by the original state constitutions were ones for property and wealth. A majority of the original states imposed such requisites for legislative service, in keeping with colonial practices. Wealth and property qualifications for membership in the U.S. Congress were rejected during the Constitutional Convention, although they engendered considerable debate. Support for exclusive qualifications at the state level dissipated following the federal Constitutional Convention. Vermont entered the union with no such membership requirements, as did Kentucky, Alabama, and Maine. Notions about Jacksonian democracy struck a fatal blow to what were seen as elitist membership standards, and most of the states that had property and wealth standards abolished them before the Civil War. Newer states never adopted them. But Rhode Island held on to its wealth and property qualifications until 1888, and Missouri required legislators to have paid county and state taxes well into the twentieth century (Luce 1924, 233–34).

One kind of qualification was added to state constitutions over time. Originally, disqualification for criminal misconduct was indirectly imposed in many states through the requirement for elected officials to be qualified voters. But during the nineteenth century, most states made criminal disqualification explicit in their constitutions and laws. Some disqualifications were broad and covered many offenses; others were more specific, often targeting bribery and dueling (Luce 1924, 258–65). The key distinction regarding disqualification for criminal misconduct today revolves around the question of permanent disqualification. A majority of states permanently bar a person convicted of a felony from ever holding office. A handful of states bar ex-felons only while they are still on parole. Fewer than ten states allow ex-felons to run for office once they are discharged from the prison system (Snyder 1988).

Historically, other qualifications were imposed for state legislative service but later abolished. As discussed in chapter 1, for example, ministers were kept from serving as legislators in many states. And military contractors and others who had business dealings with the state were prohibited from legislative service in most states, although these provisions were generally removed over the course of the nineteenth century. Other occupations were also excluded. Until 1865, Florida barred any bank officer from legislative service. Virginia did likewise from 1850 to 1870, but only for membership in its lower house. Railroad executives were prohibited from serving in the West Virginia legislature from 1872 until well into the twentieth century. And Harvard's faculty and president could not be members of the Massachusetts state legislature until 1877, because of the university's relationship with the state (Luce 1924, 253–54).

Constituency Size

Assuming single-member districts, the number of constituents in a district depends, of course, on the number of districts and a state's population. Because both the number of legislative seats and the number of people living in a state change over time, constituency sizes change as well. In the U.S. House, the Constitution (Article 1, section 2) recommended districts of 30,000 people. That number was arrived at, in part, because George Washington, in his only substantive contribution to the Constitutional Convention, argued in favor of a motion to change the number to 30,000 from 40,000 because he thought the lower figure would generate more popular support for the proposed Constitution (Keller 1993, 23). The first ratio employed was actually 33,000 constituents per representative, a figure that climbed to 47,700 constituents per representative in 1830, and 77,680 constituents per representative in 1840. After that point in time, the number of seats was set in advance of reapportionment, with the number capped at 435 in 1911 (Butler and Cain 1992, 18–19). By 2003, the average district size in the House was approximately 663,000 people. U.S. senators, of course, represent different size constituencies, ranging from fewer than 500,000 people in Wyoming, to 35,000,000 people in California. District populations for all American upper and lower houses in 2003 are given in tables 2–6a and 2–6b.

State legislative district sizes have changed over time as both populations and the size of legislatures have fluctuated. Since the Supreme Court decision in *Reynolds v. Sims* in 1964, all state legislative houses must be apportioned on the basis of population.[28] The range of constituency sizes at the state legislative level is remarkable, both longitudinally and cross-sectionally. Following the 2000 redistricting process, the 40 California state senators represent almost 878,000 people, over 200,000 more constituents than U.S. representatives, and even more constituents than U.S. senators from Alaska, Delaware, North Dakota, South Dakota, Vermont, and Wyoming represent. Members of the Texas state Senate, with 703,000 constituents, also have districts larger than U.S. House districts. At the other extreme, the 400 New Hampshire representatives have districts with just over 3,000 people in them.[29] Overall, state legislative districts in six chambers have fewer than 10,000 people, while ten chambers have districts with more than 200,000 constituents.

The effect of constituency size on legislative behavior is a relatively unexplored area. Research comparing the electoral and representational effects of constituency size has been conducted using the U.S. Senate (e.g., Hibbing and Brandes 1983; Hibbing and Alford 1990; Krasno 1994, 39–58). Little attention, however, appears to have been given to the variable in studies of the U.S. House. We do not know, for example, how, if at all, member behavior has changed as the number of people represented in a district climbed from 30,000 to 663,000. We

TABLE 2-6a Constituency Size by American Lower House Chamber, 2003

State	Lower House Seats	District Population	State	Lower House Seats	District Population
NH	400	3,188	MA	160	40,174
VT	150	4,111	KY	100	40,929
ND	94	6,746	LA	105	42,692
WY	60	8,312	AL	105	42,729
ME	151	8,573	GA	180	47,557
MT	100	9,095	NV	42	51,750
SD	70	10,872	WI	99	54,962
RI	75	14,263	TN	99	58,558
AK	40	16,095	OR	60	58,692
WV	100	18,019	PA	203	60,764
ID	70	19,159	IN	100	61,591
DE	41	19,692	WA	98	61,929
KS	125	21,727	CO	65	69,331
CT	151	22,917	NC	120	69,335
MS	122	23,539	VA	100	72,935
HI	51	24,410	AZ	60	90,941
NM	70	26,501	MI	110	91,368
AR	100	27,101	IL	118	106,785
IA	100	29,368	NJ	80	107,379
UT	75	30,883	OH	99	115,366
SC	124	33,122	NY	150	127,717
OK	101	34,591	FL	120	139,276
MO	163	34,801	TX	150	145,199
MN	134	37,461	CA	80	438,950
MD	141	38,710	**U.S. House**	**435**	**662,917**

Source: Calculated by authors using U.S. Census Bureau data for 2002.

FUNDAMENTAL STRUCTURES

TABLE 2-6b Constituency Size by American Upper House Chamber, 2003

State	Upper House Seats	District Population	State	Upper House Seats	District Population
ND	47	13,492	MD	47	116,131
WY	30	16,623	OR	30	117,384
MT	50	18,189	IN	50	123,181
VT	30	20,553	WA	49	123,857
SD	35	21,745	AL	35	128,186
RI	38	28,151	CO	35	128,758
AK	20	32,189	GA	56	152,863
NE	49	35,289	MA	40	160,695
ME	35	36,985	WI	33	164,885
ID	35	38,318	NC	50	166,403
DE	21	38,447	MO	34	166,841
NM	42	44,168	TN	33	175,675
HI	25	49,796	AZ	30	181,882
WV	34	52,996	VA	40	182,339
NH	24	53,127	IL	59	213,570
MS	52	55,227	NJ	40	214,758
IA	50	58,735	PA	50	246,702
KS	40	67,897	MI	38	264,485
OK	48	72,786	NY	62	308,992
MN	67	74,921	OH	33	346,099
AR	35	77,431	FL	40	417,829
UT	29	79,871	TX	31	702,577
SC	46	89,287	CA	40	877,901
CT	36	96,125			Entire State—
NV	21	103,500	U.S. Senate	100	498,703 to 35,116,033
KY	38	107,708			
LA	39	114,940			

Source: Calculated by authors using U.S. Census Bureau data for 2002.

can observe that members became more electorally secure as the number of people they represented increased, but the mechanism to explain that process has yet to be identified. Moreover, as the number of people (and, we would assume, number of organizations and differing interests) in a district increases, more demands are made on a legislator. How do they cope? Little light is shed on these questions by the state legislative literature, beyond learning that constituent contacts with legislators decline with increased district size (Squire 1993, 485). Such questions can be addressed both cross-sectionally and longitudinally by looking at the U.S. Senate and state legislatures. The U.S. House can, of course, only be used for over-time studies on these sorts of questions.

Currently, most American legislators are elected from single-member districts. This has not always been the case. Earlier in American history the multi-member district was the norm. Reliance on multi-member districts was imported into the colonies from England. The original development of multi-member districts was a response to the practical realities of medieval English political life. According to Klain (1955, 1111–12), "In the thirteenth century roads to London were lonely, rough, and bandit-ridden—two or three men would afford each other company and protection. Besides, once the men were safe in London the arrangement might best serve constituents—the men could watch and check each other." When the Virginia House of Burgesses was founded in 1619, it followed the districting practices of the mother parliament, and accordingly a call was issued for two burgesses to be sent from each plantation. During the colonial period most assemblies used multi-member districts, some of which were particularly large. In New Jersey, for example, both Burlington and Gloucester counties elected 20 at-large assemblymen (Klain 1955, 1112).

Multi-member districts and at-large districts were used in the past to elect members of the U.S. House, even as recently as the 1960s (Calabrese 2000). Indeed, they were prominent electoral configurations during much of the nineteenth century. At the state level the use of multi-member districts was even more pronounced, particularly in lower houses. In the 1950s, for example, 39 of the 48 states used multi-member districts to elect at least some members of their state legislatures (Klain 1955, 1106–7). In the 1990s multi-member districts were still employed, at least for some seats, in four state senates and eleven state lower houses (Jewell and Morehouse 2001, 219). In the current decade, multi-member districts are found in two state senates and eleven state lower houses. As shown in Table 2–7, at least 90 percent of all legislators are elected from multi-member districts in nine of these thirteen chambers, while the figure is greater than 50 percent in another three chambers. All told, roughly 22 percent and 3 percent of all legislators serving in the lower houses and senates respectively are currently elected from multi-member districts.

Beyond the obvious questions about the electoral ramifications of multi-member districts as opposed to single-member districts, the representational and

FUNDAMENTAL STRUCTURES

TABLE 2–7 States Using Multi-Member Legislative Districts in the 2001–2003 Elections

State	Chamber	Percentage of Members Elected from Multi-Member Districts	Number of Multi-Member Districts	Number of Members Elected per District (Range)	Type of Multi-Member District System
Arizona	Lower House	100.0%	30	2	Plurality[a]
Georgia[b]	Lower House	31.1%	33	2–4	Post or Place[c]
Idaho	Lower House	100.0%	35	2	Post or Place
Maryland	Lower House	85.1%	44	2–3	Plurality
New Hampshire	Lower House	98.5%	82	2–14	Plurality
New Jersey	Lower House	100.0%	40	2	Plurality
North Dakota	Lower House	100.0%	47	2	Plurality
South Dakota	Lower House	100.0%	35	2	Plurality
Vermont	Lower House	55.6%	42	84	Plurality
Vermont	Upper House	90.0%	10	2–6	Plurality
Washington	Lower House	100.0%	49	2	Post or Place
West Virginia	Lower House	64.0%	22	2–7	Plurality
West Virginia[d]	Upper House	100.0%	17	2	Plurality

[a] For example, if voters may vote for 5 candidates, then the top 5 vote getters are declared the winners.
[b] A federal court declared Georgia's legislative redistricting plan unconstitutional in February 2004. A new plan must be adopted for the 2004 elections.
[c] Voters cast more than 1 vote but only 1 for each place, position, or post on the ballot.
[d] In the West Virginia Senate there are 2 members in each of the 17 districts. Terms are staggered, so only 1 member is elected from each district in each election.

behavioral effects of at-large districts and multi-member districts versus single-member districts demand investigation (Hamilton 1967).[30] Institutional effects also need to be explored. Adams (1996), for example, found that political parties in the Illinois House were ideologically more diverse when the chamber was elected using multi-member districts than they were when single-member district elections were employed.

CHAPTER 2

Geographic Size

Another aspect of district size gets remarkably little scholarly attention: the geographic size of the district. Upon reflection, we might anticipate that the act of representing a large district differs from the act of representing a small district. And it is important to understand that legislative districts vary enormously in terms of space. New York Assembly districts in Manhattan, for example, are measured in city blocks. Compare that with the most extreme case in the other direction: Alaska's state Senate District C. That district covers the sparsely populated rural areas of the state and encompasses more than 240,000 square miles, making it almost the same size as Texas. Representing District C is demanding. To visit constituents the state senator has to travel by car, airplane, and ferry, and with bad weather, trips to some communities may take days and even weeks. A few years ago, the incumbent senator tried to visit every town in District C, but after having been gone from home for three months, she had managed to get to only about 75 percent of them. And as the senator observes, once she makes the trek to one of the far-flung communities in her district (McAllister 2002), "They don't expect you to go in and spend 15 minutes and you're out of there. That's rather insulting. They expect you to spend the night."

Alaska's District C may be the most extreme case, but every state in the western part of the country has very large legislative districts representing rural populations. Legislators in such districts realize the problems they face trying to represent the interests of people strewn across vast distances. A Wyoming representative with a huge district, for example, lamented (*Caspar Star Tribune* 2001), "After my first 300-plus mile campaign trip to Jeffrey City, I wondered how someone like me from Rock Springs could fairly represent those ranchers up there. And the answer then was and still is . . . I can't fairly represent those people in Fremont County." Legislators representing districts in more densely populated eastern states have very different experiences. A member in the Rhode Island House, for example, commented to her colleagues (State of Rhode Island and Providence Plantations, 2000), "I learn by listening and I listen to my voters over the fence, at the swimming pool . . . My office is a shopping cart on Sunday afternoon at Stop & Shop." It is hard to imagine many of her colleagues from large districts in the West being able to make the same claims. Although the physical size of representational units has gotten some passing attention in studies of the U.S. Senate (e.g., Krasno 1994), it seems plausible to expect that geography mediates the relationship between the representative and represented in ways that have yet to be explored.[31]

Terms of Office

Term length is thought to influence member behavior, with longer terms allowing legislators greater freedom from electoral pressures, shorter terms allowing less freedom. As Davidson and Oleszek note (2002, 378) in regard to the U.S. Senate, "Six-year terms, it is argued, allow senators to play statesman for at least part of each term before they are forced by oncoming elections to concentrate on fence mending." The implicit contrast here is, of course, between the two-year House term, and the six-year term for senators, lengths unchanged since 1789.

The experience at the state legislative level is far different. Terms for state legislators have changed over time. As noted in chapter 1, all but one of the original state constitutions gave lower house members a single-year term. Terms in upper houses were more variable; the modal term was a single year, but the terms in the other states ranged from two years to five years. As new states were created and existing states replaced old constitutions with new ones, different patterns emerged. When Tocqueville (1969, 85) observed state legislatures in the 1830s he noted, "senators have a longer term of office than the representatives. The latter seldom remain in office for more than one year, but the former usually for two or three."

In general, over the course of the nineteenth century state legislative terms were lengthened (Luce 1924, 113). In Pennsylvania, for example, members of the House of Representatives were elected to one-year terms until the 1874 constitution, when two-year terms were adopted. In that same constitution state senators were bumped up to four-year terms from three-year terms (Kennedy 1999, 2–3). In most states, lower house terms were extended from one year to two years.[32] Typically, upper house terms were extended as well, although the number of years adopted often bounced around. Maryland, for example, started with five-year terms in 1776, changed to six-year terms in 1837, and then settled on four-year terms in 1851 (Luce 1924, 119). A six-year term was also provided to state senators in Texas in 1868, but the term was switched back to the more typical four-year term in 1876 (Luce 1924, 120). Georgia kept changing the term of office for its upper house (Luce 1924, 119):

> Her first senators, provided for in 1789, were to be elected every third year. Annual election was substituted in 1795; this was changed to biennial in 1840 with the adoption of the biennial system; in 1868 the four-year term was substituted; and in 1877 return was made to the two-year term.

New York and Nevada also reduced the term of office for their state senators (Luce 1924, 119–124). By the beginning of the twentieth century, Bryce (1906, 332) noted, "In twenty-nine States [a state senator] sits for four years, in one (New Jersey) for three, in thirteen for two, in two (Massachusetts and Rhode Island) for one year only; the usual term of a representative being two years."

Terms continued to change over the twentieth century, as the current terms of office given in table 2–8 reveal. Although one- and three-year terms no longer

TABLE 2-8 American Legislative Terms, 2003

Legislature	Lower House Term	Senate Term
AZ, CT, GA, ID, ME, MA, NH, NY, NC, RI, SD, VT	2 years	2 years
NJ	2 years	2 years—4 years—4 years
IL	2 years	Three classes: 4 years—4 years—2 years 4 years—2 years—4 years 2 years—4 years—4 years
AK, AR, CA, CO, DE, FL, HI, IN, IA, KS, KY, MI, MN, MO, MT, NV, NM, OH, OK, OR, PA, SC, TN, TX, UT, VA, WA, WV, WI, WY	2 years	4 years[a]
NE		4 years[a]
U.S.	2 years	6 years
AL, LA, MD, MS, ND,	4 years[a]	4 years[a]

Source: *The Book of the States, 2003 Edition*, pages 115–16; and information from the National Conference of State Legislatures.
[a]Many, but not all, states with staggered 4-year terms employ rules to force some legislators to serve a 2-year term at some point during the decade, typically during the first election cycle following redistricting.

exist, there is still substantial variation in terms across the states. None of the terms in the states, however, emulate those in the U.S. Congress. Terms in 30 states come close, with two-year terms in the lower house, and four-year terms in the state senate. But in 12 states members of both houses are given two-year terms, and in five states both chambers get four-year terms.[33] In Illinois and New Jersey, state senators have shifting terms, with one two-year term and two four-year terms to accommodate redistricting every ten years.

Among the states with staggered four-year terms—only ten states do not stagger terms in their upper houses—there is considerable variation in how they cope with the required ten-year redistricting cycle. In one way or another, the states have to either re-stagger their terms or devise a way to assign legislators to districts that wind up with no resident representation following redistricting. In Montana, the state constitution prohibits two-year terms for senators, so following redistricting the 25 holdover senators—those in the middle of their four-year terms—are assigned to districts by the state's redistricting commission. Similarly, in Pennsylvania holdover senators continue to represent the same numbered district even if their residence is no longer in the district once the lines are changed. Delaware employs a system reminiscent of those used in Illinois and New Jersey: half the senate starts with a two-year term followed by two four-year terms, and half are given two four-year terms followed by a two-year term. Many states use district numbers to determine which districts are to be contested in the

FUNDAMENTAL STRUCTURES

first election following redistricting. In Iowa, for example, senators from even-numbered districts run in the first post-redistricting election and senators from odd-numbered districts in the second post-redistricting election. But odd-numbered districts will be contested in the first post-redistricting election if there is no incumbent elected for a term expiring after the second post-redistricting election residing in the district. Hawaii takes a senator's previous experience into account. A senator whose four-year term was reduced to a two-year term in the previous decade's redistricting is automatically assigned a four-year term following the current redistricting. Other senators are given two-year terms following redistricting. In the event that more than twelve senators are assigned two-year terms, the number is reduced to twelve by a random process designated by law. A random process is also employed in Texas, where lots are drawn to determine which half of the senate will serve an initial two-year term. The Reapportionment Commission determines which districts start with a two-year term in Colorado.[34]

All of this variation offers a better opportunity to investigate the effects of different term lengths than looking just at Congress provides. Jumping off from the congressional expectation that longer terms allow legislators greater decision-making freedom, scholars can look to see if the same pattern reveals itself in the 30 states with different terms between their two houses. The flip side of the coin is to examine such questions in the 17 states with the same terms for their two houses, to see if different perspectives are produced by different chambers and district sizes rather than by different term lengths. Perhaps even more interesting would be to investigate the behavior of state senators in Illinois and New Jersey to see if their behavior changes between their two-year term and their four-year terms. Such an analysis would have tremendous methodological advantages over looking for bicameral differences because, of course, the legislators being examined would vary only in their length of term; their constituencies and other important characteristics would remain the same. And in both Illinois and New Jersey legislators can anticipate their terms. In many other states with staggered four-year terms, legislators cannot be certain prior to redistricting whether they will have a two-year or four-year term in the following session. The behavior of those who know their upcoming term lengths can be compared with those who cannot forecast their next term length to see the behavioral consequences, if any, of this form of uncertainty.

Term Limits

One final fundamental difference across American legislatures is the existence in some of them of limitations on the number of terms a member may serve. As noted in chapter 1, the first term limits were imposed on the Pennsylvania legislature in 1776 and on the Confederal Congress a year later. These limits were, however, dispensed with when new constitutions were adopted, nationally in 1787 and in Pennsylvania in 1790. But the idea of limits on legislative service still held in various places around the country. Usually referred to as the practice of rotation, legislators in many districts were expected to serve only a term or two and then step aside so that someone else could hold the seat. Rotation was relatively common in the U.S. House during the early to mid-1800s (Kernell 1977), and there is evidence that it was also a norm in many state legislative districts during this same time period (Deming 1889, 427; Harrison 1979, 338; Luce 1924, 352–56; VanderMeer 1985, 154, 193; Wooster 1969, 42; 1975, 42–44). Indeed, it was even enshrined in West Virginia's first constitution in 1863. (The provision was not included when a new constitution was adopted nine years later.) And, although the causes for the decline of the rotation norm are not altogether clear, it appears to have vanished from the scene at both the congressional and the state legislative levels at roughly the same time in the last few decades of the nineteenth century (Kernell 1977; VanderMeer 1985, 200).[35]

Term limits were not seriously debated again until the late 1980s, and then they were adopted in over 20 states with astonishing speed. Three states adopted term limits in 1990, followed by more than ten states in 1992. The movement ran out of steam in the late 1990s, in part because the political fervor pushing them dissipated following the Republican party's great successes in the 1994 elections. Indeed, Republican-dominated state legislatures in Idaho and Utah abolished term limits in 2002 and 2003, respectively. But, it should also be noted that voters with one exception imposed term limits on legislators, and almost all the states that afford the citizenry that opportunity have availed themselves of it.[36]

There were, of course, attempts to impose term limits on members of Congress, both from within both houses, and from several states. The Supreme Court, however, held term limits to be unconstitutional at the federal level, because imposing a limit was in essence adding a fourth qualification for service, something which could only be done by constitutional amendment.[37] The Supreme Court has, however, allowed term limits to be placed on state legislators.[38]

Thus, in 2004, 15 state legislatures have term limits, as table 2–9 shows. The other 35 state legislatures and the U.S. Congress do not have them.[39] It is important to note that the term limits that are in place vary significantly one from another. One way they differ is in how many terms can be served, with some allowing as few as six years in a chamber, and others allowing twelve years. Perhaps even more importantly, some states only impose limits on consecutive terms in office, allowing members to return after a term out of office, while others place a lifetime ban on further service once the limit is reached. The differences across the states in the harshness of their limitations is in large part the result of idiosyncratic factors involving the whims of the people and groups that initially proposed the limits. But there is evidence that states where legislators had been serving for longer tenures imposed the most stringent limits (Chadha and Bernstein 1996).

FUNDAMENTAL STRUCTURES

TABLE 2-9 Term Limits in 2004 and Year of Adoption[a]

Term Limit	Consecutive Service	Lifetime Ban
6 Years Lower House 8 Years Upper House		AR (1992), CA (1990), MI (1992)
8 Years Total	NE (2000)[b]	
8 Years Lower House 8 Years Upper House	AZ (1992), CO (1990), FL (1992), ME (1993), MT (1992), OH (1992), SD (1992)	MO (1992)
12 Years Total		OK (1990)
12 Years Lower House 12 Years Upper House	LA (1995)	NV (1996)

Source: Data from National Conference of State Legislatures.
[a]State courts in Massachusetts, Oregon, Washington, and Wyoming tossed out term limit measures passed by their voters. State legislators repealed term limits in Idaho and Utah.
[b]Voters in Nebraska passed term limit measures in 1992 and 1994, but both were ruled unconstitutional by the state supreme court.

Not surprisingly, the imposition of term limits on some American legislatures prompted a number of scholars to investigate their effects. Much of the attention thus far has been devoted to assessing the electoral effects of term limits and how they influence the political career calculations of legislators. Less attention has been devoted to figuring out their effects on legislative organization and procedure, in part because the full impact of term limits has only recently been felt in many chambers. Thus we have yet to sort out how different term limits impact different chambers with different characteristics.

Conclusion

American legislatures were born from common ancestors and shared many similarities at birth. Since the eighteenth century, however, American legislatures have evolved in many different ways. The most obvious contrasts are rooted in differing fundamental organizations of activity. The U.S. Congress has operated under essentially the same Constitution since 1789, one that grants great flexibility in how each house organizes and makes decisions. Almost all state legislatures have been governed by two or more constitutions. Over time, newer state constitutions have hemmed in the legislature, reducing its ability to devise its own structures and decision-making procedures.

There are, of course, other important fundamental differences across American legislatures. Who may serve varies, as does how long they may serve. The number of chambers, number of members in a chamber, the number of districts, and the number of people in a district, all vary, both across legislatures and over time.

In the next chapter we explore how differences in the fundamental organization of activities themselves produce further differences among American legislatures. In particular, we examine legislative professionalization by looking at how American legislatures vary in terms of member pay, session lengths, and staff and resources, and how these differences came to be over time.

· 3 ·

Institutional Characteristics

In chapter 1 we established that American legislatures germinated from the same seeds. In chapter 2 we examined questions of constitutional design, to begin exploring how over time American legislatures came to look so different from each other. We continue that exploration in this chapter. More specifically, we look at the basic components of legislative professionalization: the time demands of service, the financial incentives offered to legislators, and the staff resources and facilities given them. We observe how relatively small differences among American legislatures at the beginning of the nineteenth century became major dissimilarities by the end of the twentieth century.

The U.S. Congress became fully professionalized only around the start of the twentieth century. When the process started at the national-level legislature, institutional development in the states lagged well behind. Rumblings for reforms to allow state legislatures to better respond to the increased demands being placed on them first surfaced in any significant way only in midcentury.[1] These pressures led to the legislative professionalization revolution of the 1960s and 1970s, when Jesse Unruh (1965), the Citizens Conference on State Legislatures (1971) and others (see Herzberg and Rosenthal 1971) pushed state legislatures to become more like the U.S. Congress. By the start of the 1980s, most of the significant professionalization reforms had been put in place, and as evidenced by the election of Ronald Reagan as president, support for investing in improved and expanded government institutions was coming to an end (Brace and Ward 1999; Rosenthal 1996; 1998). By the close of the century, serious questions were being raised about whether state legislatures were experiencing a process of deprofessionalization. Thus, while the U.S. Congress became progressively more professionalized during the course of the twentieth century, the process at the state level was much more varied, not only in degree of development, but also in direction.

Limitations on Sessions

The U.S. Constitution (Article 1, section 4) requires that, "The Congress shall assemble at least once in every Year," and the House and Senate have always done so. The experience at the state level, however, is very different. Initially, state legislatures were seen as a vital check on gubernatorial power and were therefore required to meet annually. In addition, annual sessions were thought to enhance representation (Keefe and Ogul 2001, 71; Zeller 1954, 89). But over the course of the nineteenth century, attitudes toward state legislatures changed, and annual sessions were replaced with biennial sessions. As Bryce observed (1906, 337; see also Luce 1924, 129–30), "the experience of bad legislation and over-legislation . . . led to fewer as well as shorter sittings." Reinsch (1907, 132) offered a similar rationale for the introduction of session limits:

> The principle of those who favor such restriction of legislative activity is that with less frequent legislative sessions, the more important matters will occupy the attention of the legislators, and individual members will recognize the futility of advancing pet schemes of a merely personal or local nature.

At the time Bryce and Reinsch wrote, only seven states still had annual sessions; the rest met biennially, except for Alabama, which met only quadrennially.[2]

The trend over the course of the twentieth century was a return to annual sessions. As table 3–1 reveals, 19 states had annual sessions by 1960. The number continued to escalate over the next four decades, in part as a response to increased demands but also because of the professionalization revolution of the 1960s and 1970s. By 2004, 44 state legislatures met annually, leaving six states with biennial sessions.[3] Thus the trend toward meeting each year was widespread, but it was not universal. It also was not irreversible. Montana's 1972 constitution established annual sessions, but the voters passed a referendum two years later returning the legislature to biennial sessions. The voters reaffirmed their decision again in 1982 and 1988 (Rosenthal 1996, 192).[4]

TABLE 3–1 Annual and Biennial Legislative Sessions in the States, 1960 and 2004

Year	Annual Sessions	Biennial Sessions
1960	19	31
2004	44	6

Sources: *The Book of the States 1960–61*, pages 40–41, and *The Book of the States, 2003 Edition*, pages 109–12.

INSTITUTIONAL CHARACTERISTICS

Even as most states have moved to meeting annually, session lengths continue to be limited in most states. As of 2004, only twelve states do not place any limit on the length of the regular legislative session.[5] In 28 states constitutional provisions establish the limits. The Wyoming Constitution (Article 3, Section 6), for example, limits the legislature to 40 legislative days in odd numbered years and 20 legislative days in even numbered years.[6] Session length limits in Alabama, Indiana, Maine, and South Carolina are imposed by statute. Chamber rules limit the number of days in session in Arizona, California, and Massachusetts. Finally, indirect limits on legislator compensation, such as cutoff dates for per diem or mileage reimbursement, are used in three states—Iowa, New Hampshire, and Tennessee. In Iowa, for example, state legislators can no longer collect their per diem after 110 calendar days in session in odd-numbered years, or 100 calendar days in even-numbered years.[7] Indirect restrictions are, of course, the easiest to violate. Similarly, chamber rules can be rewritten, albeit with some effort, as can statutes. (The latter, however, involve the governor while the former do not.) Constitutional limitations are the hardest to breach.

One other scheduling variant deserves some mention. During the first half of the twentieth century state legislatures in California (1911–1959), New Mexico (1941–1947), and West Virginia (1921–1929) employed split or bifurcated sessions (Donnelly 1947, 95–96; Driscoll 1986, 63–64; Faust 1928; Zeller 1954, 4, 92).[8] These sessions were structured so that the legislature met for a first session, took a mandated recess, and then reconvened for a second session. The first session, for example, lasted 30 days in California and 15 days in West Virginia, during which time legislation could be introduced and assigned to committees. But only "emergency" measures could be passed during the first session and only on super majority votes. After the initial session, a constitutional recess was called, of not less than 30 days in California and around 48 days in West Virginia. During the mandated recess legislators were supposed to return to their constituencies and gather input about the proposed bills from voters, interest groups, and others. In theory, the recess was intended to allow members a chance to step back and think about the legislative proposals before them (White 1927). Most legislatures at the time operated on such abbreviated schedules that little time was available to become well versed on the nuances of many bills. When reconvened, the legislature then considered the bills introduced in the first session. In both California and West Virginia, for example, only bills supported by three-fourths of the members could be introduced in the second session. Assessments of the success of the split session were mixed (for con opinions see Barclay 1931; Donnelly 1947, 96; and Faust 1928; for a pro opinion see West 1923), and ultimately all three legislatures returned to more conventional schedules.

Arguments in favor of longer sessions give us some insight into the potential differences session length makes. In promoting longer sessions, Zeller (1954, 93) observed,

Limiting sessions intensifies all evils associated with legislative halls. Taking advantage of the short time for deliberation, a strong minority may thwart the interest of the majority through delaying tactics. Bills piled up at the end of a session are rushed through without adequate consideration. This tendency to defer action on bills until the closing days does not create a situation suitable for debate and deliberation. Certainly it would be impossible to say that legislation or the quality of legislators has been improved by limiting the sessions.

Thus, session lengths are linked to bargaining and legislative strategies, to the ability of legislative minorities to exercise a veto, and ultimately to policy outcomes. Variations in session lengths allow us to rigorously test to see what, if any, differences they really make.

Pay and Pensions

The U.S. Constitution requires that members of Congress be paid (Article 1, section 6). But it leaves the amount to Congress to decide. Members of Congress earned a per diem until 1856, except for the controversial annual salary they voted for themselves in 1816 and then rescinded because of public scorn in the next Congress (Bianco, Spence, and Wilkerson 1996). Once annual salaries were adopted, for many years they tended not to change very often. Pay, for example, was set at $5,000 from 1873 through 1907. This time period is of particular interest to note because, of course, it was during this time that members of the House began to increase the length of their service (Epstein, Brady, Kawato, and O'Halloran 1997, 973–74; Brady, Buckley, and Rivers 1999, 497–98). Thus, it is questionable that pay led to careerism. In the modern Congress there is evidence that voluntary departures are related to the level of pay (Hibbing 1982), although, again, increased career lengths may not be (Parker 1992, 78–79; Witmer 1964, 528).

In contrast to the findings on Congress, there is a strong, negative cross-sectional relationship between pay and turnover in state legislatures (Rosenthal 1974; Squire 1988a). The relationship between member pay and turnover over time within legislatures is less clear, with studies of the state legislatures in California (Squire 1992a, 1036–1037) and New York (Stonecash 1993, 310) suggesting that pay increases lag behind increased member tenure rates. Member pay varies across the states in several ways. First, how member pay gets set differs.[9] Currently, constitutions in New Hampshire and Texas set specific salary figures.[10] The Rhode Island Constitution as amended in the mid-1990s sets member pay at $10,000 annually in 1995, but then provides for an automatic yearly cost of living adjustment tied to inflation.[11] In 1998 Massachusetts voters amended their constitution to link legislative salaries starting in 2001 to the change in the median household income in the state as determined by the governor.[12] Legislators set their own pay in 27 states.[13] Compensation commissions alone set pay in eight states, in conjunction with the legislature in another seven states, and in conjunction with state constitutional provisions in one state. Compensation commissions, constitutional provisions, and legislative input are all used in three states. Pay mechanisms matter. Legislators who control their own salary are paid much higher wages than are legislators whose pay is set through the state constitution (McCormick and Tollison 1978).

Second, how much legislators earn, of course, varies over time. Members of colonial assemblies were, for the most part, compensated for their services, in large part because initially there were too few members of the wealthy landed class in the colonies who could afford to serve without some form of remuneration (Luce 1924, 521). Who should finance legislative representatives was a difficult issue; in some colonies the constituency was to pay, while in others the colony covered the cost (Luce 1924, 522). What members were to be paid also varied. Initially, the burgesses in Virginia were paid in tobacco by their counties (Miller 1907, 96). Later they were paid eight or nine shillings out of the colonial treasury (Luce 1924, 525). Assembly members in Rhode Island initially received no pay, but after finding it hard to get members to attend, a credit of three shillings a day that would be offset against their taxes owed was instituted in 1666 (Luce 1924, 523). In Pennsylvania in 1683 members were paid three shillings a day if they attended, but if they "willingly" failed to attend they were fined five shillings (Young 1968, 158).[14] Not all assemblies paid their members. In Georgia (Corey 1929, 117) and South Carolina (Luce 1924, 525) members received no compensation at all, while in New Jersey they received a per diem of six shillings, which one estimate suggests covered only about half of their actual living expenses (Purvis 1986, 42).

The notion of a salary for legislative service was still somewhat suspect at the time of the newly established state legislatures during the Revolution. The Pennsylvania constitution of 1776, for example, observed in section 36:

> As every freeman to preserve his independence, (if without a sufficient estate) ought to have some profession, calling, trade or farm, whereby he may honestly subsist, there can be no necessity for, nor use in establishing offices of profit, the usual effects of which are dependence and servility unbecoming freemen, in the possessors and expectants; faction, contention, corruption, and disorder among the people. But if any man is called into public service; to the prejudice of his private affairs, he has a right to a reasonable compensation: And whenever an office, through increase of fees or otherwise, becomes so profitable as to occasion many to apply for it, the profits ought to be lessened by the legislature.

The original state constitutions generally held that legislative salaries should be drawn from the state treasuries, but failed to state what sum ought to be given.

TABLE 3-2 American Legislative Pay on Annual Basis in 1910[a]

Legislature	Salary in 1910	1910 Salary in 2003 Dollars[b]
U.S. Congress	$7,500	$139,242
NY	$1,500	$27,848
MA, PA	$750	$13,924
OH	$600	$11,152
CA, IL, NJ, WI	$500	$9,283
MS	$400	$7,426
IA	$275	$5,106
CO	$270	$5,013
NV	$240	$4,456
MD, MN	$225	$4,177
GA, NE	$200	$3,713
AR, FL, IN, MT	$180	$3,342
MO	$175	$3,249
SC	$160	$2,971
CT, DE, ID, KY, LA, ME, NM, ND, RI, SD, TN, TX, WA	$150	$2,785
MI	$125	$2,321
AZ, NC, OK, UT, VA, WV	$120	$2,228
NH, WY	$100	$1,857

Sources: State legislative data were calculated from the *Official Manual of Kentucky,* 1910, page 147. In addition, Driscoll (1986, 79), Bryce (1906, 336), and legislative staff in several states were consulted. Data on the U.S. Congress were taken from Fisher (1980, 40–41).
[a] Pay includes salary or per diem only.
[b] Current dollars calculated using the inflation calculator on the Bureau of Labor Statistics Web page. The calculator calculated the value of the dollar in 1913 (the first year for which the Bureau figured the Consumer Price Index) as of 2003.

Specific salary figures only began to be incorporated into state constitutions at the end of the eighteenth century, starting with the admission of Kentucky and Tennessee into the Union.

Once the notion of a salary was accepted, the amounts still varied considerably across states and over time. In California, for example, legislators originally earned a $16 per diem, a sum Bancroft (1888, 311) notes was "no inducement, as they could make thrice as much elsewhere."[15] The Constitution of 1879 reduced that sum to a per diem of no more than $8. A constitutional amendment in 1908 provided legislators a salary of $1,000 biennially. Subsequent amendments in 1924, 1949, and 1954 increased member pay to monthly salaries of $100, $300, and $500 respectively. The $6,000 annual salary paid California state legislators in 1954 generally compared favorably to those offered to their counterparts in other states, less than the $7,500 given legislators in New York, but more than the $5,000 salaries for Illinois legislators, or $3,000 salaries for Pennsylvania legislators. But the pay for California state legislators paled in compar-

INSTITUTIONAL CHARACTERISTICS

TABLE 3-3 American Legislative Pay on Annual Basis in 2003

Legislature	Annual Salary	Legislature	Annual Salary
U.S. Congress	**$154,700**	LA	$16,800
CA	$99,000	TN	$16,500
NY	$79,500	GA	$16,200
MI	$77,400	*KY*	$16,135
PA	$64,638	ID	$15,646
IL	$55,788	OR	$15,396
OH	$53,707	WV	$15,000
MA	$53,380	NC	$13,951
NJ	$49,000	AR	$13,751
WI	$45,569	*VT*	$12,864
OK	$38,400	NE	$12,000
DE	$34,800	IN	$11,600
WA	$33,556	RI	$11,236
HI	$32,000	SC	$10,400
MO	$31,561	MS	$10,000
MD	$31,509	ME	$9,555
MN	$31,140	KS	$8,426
CO	$30,000	TX	$7,200
AL	$28,350	*NM*	$6,525
CT	$28,000	SD	$6,000
FL	$27,900	*ND*	$4,813
AK	$24,012	*UT*	$4,500
AZ	$24,000	*NV*	$3,900
IA	$20,758	*MT*	$3,456
VA Senate	$18,000	*WY*	$2,875
VA House of Delegates	$17,640	NH	$100

Sources: Calculated from data in National Conference of State Legislatures, "2003 State Legislator Compensation." States in italics pay per diem, not annual salaries. Annual salary in per diem states is estimated using number of days in session for the previous year.

ison to salaries for other elected officials in the state. City council members in Los Angeles, for example, earned $12,000 annually, and Los Angeles County Supervisors received $18,000 a year (Cloner and Gable 1959, 723). A voter approved constitutional amendment in 1966 gave California legislators an immediate pay increase to $16,000, and, more importantly, the power to determine their own raises. Members of the legislature used that power to make themselves among the best paid state legislators in the country. The voters, however, took that power away in 1990, creating a California Citizens Compensation Commission to set salaries for many state offices, among them the state legislature.[16] The Compensation Commission, however, continued to treat legislators well and the legislature maintained its place atop the salary rankings.

Finally, member pay varies across the states and between Congress and the states. A gap between what members of Congress get paid and what state legislators make has long existed, as table 3–2 demonstrates. In 1910, members of Congress received $7,500 annually, or the equivalent of over $139,000 in 2003 dollars. The highest paid state legislature at that time—New York—lagged far behind. But New York legislators were much better paid than any of the counterparts in the rest of the states.

In 2003, members of Congress received $154,700 annually, far more than any state legislator, as table 3–3 shows. Legislators in 40 states are paid an annual salary, with those in California earning the most at $99,000 year and those in New Hampshire earning the least at $100 a year. Legislators in nine states are paid daily wages, ranging from $76.80 a day in Montana to $166.34 a day in Kentucky. A weekly salary is paid to Vermont legislators. Legislators in New Mexico are only paid a per diem. Overall, the current mean legislative pay for state legislators is roughly $25,400; the median is $16,800. Beyond New Mexico, however, all but six states supplement their salaries with per diems, ostensibly to cover daily expenses.[17] Thus, in most states, legislators actually pocket more money than their listed salaries. The accounting challenges in trying to calculate how much more money is pocketed are, however, considerable. Some per diems are calculated by legislative days, others by calendar days, a few by month. Some are vouchered while others are unvouchered. In many states, legislators representing districts closer to the capital get lower per diems than do those living farther away.

Retirement benefits represent a second and often ignored financial incentive offered to legislators. They are, of course, an added inducement for long-term service. Members of Congress were first given a pension plan only in 1946, as part of the Legislative Reorganization Act of that year (Fisher 1980, 43; Hibbing 1982, 1025–1026). No state legislature had a pension plan in 1946, but after Congress established one, a number of them followed suit. By 1954, 16 states extended retirement benefits to their legislators (Zeller 1954, 80). Currently, 40 states offer state legislators retirement plans.[18] The trend toward providing them is not absolute and not necessarily popular with the public. California voters took away their state legislators' pension plan in 1990, and legislators in Rhode Island had to give up their pension system as part of a deal to get voter support to dramatically increase their salaries in the mid-1990s.[19]

Over time, members of Congress have made their pension plan very generous (Hibbing 1982, 1025–1026). The level of retirement benefits varies across the states. After twelve years of service in the Idaho state legislature, a retiree would receive $305 monthly, collectable starting at age 65. After twelve years of service in the Texas state legislature, a retiree would receive $2,288.25 monthly, collectable at age 50, or after only eight years of service at age 60. Legislative pensions in Texas are of particular note because they are far more generous than the annual salary of $7,200 would suggest. The reason pensions are so much higher is because they are tied to the salaries of district court judges, not to legislative salaries. Looking only at state legislative pay in Texas without taking pension benefits into account might easily mislead a scholar investigating the nature of legislative careers in that state.

Remuneration levels are clearly important in explaining how legislative careers unfold. Not surprisingly, where pay is higher, careers are longer, and where pay is lower, careers are shorter. This simple observation is more important than it might initially seem, however, because legislative careers are linked to legislative organization (Polsby 1968; Price 1975; Squire 1988b; 1992a).

Staff and Facilities

Staff and facilities are linked to the ability of legislators to do their job. As Malbin (1980, 5) observed, "Congress needs staffs . . . to help it evaluate the flood of material from the outside and perhaps even come up with ideas of its own." With the creation of staffs comes the need for facilities in which to house and make use of them. Staff and facilities have changed over time for Congress and for most state legislatures. Even with changes, however, there is still substantial variation between Congress and the states, and among the states.

Extensive staffing is a relatively recent development in American legislatures. Congressional committees began hiring part-time staffs in the 1840s. Money for the first full-time staff was appropriated in 1856, but only for the House Ways and Means Committee and the Senate Finance Committee. All committees had full-time staff by the end of the nineteenth century (Fox and Hammond 1977, 15; Malbin 1980, 11; Rogers 1941, 3). Personal staff for members other than committee chairs was first allowed in the Senate in 1885 and in the House in 1893 (Fox and Hammond 1977, 15). Prior to that, members either did the work themselves or hired assistants with their own money. Even after staff became accepted, funds for personal and committee staffs were in short supply until after the Legislative Reorganization Act of 1946 (Davidson 1990, 367–69; Malbin 1980, 9–14). From 1947 to the mid-1980s staff numbers exploded in both the House and Senate. Since then, the number of staffers has declined a bit (Ornstein, Mann, and Malbin 2000, 131–132). Even with the recent cutbacks, however, members of Congress still enjoy unparalleled support from committee and personal staffs, as well as institutional staff support from the Congressional Research Service and the Government Accountability Office.

Members of the House and the Senate had no office space until 1908 and 1909 respectively, when the first House and Senate office buildings were opened. Until that time members used their desks, rented private offices, or maneuvered to borrow space in committee rooms. Now, members have office suites—albeit cramped—to house their burgeoning personal staff. Congressional offices in the home state or district also appear to be a relatively recent innovation. Evidence suggests that they first appeared in the early 1940s, and every member had at least one by the 1970s (Macartney 1987, 102.)

Thus, over time it developed that (Salisbury and Shepsle 1981, 559) "each member of Congress has come to operate as the head of an enterprise," with offices and employees. But have state legislators come to head similar sorts of enterprises? Like Congress, state legislatures started with little in the way of staff. In California, for example (Driscoll 1986, 125), "In 1850, legislative staff consisted of a parliamentarian, a recorder of minutes, a chaplain, a sergeant of arms, and an occasional supernumerary. This level of support remained relatively unchanged for almost 70 years." Other states offered similarly meager staff resources. In New York (Gunn 1980, 284), "In 1852 the senate employed only 15 people in addition to its members, and the assembly employed only 36. Almost all of these performed routine clerical and housekeeping chores and had no discernible impact on public policy." Campbell (1980, 45) found that, "The 1887 Wisconsin Assembly listed only 50 employees, including just 5 committee clerks. . . . In the early nineties Illinois representatives hired 101 people, 22 of whom clerked for committees at three dollars a day."

Around the beginning of the twentieth century state legislatures began to develop institutional staff resources. The New York State Library in 1890 and the Massachusetts State Library in 1892 first provided legislators with informational assistance. The establishment of the Wisconsin Legislative Reference Bureau in 1901 supplied legislators additional sorts of expertise (McCarthy 1911). By 1913, 23 states had a legislative reference bureau of some sort (Cleland 1914; Freund, Lapp, and Updyke 1913, 271); by 1930, 42 states had such services (Jones 1952, 443). The U.S. Congress actually followed the lead of the states in providing centralized research assistance by establishing the Legislative Reference Service in 1914. (The organization was renamed the Congressional Research Service in 1970.) Within a few decades state legislatures were well provided for with centralized staff for research and bill drafting (Crane and Watts 1968, 67–76; Perkins 1946, 515–17; Zeller 1954, 142–50). The provision of other sorts of staff resources, however, lagged. By the early 1950s (Zeller 1954, 156–59),

> About one fourth of the states provide[d] special research or technical assistance to serve the committees during the sessions. . . . most states provide[d] clerical and secretarial assistance for their standing committees. . . . The provision of secretarial

INSTITUTIONAL CHARACTERISTICS

TABLE 3-4 State Legislative Staff Compared to Congressional Staff in the 1990s

State Legislature	State Legislative Staff as a Percentage of Congressional Staff	State Legislature	State Legislative Staff as a Percentage of Congressional Staff
CA	66.92	GA	9.67
NY	56.86	AL	9.10
FL	41.79	SC	8.92
TX	41.14	OK	8.57
NJ	38.82	NC	8.40
PA	32.86	MO	8.18
HI	30.04	WV	8.17
MI	28.21	DE	8.14
NV	23.93	CO	8.00
AK	20.77	IA	7.51
AZ	19.38	KS	6.77
WA	18.88	IN	6.69
IL	18.37	UT	6.66
VA	18.09	TN	6.60
OR	16.55	MT	4.70
WI	16.11	RI	4.68
NE	15.70	ID	4.54
KY	13.00	WY	4.27
MN	12.87	ND	3.60
OH	12.87	MS	3.18
MD	12.06	ME	2.98
MA	12.03	SD	2.75
LA	11.20	NM	2.58
AR	10.39	NH	1.15
CT	10.25	VT	0.99

Source: Data on state legislative staff taken from National Conference of State Legislatures, "Size of State Legislative Staff: 1979, 1988 and 1996, Total Staff during Session" (June 1996). Data on Congressional staff taken from Ornstein, Mann, and Malbin (2000, 129–31).

and stenographic assistance to the individual member of the legislature [was], on the whole, less adequate. Fewer than twenty of the states assume[d] the responsibility for providing the individual legislators with needed assistance in adequate quantity.

In 1957, for example, the Washington state legislature had one permanent employee who worked full-time, the chief clerk of the House. One staff member remembers that at the end of the legislative session (Seeberger 1997, 150), "they turned out the lights, locked the doors, and went home." Legislative facilities in the states were poor as well. No state gave individual offices to all of its legislators. In 36 states not even shared office space was provided (Zeller 1954, 159).

The professionalization revolution of the 1960s and 1970s produced dramatic changes in staff and facilities in most, but not all, state legislatures (Rosenthal 1981, 206–7). By the end of the 1990s, almost every state legislative chamber provided professional and clerical staff to committees. Roughly half of the states provided members with year-round personal staff, but fewer than ten provided district staff and offices.[20] Many state legislators are still without individual offices. Overall, some states, such as California, Florida, New York, and Texas, operate with staff and facilities comparable to those of Congress, as table 3–4 reveals. Many others states provide remarkably little in the way of assistance.

Thus, the role staff and facilities play in the legislative experience varies dramatically across the states. When Hilda Solis moved from the California state Senate to the U.S. House following the 2000 elections, for example, she (Merl 2000) "decided to keep the same field offices, in El Monte and East Los Angeles, to provide continuity to her constituents." Her counterparts in Wyoming would not enjoy such advantages (Citizen's Guide to the Wyoming Legislature 2001):

> legislators in Wyoming do not have individual staff. . . . staff services for Wyoming legislators are provided by a small permanent central staff agency . . . and by temporary session staff. Office accommodations are similarly austere. Except for a few officers of the House and Senate, members of the legislature are not provided offices in the Capitol nor do they maintain full-time offices in their districts. While in session, the "office" of a typical Wyoming legislator consists of the legislator's desk on the floor of the House or Senate and one or two file cabinet drawers in a committee meeting room.

There have been occasional comparisons between how members of Congress and state legislators employ their staffs (Monroe, 2001) and how much contact is initiated with constituents (Jewell 1982, 169–71). Differences in casework conducted by state legislators and their offices have been shown to vary by institution and resource level (Freeman and Richardson 1994; 1996), but state legislators who successfully provide constituent services are rewarded by voters in the same way members of Congress are (Serra and Pinney 2001). Legislative scholars, however, have failed to take full advantage of the range of informational resources employed across the states. If informational needs drive legislative organization (Krehbiel, 1991), scholars have a great opportunity to test this theory across the range of informational resources provided legislators. Do informational theories that work in the Congressional setting work in other legislatures that are like Congress in terms of staff and facilities? Do they work in legislatures that look little like Congress in terms of staff and facilities? If information and expertise resides only in legislators without reference to institutional information resources, there may be little difference across legislatures. If, however, staff and facilities influence expertise levels, then there should be differences. Taking important and innovative theories such as Krehbiel's that are couched in general terms but developed with Congress in mind and tested with congressional data, and examining them in light of differing informational resources across legislative bodies, is the best way to rigorously test them.

Professionalization in American Legislatures

Institutional characteristics of the sort we have examined in this chapter comprise the attributes American scholars typically associate with the concept of legislative professionalization (Citizen's Conference on State Legislatures 1971; Grumm 1971; Rosenthal 1998, 54–55; Squire 1988a; 1992a; 1992b; 1997; 2000). Legislatures deemed professional meet in unlimited sessions, provide superior staff resources and facilities, and pay members well enough to allow them to pursue service as their vocation. Thus, a professionalized body shares the attributes that the U.S. Congress has enjoyed since the early twentieth century. But, it is important to note that a professionalized body does not have to be a career body, one where members want and expect to serve for many years. Even when all professionalization standards are met, members might of their own volition opt to serve for only short periods of time. The California Assembly, for example, has long been considered a paragon of legislative professionalization, yet it was described as a "springboard legislature" even before term limits because its members often left quickly to seek higher office (Squire 1988a; 1988b; 1992a).[21]

Over the last three decades a number of measures of legislative professionalization have been developed (Berry, Berkman and Schneiderman 2000; Bowman and Kearney 1988; Carey, Niemi and Powell 2000, 694–97; Citizens Conference on State Legislatures 1971; Grumm 1971; King 2000; Moncrief 1988; Morehouse 1983; Squire 1992b; 2000). In general, such indices are composed of three main components (Squire 1988, 69–70; 1992b, 70–71): level of member remuneration, staff support and facilities, and the time demands of service. Squire's (1992b; 2000) measure, which is the most commonly employed, uses an index of Congress's member pay, average days in session, and mean staff per member as a baseline against which to compare an index composed of those same attributes of other legislative bodies. In essence, this measure shows how closely a state legislature approximates the professional characteristics of the Congress, with 1 representing perfect resemblance, and 0 no resemblance (Squire 1992b; 2000).

TABLE 3-5 Legislative Professionalization in the American States Compared to Congress in the Late 1990s.

Rank	Legislature	Professionalization Score	Rank	Legislature	Professionalization Score
	U.S. Congress	**1.000**			
1.	CA	0.571	26.	DE	0.151
2.	MI	0.516	27.	VA	0.150
3.	NY	0.515	28.	NC	0.149
4.	WI	0.459	29.	LA	0.144
5.	MA	0.332	30.	SC	0.135
6.	NJ	0.320	31.	MS	0.127
7.	OH	0.315	32.	TN	0.117
8.	PA	0.283	33.	VT	0.117
9.	HI	0.252	34.	WV	0.116
10.	FL	0.249	35.	RI	0.113
11.	IL	0.236	36.	ID	0.110
12.	AK	0.232	37.	KS	0.109
13.	TX	0.215	38.	GA	0.107
14.	WA	0.198	39.	IN	0.106
15.	MO	0.198	40.	AR	0.104
16.	MD	0.189	41.	ME	0.098
17.	OK	0.188	42.	KY	0.087
18.	AZ	0.185	43.	MT	0.073
19.	MN	0.179	44.	UT	0.067
20.	CT	0.178	45.	AL	0.067
21.	CO	0.172	46.	SD	0.065
22.	NE	0.172	47.	ND	0.058
23.	NV	0.171	48.	WY	0.057
24.	OR	0.152	49.	NM	0.053
25.	IA	0.164	50.	NH	0.034

Source: Scores taken from Squire (2000).

But despite some differences in the details—other measures use legislative expenditures or legislative operating budgets as a substitute for staffing data—all the major professionalization measures produce remarkably consistent state rankings (Berkman 1991, 675; Maestas 2003, 448; Mooney 1994). And the results produced by the quantitative measures square quite nicely with qualitative assessments of professionalization in the states (e.g., Rosenthal 1993, 116–17; Kurtz 1992, 2).[22]

All measures of American legislative professionalization show that over recent decades most state legislatures are *professionalizing* (King 2000; Mooney 1995; Squire 1992; 2000). But it is hard to argue that more than a handful of them are *professionalized*. Data from one recent study (Squire 2000), presented in table 3–5, reveal that three legislatures are clearly far more professionalized than the other 47: California, New York, and Michigan. Each of these bodies pays well, meets in unlimited sessions, and provides ample staff. Only these states could be argued to be comparable to Congress. A few other legislatures, such as Massachusetts, New Jersey, Ohio, Pennsylvania, and Wisconsin are substantially professionalized. Most state legislatures, however, are not close to being professionalized. Indeed, some legislatures, particularly New Hampshire, New Mexico, North Dakota, South Dakota, and Wyoming, are deficient across the board.

The Coming of Legislative Professionalization

What has been the course of professionalization of American legislatures across the twentieth century? In this section we explore American legislative professionalization by examining how state legislatures compared to Congress at five points in time: around 1910, 1930, 1960, 1980, and 1999. The professionalization of Congress occurred roughly in the first decade of the twentieth century. As noted earlier in this chapter, congressional pay was set at $5,000 from 1873 until 1907, at which point it was raised to $7,500. From that point on, salary adjustments (almost always increases) occurred with much greater frequency. In session length, the Congress was only becoming a year-round institution in 1910 (Galloway 1961, 122). The Sixty-first Congress, for example, was in session from March 15, 1909 to August 5, 1909, again from December 6, 1909 to June 25, 1910, and then finally from December 5, 1910 to March 3, 1911. Over that two-year period it met 435 days, or an average of 217 days a year, a substantial figure although far less than the 280 days or more spent in session toward the end of the century.[23] Finally, again as noted above, staff and facilities were becoming widely available to members of both houses around this time. Thus around 1910 seems to be a good point at which to begin to assess American legislative professionalization if the U.S. Congress is the baseline to be used.[24]

The next snapshot is around 1931, after the boom years of the 1920s and at the beginning of the Great Depression, a point at which the traditional notions of federalism had not yet been altered and Congress and state legislatures each still pursued their long-held responsibilities. Thus, from 1910 to 1931, there is no significant pressure on state legislatures for organizational change. But rumblings for reform to allow state legislatures to better respond to increased demands on them surfaced by 1960 (Teaford 2002, 163–69). These pressures led to the legislative professionalization revolution, which occurred between the early 1960s and the late 1970s. By 1981, most of the significant professionalization reforms had been put in place, and as evidenced by the election of Ronald Reagan as president, support for investing in improved and expanded government institutions was coming to an end (Brace and Ward 1999; Rosenthal 1996; 1998). The final snapshot year, 1999, is appropriate not simply because it closed the century, but also because by that time term limits had taken root in many state legislatures and questions about whether state legislatures were experiencing a process of deprofessionalization had been raised.

Member Pay in Comparison

If Congress professionalized around 1910, what was the status of state legislatures in comparison? The range and mean of annual state legislative salaries as a percentage of the annual congressional salary at five points in time across the twentieth century are shown in figure 3–1.[25] As table 3–2 revealed, state legislative salaries lagged far behind the $7,500 paid to members of Congress in 1910. The highest state legislative salary was $1,500 for New York state legislators; the lowest was $50 in Alabama. The mean salary across state legislatures was just under $250, slightly over 3 percent of the congressional salary.

FIGURE 3–1 Range and Mean of State Legislative Salaries Compared to Congress, 1910–99

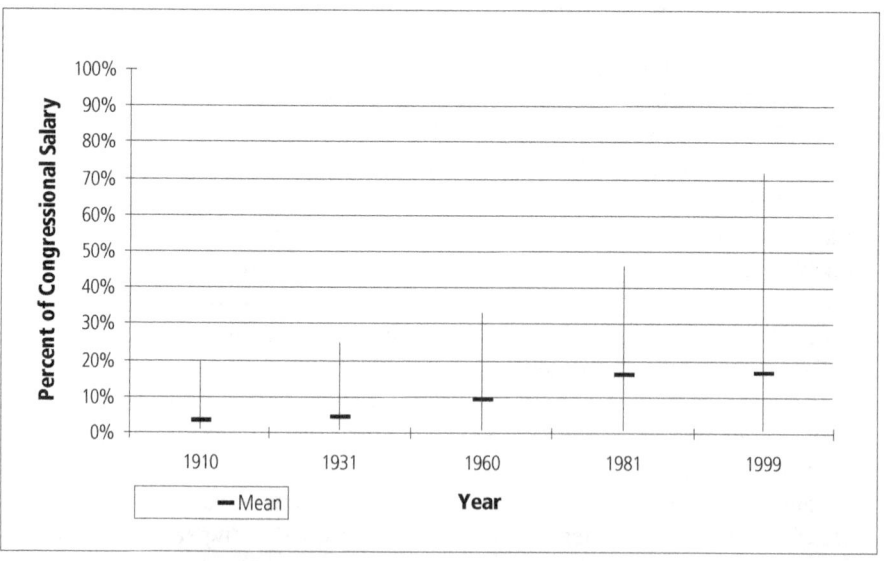

Sources: Data from *The Official Manual of Kentucky,* 1910, p. 147; Schumacker (1931, p. 10); *The Book of the States;* and the Dirksen Congressional Center's CongressLink Web page.

INSTITUTIONAL CHARACTERISTICS

State legislatures made scant progress in closing the gap with Congress over the next 20 years. In 1931, the range and mean of state legislative salaries had barely budged compared to Congress. The mean salary was up to $453, but that still represented only 4.5 percent of congressional pay. More progress was recorded over the next thirty years. In 1960, the median salary was a bit over $2,150, or 9.6 percent of what members of Congress were paid. A similar jump was registered from 1960 to 1981. In the latter year, state legislators earned an average $9,808, or 16.1 percent of the congressional salary. But progress for most state legislators stopped at that point. Although the range of state legislative salaries increased, meaning that some state legislatures continued to close the gap with Congress, most simply treaded water. The 1999 mean salary of $20,398 was only 16.6 percent of congressional pay.

In figures 3–2 and 3–3, we disaggregate state legislative salaries by looking at the over-time progress of the 16 bodies deemed among the most professionalized in 1999 (Squire 2000). (There is little reason to look at the change over time among the lowest ranking institutions because they hover at the very bottom throughout. Legislative salaries in New Hampshire, for example, were set at $200 biennially by a constitutional amendment in 1889; that sum has not been changed

FIGURE 3–2 Salaries in Most Professional States Compared to Congress, 1910–99

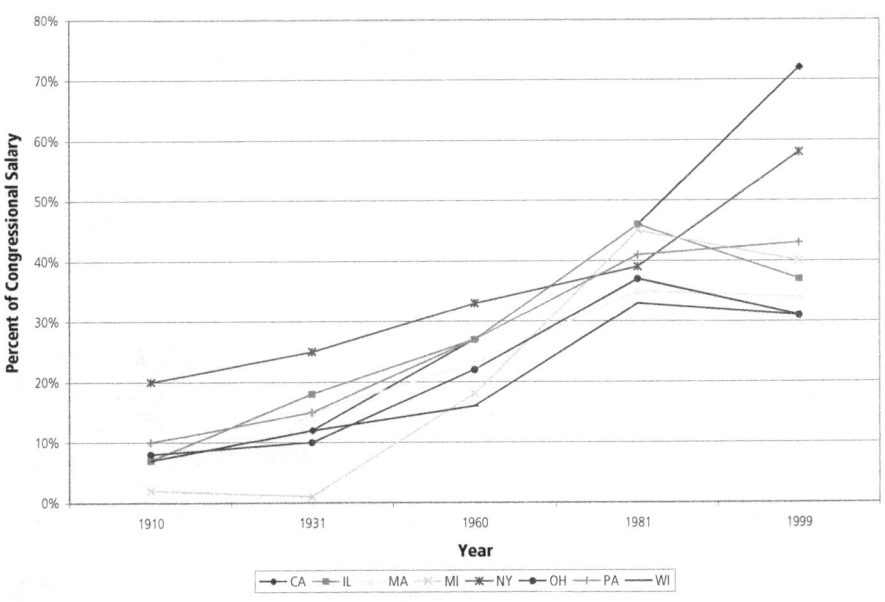

Sources: Data from *The Official Manual of Kentucky*, 1910, p. 147; Schumacker (1931, p. 10); *The Book of the States;* and the Dirksen Congressional Center's CongressLink Web page.

FIGURE 3-3 Salaries in Professionalizing States Compared to Congress, 1910–99

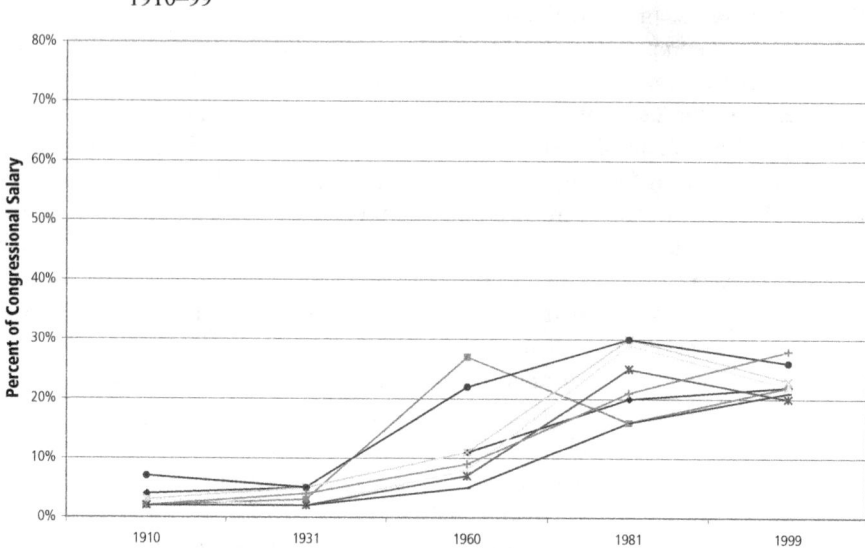

Sources: Data from *The Official Manual of Kentucky,* 1910, p. 147; Schumacker (1931, p. 10); *The Book of the States;* and the Dirksen Congressional Center's CongressLink Web page.

since.) The eight most professionalized state legislatures, shown in figure 3–2, evidence the same basic trends. The salary compared to Congress of almost all of the legislatures improved between 1910 and 1931, and then improved at an even greater rate over the next 30 years. But, as we would expect, the period of greatest progress was during the professionalization revolution between 1960 and 1981. After 1981, however, more states lost ground than gained compared to Congress.

The eight professionalizing legislatures in 1999 evidence slightly different patterns. The relative standing of these states compared to Congress changed little between 1910 and 1931. All of them, however, closed the gap a bit over the next thirty years, Delaware and New Jersey in particularly impressive fashion. As with the most professionalized state legislatures, the professionalizing legislatures all gained the most ground during the professionalization revolution, save for Delaware, which fell behind. After 1981, about half the professionalizing states continued to make progress compared to Congress, while the other half failed to do so.

Overall, state legislative salary patterns over the twentieth century reveal the same general pattern, whether examined in the aggregate or individually with the 16 most professionalized legislatures. The great difference found between the

INSTITUTIONAL CHARACTERISTICS

states and Congress in 1910 was still present in 1931. State legislative salaries closed the gap a little with the congressional salaries between 1931 and 1960, and even more ground was gained during the professionalization revolution of the 1960s and 1970s. After 1981, however, overall progress essentially stopped, although a few states continued to close the disparity. Overall, however, the mean state legislative salary still lags far behind what members of Congress get paid.

Time Demands in Comparison

What about the number of days in session? Legislative salary and the time demands of service are typically thought of as linked, with legislators serving more days in session receiving more money in return. The relationship between congressional and state legislative time demands over the twentieth century are, however, very different from those for member pay. As figure 3–4 reveals, in 1909, virtually no state legislature met for very long compared to Congress.[26] The mean number of days in session for state legislatures was 28, compared to 210 days for Congress. That relationship began to change over the next two decades. By 1926 to 1929, the mean percentage of days in session compared to Congress

FIGURE 3-4 Range and Mean of State Legislative Days in Session Compared to Congress, 1909–99

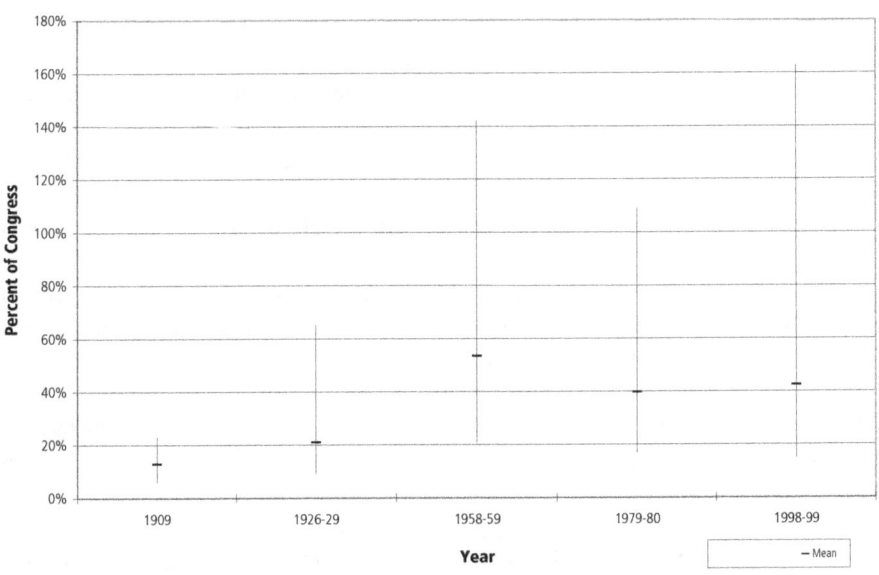

Sources: Data collected by authors from Christensen (1931, p. 6); *The Book of the States; Congressional Quarterly* (1993, pp. 483–87); and Ornstein, Mann, and Malbin (2000, pp. 154–57).

85

increased, and the range across state legislatures grew substantially. The biggest change, however, occurred between 1930 and 1960. By 1958 and 1959 a few state legislatures were meeting for many days more than the U.S. Congress, although most were meeting for only half as many days.[27] Since 1960, even during the height of the professionalization revolution, the mean number of days in session has declined, while the range has fluctuated.

Why are the patterns for days in service so different from those for member pay? As discussed above, the fundamental rules governing how long American legislatures can meet in session differ across American legislatures. Congress is free to meet every year for as long as deemed necessary, while most state legislatures face substantial constraints. Many states moved to annual meetings through the first half of the twentieth century, thereby increasing their number of days in session. That trend, however, slowed over the second half of the century. Moreover, session limits were still imposed on many state legislatures. In Congress, the number of days in session increased substantially over the first seven decades before trailing off slightly. Thus, while Congress clearly became a full-time institution year-in and year-out, most state legislatures still met for far fewer days and not necessarily every year.

Professionalization and Population

Our examination of legislative pay and the number of days in legislative session over the course of the twentieth century documents the trend toward the professionalization of state legislatures. The average state legislature became more like Congress; a few legislatures made particularly impressive strides. But, which legislatures tended to close the gap with Congress and which continued to lag?

Studies of state legislative professionalization trends since the 1960s by Mooney (1995) and King (2000) reach very similar conclusions on this question. The one variable that is consistently associated with legislative professionalization is state population. That population is so critical to professionalization makes sense. From an economics perspective, the membership sizes of American legislatures do not vary much (Stigler 1976), even taking into account the current range from 60 legislators in Alaska, to 424 in New Hampshire, and 535 in Congress. The important relationship for our discussion here is between the number of legislators and the size of the population that finances them. It is very easy to understand how 35 million Californians can more easily finance their 120 member state legislature at a generous level than 500,000 Wyomians can support their 90 legislators. Large populations generate more income that can be used to finance the legislature, and the costs are spread across more people. So the critical variable then is not really population, but rather the wealth they generate. A small but poor state, for example, will not be able to support its legislature at the same level as a similarly small but much wealthier state can. But the very high correlation between state wealth and state population renders them essentially the same in statistical analyses. Consequently, in our analyses we use measures of total state income when they are available, and state population when they are not. We would expect state wealth to positively influence the level of legislative professionalization across the twentieth century.

Other theories can be advanced to explain a state's willingness to subsidize a more professionalized legislature. State partisanship, for example, seems like a plausible challenger. Over the course of the twentieth century, Democrats generally were more supportive of increasing the power of governmental institutions than were Republicans. Such support may translate into backing for increased legislative professionalization. We test this idea by measuring Democratic voting strength as represented by the average state vote for the Democratic presidential candidate in the previous two elections rather than by using the percentage of state legislative seats held by the Democrats. We do this because we think the presidential vote is a better control for public sentiment for national Democratic party ideals than the percentage of state legislative seats would be. We would not, for example, expect Democratic state legislators in the South for much of the twentieth century to believe in the same things or to manifest the same behavior as their party counterparts in state legislatures in the rest of the country. And we also would not expect Democratic state legislators in more rural Western states to behave just like Democratic state legislators in the urban Northeast. Using support for the party's presidential candidate gives us a more consistent measure across the country at each point in time.[28] In 1910 we might not expect any relationship between support for the Democratic party and professionalization level because at that point in time the Democrats had not yet articulated a program intended to grow government power. But, at each subsequent time period support for professionalization should increase with Democratic party voting strength.

State political culture also might influence professionalization. One might, for example, use Elazar's (1984) typology to argue that traditionalistic states ought to prefer citizen legislatures because of their strong sense of *noblesse oblige,* while the tolerance of individualistic states for professional politicians would lead them to support professional legislatures. Where moralistic states would fall between the professionalized and citizen legislature ends of the dimension is, however, not clear. On the one hand, a major argument advanced by professionalization supporters in the 1960s was that increasing member pay would allow more people from modest financial circumstance to run for office (e.g., Unruh 1965), a value consistent with the moralistic culture's emphasis on participation. On the other hand, Elazar observes (1984, 117) that in the moralistic culture there is a "general rejection of the notion that the field of politics is a legitimate realm for private enrichment." Using this typology raises other concerns as well. As Elazar notes, most states are blends of all three cultures. In addition, employing his measure of culture over time requires rather heroic assumptions about its stability. Keeping these potential limitations in mind, we coded dummy variables for individualistic and traditionalistic states, including those states in each category that were predominately of that cultural strain. Moralistic states were the excluded category. Our hypotheses are straightforward: individualistic states should be positively associated with professionalization levels while traditionalistic states should be negatively associated with professionalization levels. Given how these cultures become less pronounced in the states over time, we might anticipate that their effects are more powerful earlier in the twentieth century than later.

We also employ a simple dummy variable for the South, measured as the eleven states of the Confederacy. This is, in most important respects, an alternative measure of political culture. Indeed, it overlaps substantially with the traditionalistic states in Elazar's (1984) typology. All of the former states of the Confederacy are deemed traditionalistic, but other border and a few southwestern states are as well. This variable will also pick up any residue of the "South is different" argument for reasons other than political culture (Fiorina 1997, 156–57). The expectation for this variable is the same as for the Elazar measure; the South should be less supportive of professionalization than is the North. But, again, these differences may disappear later in the century as American politics become more nationalized.[29]

Finally, several scholars argue that citizen demands, rather than political culture, drive the adoption of state policies. Generally speaking, where state populations are more diverse along social, racial, and economic dimensions, greater policy demands are made on government. In turn, these increased demands might produce greater support for legislative professionalization. Thus, where appropriate data are available we explore whether Sullivan's diversity index (1973; Morgan and Wilson 1990) and Hero and Tolbert's (1996) ethnic and racial diversity measures are associated with level of legislative professionalization.

We test our state wealth theory against its competitors using two different sets of OLS regression equations to assess the effect of each approach on salary and number of days in session compared to Congress at each of our five points in time. In both sets the equations are run separately for each period rather than in a pooled time series model to allow for the real possibility that particular variables influence professionalization level in different ways at different points in time (Pindyck and Rubinfeld 1991, 223). The first set of equations for pay and session length is static, assessing the influence of the independent variables at each time point. The second set of equations for each is more dynamic, assessing the influence of the change in state wealth and other variables on the change in professionalization level in each of the last four time periods.

The results of the static equations explaining legislative pay in each time period presented in table 3–6 are clear and consistent. In every equation at each point in time, state wealth is both statistically and substantively of overwhelming

TABLE 3-6 Explaining State Legislative Pay Compared to Congress, 1910–99

	1910 I	1910 II	1931 I	1931 II	1960 I	1960 II	1960 III	1981 I	1981 II	1981 III	1981 IV	1999 I	1999 II
Total State Income in Billions[a]	.002*** (.0001)	.001*** (.0001)	.218*** (.019)	.220*** (.021)	.065*** (.007)	.061*** (.007)	.055*** (.008)	.015*** (.002)	.014*** (.002)	.014*** (.002)	.015*** (.003)	.006*** (.001)	.006*** (.001)
Democratic Party Support	.027 (.031)	.030 (.030)	.034 (.038)	.025 (.037)	.094 (.127)	-.006 (.129)	.001 (.001)	.637* (.258)	.586* (.262)	.006* (.003)	.0058 (.0030)	.632** (.186)	.658** (.213)
South	-2.579* (1.268)		-1.371 (1.502)		-4.198 (2.234)			-6.217* (2.888)				-12.024*** (2.478)	
Individualistic Culture		.204 (.786)		-.024 (1.031)		3.717 (1.852)			2.369 (3.049)				-.293 (2.948)
Traditionalistic Culture		-2.585* (1.281)		-.148 (1.424)		-.491 (2.274)			-4.701 (2.922)				-8.359** (2.829)
Sullivan Diversity Index							.428** (.164)			.178 (.420)			
Ethnic Diversity											.117 (.234)		
Minority Diversity											.074 (.099)		
Constant	-.066 (1.193)	-.063 (1.085)	.539 (1.349)	1.422 (1.189)	1.017 (5.140)	3.677 (4.983)	-.190 (.106)	17.240 (10.775)	-15.345 (10.893)	-.266 (.189)	-.157 (.123)	-18.286 (8.071)	-18.804* (9.057)
N	45	45	48	48	48	48	48	48	48	48	48	48	48
Adjusted R^2	.67	.68	.75	.74	.65	.66	.68	.61	.60	.57	.56	.77	.71

[a] State population is substituted for total state income in the 1910 equations because of a lack of data.
*$p < 0.05$, two-tailed test; **$p < 0.01$, two-tailed test; ***$p < 0.001$, two-tailed test.

importance in explaining legislative salary in comparison to Congress.[30] In stark contrast, the effects of the other variables are inconsistent over time. The shifting parameters over time validate our decision to examine each period separately.

Although in each equation state wealth is statistically significant, the size of the state wealth coefficients decline over time. This is only because total state incomes grew dramatically, from a mean of $1.3 billion in 1931 to a mean of $160 billion in 1999. The dependent variable, however, is always measured as a percentage. Thus the effects of state wealth are consistently large. Indeed, they actually increase over time. The difference between the wealthiest state and the poorest state in 1909 was almost 22 percentage points. By 1999 that gap had increased to over 50 percentage points. Thus, the larger the state income level, the more money paid to state legislators relative to congressional pay.

Democratic party support matters only in the post-professionalization revolution time period. In both 1981 and 1999, increased support for Democrats is associated with higher levels of state legislative pay compared to Congress. The difference between the most Democratic and least Democratic states in these two years translates into about a 16 percentage point difference in salary. In earlier eras, the relationship, although almost always in the expected direction, is substantively much weaker and always far from achieving statistical significance.[31]

The effect of political culture is, at best, inconsistent over time. The coefficients for the individualistic states occasionally take the wrong sign. More importantly, they are always substantively small and statistically insignificant. The coefficients for the traditionalistic states behave in a more consistent and expected fashion. They always take the anticipated negative sign, but they are only statistically significant in two of the five time periods, while coming close in a third. Even when the coefficient is statistically significant, its impact is impressive only in the 1999 equation, when traditionalistic states are over 8 percentage points lower in their pay compared to Congress than are the nontraditionalistic states. Not surprisingly, the coefficient for the South dummy variable behaves in virtually the same way as the traditionalistic dummy variable. Its biggest impact also appears in 1999, when southern states lag their nonsouthern counterparts by over 12 percentage points compared to Congress.

The policy demand variables exert limited influence at best. The Sullivan diversity index is statistically significant in 1960, suggesting that demands for increased legislative capacity in the time period prior to the professionalization revolution were driven in part by greater social and economic diversity. In the 1981 equations, however, the Sullivan diversity index and the measures of ethnic and racial diversity fail, both statistically and substantively.

Equations explaining the change in legislative professionalization level between time periods are given in table 3–7. We lag the previous time period's salary percentage for each state in each equation. Looking at the change between time periods and using the lagged salary variables constitutes a more stringent

TABLE 3-7 Explaining Change in State Legislative Pay Compared to Congress, 1910–99

	1931 I	1931 II	1960 I	1960 II	1960 III	1981 I	1981 II	1981 III	1981 IV	1981 V	1999 I	1999 II
Lagged Salary Percentage from Previous Time Period	26.391 (13.642)	31.552* (14.068)	-23.841 (20.645)	-28.057 (20.027)	-27.451 (19.602)	-11.617 (19.688)	-4.694 (20.268)	3.909 (19.443)	-5.585 (20.058)	5.509 (19.927)	-36.608*** (8.426)	-30.123** (9.764)
State Income Increase from Previous Period in Billions[a]	.0007 (.0005)	.0006 (.0006)	.444*** (.123)	.414** (.116)	.362** (.116)	.077* (.030)	.067* (.029)	.080* (.031)	.069* (.030)	.077* (.032)	.046*** (.008)	.039*** (.009)
Democratic Vote	-.014 (.034)	-.038 (.034)	.007 (.078)	.019 (.120)	.106 (.106)	.415 (.257)	.466 (.250)	.306 (.243)	.323 (.250)	.414 (.256)	.119 (.164)	.114 (.189)
Democratic Vote Change from Previous Period	.060 (.058)	.068 (.057)	.068 (.122)	.069 (.069)	.035 (.055)	-.182 (.192)	-.300 (.195)	.115 (.182)	-.063 (.195)	-.138 (.194)	.385 (.249)	.398 (.288)
South	.436 (1.382)		-2.994 (2.954)			-4.290 (3.465)					-7.704*** (1.870)	
Individualistic Culture		.003 (.792)		3.263 (1.787)			-2.684 (2.778)					-1.832 (2.092)
Traditionalistic Culture		1.563 (1.563)		.857 (2.619)			-6.893* (3.294)					-4.570* (2.145)
Sullivan Diversity Index					32.195* (15.618)			-60.044 (44.665)				
Change in Diversity Index from 1960									-15.701 (56.821)			
Ethnic Diversity										-20.503 (20.536)		
Minority Diversity										-11.106 (10.521)		
Constant	.493 (1.217)	1.086 (1.106)	.724 (4.787)	2.663 (4.547)	-15.069 (9.716)	-12.422 (10.328)	5.565** (1.975)	17.314 (22.127)	-9.309 (10.178)	-10.488 (10.212)	-2.925 (6.657)	-2.687 (7.591)
N	45	45	48	48	48	48	48	48	48	48	48	48
Adjusted R^2	.29	.24	.29	.32	.34	.16	.21	.18	.14	.17	.43	.26

[a] Change in state population is substituted for change in state income in the 1931 equations because of a lack of appropriate data.

*$p < 0.05$, two-tailed test; **$p < 0.01$, two-tailed test; ***$p < 0.001$, two-tailed test.

test of our theory. The independent variable of greatest theoretical interest to us in these equations is the increase in state wealth from the preceding time period. The coefficients for increase in state wealth are large and statistically significant in each of the equations for 1960, 1981, and 1999, failing only in the 1931 equations where they still take the predicted sign. As in table 3–6, the effect of the change in wealth coefficients increases over time. The difference between the largest and smallest increases in 1960 was a bit over 20 percentage points of salary compared to Congress. The difference in 1999 was around 45 percentage points.

Little support for the competing theories is found in table 3–7. Neither Democratic party support nor the change in support for the party matters at any point in time. Political culture is influential only on the margins and, contrary to what we might expect, only in the most recent time periods. Traditionalistic states lag the other states in the 1981 and 1999 equations by between 4 and 7 percentage points. Similarly, states in the South trailed the rest of the country by about 8 points in 1999. The citizen demand variables are again relatively weak. Statistically, the Sullivan diversity index performs well in the 1960 equation, but the difference between the least diverse and most diverse states is less than 8 percentage points. In the 1981 equations, the Sullivan diversity index, the change in the diversity index between 1981 and 1999, and the ethnic and racial diversity measures all take the incorrect signs and fall far short of reaching statistical significance.

The results presented in tables 3–6 and 3–7 demonstrate that state wealth exerts a powerful effect on legislative pay over time. But does wealth also influence legislative session length? The relationships are different, as table 3–8 shows. None of the independent variables comes close to exerting a statistically significant effect on session length through 1960, save for the Sullivan diversity index. But substantively, the effect of that variable is trivial; the difference in session length between the least diverse and most diverse states is only half of one day. It is only in the post-professionalization revolution era that any consistent effects are seen. In both 1981 and 1999, a positive relationship between state wealth and session length develops. But its effect also is substantively trifling. Partisanship, political culture and the other citizen demand variables all fail to register any impact at all.

The results for equations examining the change in session length from one time period to the next are presented in table 3–9. At first glance table 3–9 appears to tell the same story as table 3–8. There is, however, a very important difference between the results reported in the two tables. The statistically significant coefficients in table 3–9 produce much bigger effects than they did in table 3–8. Again, the Sullivan diversity index is statistically significant in the 1960 equation but this time the change in days in session as compared to Congress between the least diverse states and the most diverse states is large: 50 percentage points,

TABLE 3–8 Explaining State Legislative Days in Session Compared to Congress, 1910–99

	1910 I	1910 II	1931 I	1931 II	1960 I	1960 II	1960 III	1981 I	1981 II	1981 III	1981 IV	1999 I	1999 II
Total State Income in Billions[a]	.000006 (.000006)	.000007 (.000007)	.005 (.007)	.003 (.001)	.008 (.005)	.005 (.005)	.002 (.005)	.002*** (.0005)	.002** (.0006)	.001** (.0004)	.002** (.0004)	.0005* (.0002)	.0005* (.0002)
Democratic Party Support	-.0004 (.001)	.0001 (.001)	.0008 (.001)	.0008 (.001)	-.006 (.008)	-.006 (.008)	.0003 (.008)	.004 (.006)	.004 (.006)	.003 (.006)	-.001 (.006)	.006 (.006)	.007 (.007)
South	-.007 (.034)		-.067 (.055)		-.100 (.149)			-.113 (.062)				-.142 (.085)	
Individualistic Culture		-.007 (.022)		.010 (.037)		.195 (.123)			-.004 (.066)				-.027 (.091)
Traditionalistic Culture		-.033 (.034)		-.065 (.051)		-.048 (.148)			-.103 (.063)				-.157 (.087)
Sullivan Diversity Index							2.338* (1.084)			.838 (.879)			
Ethnic Diversity											.821 (.476)		
Minority Diversity											-.208 (.201)		
Constant	.137*** (.031)	.123*** (.029)	.187*** (.049)	.193*** (.042)	.772* (.340)	.726* (.326)	-.488 (.698)	.151 (.230)	.175 (.235)	-.206 (.395)	.299 (.250)	.127 (.277)	.123 (.278)
N	34	34	47	47	47	47	47	48	48	48	48	48	48
Adjusted R^2	.00	.00	.00	.01	.06	.10	.14	.29	.27	.25	.29	.14	.14

[a] State population is substituted for total state income in the 1910 equations because of a lack of appropriate data.
*$p < 0.05$, two-tailed test; **$p < 0.01$, two-tailed test; ***$p < 0.001$, two-tailed test.

TABLE 3–9 Explaining Change in State Legislative Days in Session Compared to Congress, 1910–99

	1931 I	1931 II	1960 I	1960 II	1960 III	1981 I	1981 II	1981 III	1981 IV	1981 V	1999 I	1999 II
Lagged Days in Session Percentage	76.709** (27.143)	73.211** (28.935)	41.821 (53.229)	32.996 (53.146)	35.713 (49.834)	-87.849*** (8.677)	-87.873*** (9.154)	-87.068*** (9.131)	-88.018*** (8.949)	-91.295*** (9.541)	-30.766 (17.888)	-31.817 (18.125)
State Income Increase from Previous Period in Billions[a]	.0001 (.002)	.0001 (.002)	.857 (.567)	.550 (.580)	.199 (.618)	.190** (.055)	.183** (.056)	.188* (.069)	.186** (.056)	.196** (.071)	.018 (.030)	.017 (.030)
Democratic Party Support	.236 (.130)	.164 (.135)	-.680 (.846)	-.816 (.844)	-.134 (.730)	.354 (.640)	.361 (.657)	.146 (.629)	.177 (.630)	-.091 (.668)	.607 (.670)	.624 (.688)
Democratic Vote Change from Previous Period	-.347 (.242)	-.265 (.246)	-.364 (.528)	-.184 (.473)	-.328 (.372)	-.072 (.505)	-.085 (.528)	.336 (.482)	.161 (.506)	.154 (.507)	-1.301 (1.081)	-1.197 (1.113)
South	-8.537 (5.173)		-10.926 (20.176)			-10.529 (8.536)					-3.942 (7.934)	
Individualistic Culture		-.073 (3.161)		18.360 (12.401)			-1.861 (7.210)					-1.816 (7.998)
Traditionalistic Culture		-5.148 (5.573)		-.217 (18.526)			-10.043 (8.802)					-5.556 (8.226)
Sullivan Diversity Index					220.004* (104.618)			-2.789 (117.254)				
Change in Diversity Index									-74.391 (141.322)			
Ethnic Diversity										62.425 (55.098)		
Minority Diversity										-11.361 (27.771)		
Constant	-10.161 (6.121)	-7.171* (5.921)	53.581 (33.649)	55.177 (31.942)	-62.793 (65.800)	11.956 (26.211)	13.486 (26.463)	19.530 (56.747)	18.823 (26.097)	26.941 (27.084)	-10.205 (27.951)	-9.155 (28.507)
N	34	34	46	46	46	47	47	47	47	47	48	48
Adjusted R^2	.17	.09	.01	.05	.11	.70	.69	.69	.69	.69	.00	.00

[a] State population is substituted for total state income in the 1931 equations because of a lack of appropriate data.

*$p < 0.05$, two-tailed test; **$p < 0.01$, two-tailed test; ***$p < 0.001$, two-tailed test.

suggesting that societal pressures building in the period leading up to 1960 motivated the most diverse states to increase the number of days the legislature met. But the diversity index, the change in the index, and the other citizen demand variables, as well as the political culture and partisanship variables, all fail in the 1981 and 1999 equations.

Change in state wealth is both statistically and substantively significant only in the 1981 equations. The difference between the states with the greatest increase in wealth and the least increase in wealth is around 51 percentage points in 1981. Although the coefficients in the equations for the other years always take the correct sign, none achieves statistical significance. Thus, during the period of the professionalization revolution, the wealthiest states were the ones that pushed the hardest to have their legislatures become more like Congress.

The Consequences of Professionalization for Legislators and Legislative Institutions

Why should professionalization be of interest to legislative scholars? Professionalization has been found to impact an extensive web of relationships involving legislators and the organizations in which they serve. Professionalization, for example, alters the relationship between the representative and the represented. Legislators in more professionalized legislatures have more contact with their constituents (Squire 1993) and are more attentive to their concerns (Maestas 2003) than are their counterparts in less professionalized legislatures. At the same time, legislators enjoy increasing electoral isolation from political tides as professionalization levels rise (Berry, Berkman, and Schneiderman 2000). And the relationship between interest groups and legislators is mediated by professionalization (Berkman 2001).

A related and important question is whether legislative professionalization attenuates or enhances the linkage between public opinion and public policy. One argument has been that professionalization of state legislatures insulates members from their constituencies, resulting in legislative policies that are less representative of the interests of individual districts and or the interests of the state (Luttbeg 1992; Weber 1999). Maestas (2000), however, has shown that states with more professional legislatures and with more opportunities for members to progress to higher office have greater aggregate public opinion–policy congruence. This is the case even after controlling for the effects of electoral competition and other variables that might influence policy decisions.

The internal organizational arrangements of legislatures also have been linked to professionalization. As legislatures become more professionalized, for example, committee systems change more frequently (Freeman and Hedlund 1993), and power becomes less centralized in the hands of legislative leaders (Squire

1988a; 1988b; 1992a). Leadership styles are associated with legislative professionalization, with less collaborative approaches being found in more professionalized chambers (C. Rosenthal 1998). And career paths to the speakership are not as defined in more professionalized chambers as they are in less professionalized chambers (Freeman 1995).

Finally, there is a clear relationship between professionalization and legislative output. Legislative efficiency—the percentage of bills passed and the number of bills enacted per legislative day—is positively related to professionalization level (Squire 1998). The independence of legislative decision making from executive influence rises with professionalization (Thompson 1986). The propensity to reform government personnel practices increases with legislative professionalization (Kellough and Selden 2003), as does the willingness to adopt increasingly complex and technical policies (Ka and Teske 2002). And there is evidence that per capita government spending increases with the level of legislative professionalization (Owings and Borck 2000).[32]

The level of professionalization also appears to impact how legislators decide to design legislation covering the same policy issue. For example, why do different legislatures delegate different levels of authority to bureaucratic agencies? The literature on legislative–bureaucratic relations is extensive and has come to be dominated by the principal–agent framework from economics. After reviewing the theoretical work in this area, Huber and Shipan (2002, 40) contend that, "There exists a bias, then, in our theories of delegation, one that emphasizes explanatory factors that vary within polities—and particularly within the U.S. Congress—at the expense of explanatory factors that vary across polities." They suggest that the broader political environment in which legislators find themselves affects the strategies they use for controlling bureaucracies, arguing that where such environmental features do not vary, as in studies of the U.S. Congress, these aspects cannot become part of any theory of delegation. Huber and Shipan posit legislative professionalism as one potential factor that would affect the willingness of legislators to exercise control over the bureaucracy. Their findings are particularly instructive. They show that in the least professional legislatures—in their case measured by lower compensation levels, fewer staff, and fewer committees—there is relatively little difference in the degree of direction given to bureaucrats in legislatures with unified party control versus those in legislatures with divided party control. Legislators in legislatures with divided party control, however, are more likely to write laws that give bureaucrats less direction in implementing policies than are legislators in legislatures with unified party control, and this difference increases with the level of legislative professionalism (Huber and Shipan 2002, 159).

Overall, it seems clear that the cumulative effects of professionalization on a particular legislature can be profound. Rosenthal (1986, 135–36), for example, observes of New Jersey that,

> During the late 1960s and 1970s the legislature increased its capacity markedly and developed as a political institution. Standing committees became significant in the process, specialization began to be taken seriously, the legislative workload grew heavier, and more time and energy were devoted by members to their tasks. As important as anything else in the development of the legislature and its enhanced capacity was the expansion in the size and competence of its professional staff. . . . As a result, the legislature today insists on sharing not only in the credit for state policy, but also in its formulation.

The research questions raised by looking at professionalization both dynamically and comparatively are intriguing. Certainly, tracing the effects of reform on legislative organization and behavior in particular bodies is of interest. But thinking of professionalization in state legislatures as an attempt to emulate the development of the U.S. Congress suggests another research agenda. Consider this question: should legislative organizations that develop like one house of Congress come to operate in the same way as that chamber? Should rules, procedures, and structures develop to look the same? If professionalization leads to legislative chambers coming to look alike, then there is a strong argument to be made that professionalization is a path-dependent phenomenon. But if legislatures develop or maintain different organizational schemes and procedures as they professionalize—and a cursory look at American legislatures would suggest that this is the case—that observation creates a challenge for theories developed to explain the evolution of one chamber of Congress. The limitations of theories that work only to explain the result of evolution found, say, in the U.S. House will be exposed and scholars will be set on a hunt for variables, hypotheses and theories that can better account for the wider range of outcomes found in American legislatures.

Conclusion

Over the course of the twentieth century, nearly all state legislatures became more like the U.S. Congress, albeit most of them only marginally so. At the beginning of the twentieth century, the vast majority of state legislatures were very similar to each other in terms of pay and days in session. Over the next 90 years, substantial differences emerged. A few states became well-paid, full-time bodies much like Congress. Most states improved their lot relative to Congress, at least a little bit. But some failed to make up any ground at all.

We argued that the explanation for the growing disparity across the states is rooted in a simple explanation. State wealth—effectively the same thing as state population—made the biggest and most consistent difference. The relationship between state wealth and member pay over time, as revealed in tables 3–6 and

3–7, is straightforward and unambiguous. There has always been a very strong, positive relationship between member pay and state wealth. Indeed, the correlation between *state population in 1910 and legislative salary in 1999* is 0.638 ($p > 0.01$). Thus, the professionalization revolution did nothing to alter that basic association.

The reforms of the 1960s and 1970s did, however, link legislative session length with state wealth. By the last part of the twentieth century legislatures in wealthier states were meeting for more days than their poorer state counterparts. But that relationship is highly constrained by the various session length and meeting limits still imposed on many state legislatures today.

The evidence in support of competing theories to explain legislative professionalization is, at best, very weak and inconsistent. Support for the Democratic party manifested only an effect on member pay, and that only in the post-reform period. Similarly, there is mixed evidence suggesting that southern or traditionalistic states were more reluctant to pay their state legislators more than were other states, the most notable effect only surfacing in the most recent time period. Other than the Sullivan diversity index in the 1960 equation, none of the political culture or citizen demand variables influenced the move to longer state legislative sessions.

Finally, our findings point to the important effects that the professionalization revolution had on state legislatures between 1960 and 1981. Although some professionalization characteristics were already present by the time Jesse Unruh and the Citizens Conference rallied state legislatures to become more like Congress in the 1960s, their efforts did make a difference. But our data also reveal how the professionalization fervor dissipated by 1981. Indeed, many state legislatures lagged as far behind Congress in 1999 as they had in 1960. Thus, by the end of the twentieth century only a few state legislatures had professionalized to the extent that they were in any way akin to the U.S. Congress.

Unfortunately, the scholarly study of professionalization and its consequences is almost exclusively focused on state legislatures and not on Congress (Price 1975 being the notable exception). Exploring the differences in institutional attributes across legislatures gives us greater leverage on answering important questions about the organizational evolution of legislatures. An exclusive focus on the evolution of a single legislature, even one as important as the U.S. House, may well lead us astray if we fall into the trap of thinking its evolutionary path tells us very much about the evolutionary path of legislative bodies in general (e.g., Hibbing 1999).

·4·

Organizational Characteristics

We take organizational characteristics to include leadership, political parties, committees, and procedures. As noted in chapter 2, constitutional provisions establish some of these characteristics, but legislators have created most over time. Each characteristic is a central component in current theories of legislative organization and behavior. And, importantly, examining each beyond the confines of the U.S. Congress reveals considerable variation across chambers and over time.

The process of impeachment is but one example of a procedure that varies, both over time and across legislatures. Impeachment was imported from the English system, where the House of Commons bring charges against government officials and the House of Lords try them. American colonial assemblies in Maryland, Pennsylvania, and Virginia impeached high-ranking officials in the seventeenth century, although only Pennsylvania's charter explicitly granted that power (Hoffer and Hull 1978). In the 75 years prior to 1776, six more impeachment cases were tried in the colonies (Hoffer and Hull 1979). As with the British model, in each colonial case impeachment charges were brought by the lower house and tried by the upper house. This procedure was formally incorporated into the original state constitutions in eight states and, of course, in the U.S. Constitution as well.[1] Today, every state constitution, save for Oregon's, provides for an impeachment process.[2] The impeachment procedures, however, vary across the states. In Missouri judges, not legislators, try impeachment articles. In New York those impeached by the Assembly are tried by a combination of judges and state senators. And the process as we usually see it is reversed in Alaska, where impeachment articles are brought by the state senate and tried by the lower house, the rationale being that the latter with their two-year terms are, in theory, closer to the people and thus better equipped to serve as a jury (McBeath and Morehouse 1994, 147).

The major reason differences in organizational characteristics emerge across American legislative chambers is that, as was noted in both chapters 1 and 2, virtually all of them are empowered to establish their own rules and procedures. This flexibility allows for organizational characteristics to change over time. Some of the changes are truly evolutionary. Parliamentary procedures in the U.S. House, for example, have been slowly accreted over time. Some organizational changes, however, are—or at least appear to be—revolutionary. When, for example, the Republicans took control of the U.S. House for the first time in 40 years following the 1994 election, they instituted a number of significant changes in rules and organization (Evans and Oleszek 1997). From time to time, state legislative chambers also experience very quick reforms. Following the GOP's takeover of the Florida House of Representatives in 1998—the first time the party took control of the chamber since Reconstruction—the new majority (Jewett and Handberg 1999, 27),

> abolish[ed] subcommittees; increase[d] the number, but [shrank] the size, of standing committees; eliminate[d] the calendar committee and change[d] the calendar system; create[d] policy councils to organize the various committees and to rank all bills in priority order that have cleared committee for floor consideration; limit[ed] members to four bills referred at one time; allow[ed] bills to be carried over to the second year; increase[d] notice requirements; . . . limit[ed] what can be considered in the last days of the session; establish[ed] strong germanity rules; and permit[ed] closed bills under certain circumstances.

Thus, over time differences in organizational characteristics appear both within a legislative chamber, and across all legislative chambers.

Leadership

Every legislature has leaders. Yet, despite being ubiquitous, leadership is one of the least studied and least understood aspects of the legislative process. One obvious reason for the lack of progress on understanding legislative leadership is that there are relatively few legislative leaders in a chamber at any one time, giving us too few cases for rigorous analyses. And diachronic analyses of leadership in a single body leave us at the mercy of the vagaries of institutional and political change. Thus, as Peabody (1985, 239) noted over 15 years ago, "But, unless each legislature is *sui generis,* and some seem to argue so, there is much that remains to be done by way of comparative analysis. Leadership, which is common to all legislatures, seems to provide an appropriate vehicle for developing comparisons and generalizations beyond single-nation settings." We would, of course, extend the final comment to beyond single-chamber settings. State legislatures

ORGANIZATIONAL CHARACTERISTICS

provide the number of cases and the variation on important variables needed to advance the study of legislative leadership.

One source of variation is the size of the leadership structure. The U.S. House and Senate have relatively few leaders. The House has 14 leadership positions and the Senate has 13 positions.[3] The number of leaders in state legislative chambers varies considerably.[4] Among lower houses, Louisiana and Mississippi have just two leaders: a speaker (a position found in every lower house), and a speaker pro tem. The other extreme is represented by the 151-member Connecticut House which has 49 leadership posts: a speaker, 3 deputy speakers, a majority leader, 4 deputy majority leaders, 14 assistant majority leaders, a majority whip-at-large, a deputy majority whip, 3 assistant majority whips, a minority leader, 3 deputy minority leaders, a deputy majority leader-at-large, 12 assistant minority leaders, and 4 minority whips.

State senate leadership structures also vary. The lieutenant governor is the president of the senate in 26 states, at least superficially holding the same position as the vice-president in the U.S. Senate. But some, such as the lieutenant governors in Georgia and Texas, exercise enormous power within their state senates (Halter 1997, 104–5; Rosenthal 1998, 248). In the other 24 state senates the president is elected by the membership. And, again, the size of the leadership structures varies. In four states (Louisiana, Mississippi, South Carolina, and Texas) only a president pro tem supplements the president. Other senates operate with far more leaders. In the 36-member Connecticut state senate, for example, there are 28 designated leadership positions.[5]

Leadership positions also vary in tenure. Speaker careers in the U.S. House were short until the twentieth century (Polsby 1968, 150–51), at which time they became considerably longer. A similar story unfolds in many, but not all, state lower chambers. In California, for example, no speaker served in successive sessions until C. C. Young did between 1913 and 1919 (Driscoll 1986, 199–200). Longer tenures became the norm from that point on, with Willie Brown setting the record, serving as speaker from 1981 to 1995. Many other state legislative chambers saw similar changes, with regular turnover among top leaders being replaced by longer careers (Squire 1992c, 180–185). Chambers in some states, however, continue to change leaders regularly. Indeed, constant change is essentially mandated by the imposition of legislative term limits in the 15 states that have them. The effect can be dramatic. The California Assembly, for example, which first had term limits take effect in 1996, had six different speakers in the six years after Willie Brown left in 1995.

A final source of variation is the power or authority accorded to legislative leaders. Leadership power varies over time as studies of the U.S. House speakership reveal (e.g., Cooper and Brady 1981a; Peters 1997). Examining change in leadership power over time in one chamber is, however, daunting because, of course, so many other things change as well. The political worlds in which

CHAPTER 4

TABLE 4-1 Institutional Power Index of Lower House Speakers

Chamber	Appoint	Committee	Resource	Procedure	Tenure	Total
WV	5	4	5	4.5	5	23.5
NH	5	4	5	4	5	23
AZ	3	5	5	4.5	5	22.5
MI	3	4	5	4.5	5	21.5
OR	3	4.5	5	4.	5	21.5
UT	3	4	5	4.5	5	21.5
WI	3	4	5	4.5	5	21.5
IL	5	3.5	5	2.5	5	21
NM	3	4	5	4	5	21
NY	5	4	3	4	5	21
OK	4	4	5	4.5	3	20.5
HOUSE CANNON	5	4	1	5	5	20
ID	3	5	3	4	5	20
IA	3	5	3	4	5	20
MO	3	2.5	5	4.5	5	20
NC	3	5	3	4	5	20
OH	3	4	5	3	5	20
IN	3	4	3	4.5	5	19.5
MN	3	5	3	3.5	5	19.5
TX	4	1	5	4.5	5	19.5
ME	3	4	5	2	5	19
MT	3	4	3	4	5	19
TN	3	4	3	4	5	19
VT	3	4	3	4	5	19
VA	3	4	3	4	5	19
RI	3	4	3	3.5	5	18.5
WA	2	4	5	2.5	5	18.5
CO	3	2.5	3	4.5	5	18
GA	3	4	3	3	5	18
PA	3	1	5	4	5	18
DE	3	5	0	4.5	5	17.5
MD	4	4	0	4.5	5	17.5
NV	3	4	3	2.5	5	17.5
NJ	3	5	3	4.5	2	17.5
CT	4	4.5	3	3.5	2	17
LA	3	4	1	4	5	17
MA	5	2.5	3	2.5	4	17
ND	3	4	5	4	1	17
SC	1	4	3	3.5	5	16.5
AL	3	4	0	4	5	16
KS	3	4.5	3	3.5	2	16
AR	3	0	3	4.5	5	15.5
CA	2	1.5	3	3.5	5	15
SD	3	4	3	3	2	15
HOUSE HASTERT	2	1.5	3	4	4	14.5
FL	4	5	0	4	1	14
KY	2	1	3	3	5	14
AK	2	1	3	2.5	5	13.5
MS	2	1	0	4.5	4	11.5
HI	1	0	0	4.5	5	10.5
WY	2	1	0	3.5	1	7.5

Sources: Data on state legislative speakers are from Clucas (2001, 326–27). Data on U.S. House Speakers Cannon and Hastert coded by the authors using Clucas's (2001, 335–36) coding scheme.

ORGANIZATIONAL CHARACTERISTICS

speakers Joe Cannon and Dennis Hastert operated are hard to compare. An alternative strategy made possible by the existence of a large number of similar legislative chambers is cross-sectional comparison. One recent effort along these lines is Clucas's (2001) attempt to test hypotheses generated by principal–agent theory using speakership powers in lower state legislative chambers. Clucas measured speakership power by looking at several different aspects of it, among them the ability to appoint other leaders, committee chairs, and committee members, as well as the office's tenure potential and control over various resources and procedures. Using his coding scheme we supplement Clucas's scores for speakership power in the 49 lower state houses with scores for U.S. House speakers Cannon and Hastert. As table 4–1 reveals, speakers in several states currently employ great powers along the lines of those enjoyed by Cannon. Indeed, several speakers exercise even greater powers, mostly because of their greater control over campaign finance resources. And Hastert's less impressive institutional powers are similar to those of speakers in a handful of state houses. To us, this suggests the possibility that examining the relatively large number of state legislative chambers can significantly advance our understanding of how legislative leaders operate in presidential or transformational legislatures.

Political Parties

Political parties organize every American legislature, save for Nebraska (and, in recent history, Minnesota from 1914 to 1973). Except in the very earliest Congresses, it has always been the case that the majority party votes as a bloc and organizes the chamber. A similar process usually unfolds in the states. As Jewell and Patterson (1986, 119) observe, "In most two-party legislatures, the presiding officer is selected by the majority party caucus, the members of which will normally unite behind that choice in balloting on the floor of the house or senate." While that is certainly what happens in most legislatures most of the time, the last 25 years has witnessed a rash of bipartisan coalitions electing state legislative leaders. Chambers in Alaska, California, Connecticut, Illinois, Massachusetts, New Mexico, North Carolina, Tennessee, Vermont, and Washington experienced one or more such coalitions (Hansen 1989, 11; Jewell and Patterson 1986, 120; Rosenthal 1981, 155–156; 1998, 248). Why majority party unity dissolves is not clear; examination of coalition cases suggests strong issues differences within the majority party can be important, but the more typical case is one where deep dissatisfaction with the actions and conduct of an incumbent majority party leader leads those in his or her party who are disaffected to seek an accommodation with members of the opposition party. Some of these coalitions last over a full session or two; others are, in the words of a Connecticut representative, only (Jacklin 1989) "one-day dates." But, the important point is that coalitional government does occasionally occur in the American legislative system, the congressional experience notwithstanding.

Another difference in the role of party in the two sorts of institutions is that in modern American history, neither the U.S. House nor the Senate can be said to have ever been a one-party legislature. The experience in many state legislatures is, of course, dramatically different. As recently as 1960, for example, there were *no* Republican state legislators in Alabama, Arkansas, Georgia, Louisiana, Mississippi, South Carolina, and Texas, and only a handful in Florida, Maryland, New Mexico, North Carolina, Oklahoma, Tennessee, and Virginia. Over the course of the next 40 years, the situation changed, in some cases dramatically (Martorano, Anderson, and Hamm, 2000). By 2001, both parties were represented in every legislature, although each had a few chambers in which it dominated. The process of moving from a one-party to a two-party chamber has important consequences for leadership power and the committee assignment process (Hamm and Harmel 1993; Harmel 1986).

Parties in state legislative chambers vary from those in Congress and among each other in several additional ways. First, they vary in the power exercised by party caucuses. In some legislative chambers party caucuses are powerful, even to the point of making votes binding on certain important issues as in the New Mexico and Oklahoma legislatures (Rosenthal 1998, 281). Yet in other state legislative chambers caucuses are very weak or even essentially nonexistent. The importance of caucuses also seems to vary over time. According to Hamm and Hedlund (1994, 968), as many as one-quarter of the strong-party caucuses in the 1950s were not powerful by the 1980s. The importance of party caucuses appears to be a function of size and the degree of party competition in the chamber. The more evenly matched the parties and the smaller the chamber, the greater importance of caucuses (Francis 1989, 45).

Second, parties vary in the power and influence exercised by legislative campaign committees (Gierzynski 1992, 48–50; Rosenthal 1995). In some states, party campaign committees controlled by the leadership are responsible for raising the bulk of the money members spend on their reelection efforts. In other states campaign fundraising falls almost exclusively on the members themselves. Overall, the power and influence state legislative leaders have to affect the ability of their members to achieve their policy or career goals vary substantially.

The variation in party power across state legislatures offers legislative scholars a different and potentially critical venue in which to test the most significant hypotheses about the effects of party on member behavior. Whether and to what extent party actually influences member behavior, particularly voting behavior, is perhaps the most important and contentious current debate among congressional scholars. Some, most notably Krehbiel (1993; 1998; 1999a; 1999b), argue that leaders find the majority pivot point, consequently party evidences little independent influence. Others (e.g., Binder, Lawrence, and Maltzman 1999; McCarty, Poole, and Rosenthal 2001) have struggled to find evidence and tests to dispute Krehbiel's ideas. Unfortunately, although the theories are couched in very general terms, their data and tests are focused exclusively on Congress. Thus, the critical tests they offer employ data on activities that can only be described as congressional minutiae: a rare discharge petition (Krehbiel 1995; Binder, Lawrence, and Maltzman 1999) or the handful of congressional party switchers over the last half-century (McCarty, Poole, and Rosenthal 2001).

Because state legislatures offer variation on a number of relevant institutional variables, they offer an exceptional opportunity for scholars to develop a wide-ranging set of tests to try and uncover the effects of party in more common procedural activities. Indeed, it seems reasonable to think that if you are looking for evidence of party discipline, you should look for it in places where you have reason to think that its presence might vary. Trying to uncover evidence of party influence in a single institution is difficult, even if looking over time. Thus, if Krehbiel is correct and American legislatures are majoritarian institutions, we should not find clear and convincing evidence of party influence across state legislative chambers. If we do uncover evidence of party influence, the variation on important variables supplied by state legislatures should allow us to determine the conditions under which party power surfaces.

Such analyses can be done. It is essentially what Jenkins (1999) does in his creative comparison of voting in the party organized U.S. House and the non–party organized Confederate House during the Civil War. Perhaps even more importantly, the same sorts of votes and voting data exist for state legislatures as for Congress, although the former may be harder to gather than the latter. Data on state legislatures will not, of course, necessarily solve the thorny methodological and theoretical puzzles that plague this line of research. But, again, it is hard to argue against the notion that more data and more variation on key variables will be of major assistance. The recent work by Wright and Schaffner (2002), comparing the impact of party on party polarization and dimensionality of campaign issue stances on roll call voting in the Kansas Senate and the largely comparable, but nonpartisan, Nebraska Unicameral, provides evidence for the utility of such studies.

Legislative Committees

Recently, an authoritative textbook on Congress noted (Stewart 2001, 275), "In the century since [Woodrow] Wilson wrote, political scientists have written volumes about the behavior of congressional committees. . . . Corresponding with their critical positions in the legislative process, congressional committees are the most-studied part of Congress." No similar statement can be made about the role that committees play in the fifty states. Moreover, it is also clear that committees are not the most-studied aspect of the state legislative process. What recent work that there has been, however, has tended to be comparative in nature, encompassing committees in several legislatures (e.g., Battista 2000; Francis 1989; Hamm and Hedlund 1995; Squire, Hamm, Hedlund, and Moncrief n.d.).

Theoretical progress in the congressional area has been nothing short of remarkable, including Shepsle and Weingast's (1981) structure-induced equilibrium concept, Krehbiel's (1991) informational model, and Cox and McCubbins' (1993) partisan theory. Recently, scholars are beginning to apply the theories developed in the study of Congress to state legislatures (e.g., Battista 2000; Overby and Kazee 2000; Overby, Kazee, and Prince 2004; Martorano, Hamm, and Hedlund 2000; Martorano 2001). While we applaud these efforts and want to encourage more, we suggest that investigators, after formulating research questions, be cautious in choosing the state legislatures in which to conduct their research. In the following section, we compare committees in Congress and the state legislatures, identifying differences that both offer research opportunities and create important obstacles to comparative research.

The Rise of Committee Systems

As noted in chapter 1, standing committee systems were a regular feature of many colonial assemblies. And the Congress under the Articles experimented with standing committees (Jillson and Wilson 1994, 99–106). Standing committees were not, however, initially part of the organizational scheme in either the U.S. House or Senate.[6] The transformation of those committee systems from ones of ad hoc special or select committees to standing committees has received a fair amount of scholarly attention over the years (e.g., Galloway 1959; Gamm and Shepsle 1989; Harlow 1917; Jameson 1894; Jenkins 1998; Risjord 1992; Skladony 1985; Stewart 2001, 284–87; Swift 1989) and the storyline is pretty well understood even if debate over theoretical explanations for it continues.

Relatively little is known about the development of committee systems in state legislatures. What scraps of information we can find suggests their development generally parallels that in Congress, or precedes it in a few cases.[7] According to Harlow (1917, 66; see also Jameson 1894, 267), standing committees appeared in Massachusetts in 1777, and a "fairly elaborate system had developed by 1790." Standing committees were a prominent part of the South Carolina legislative system by 1791, and they were also found in Georgia, Maryland, New Jersey, and Virginia. Dodds (1918, 36–37) reports that in 1800 there were 7 standing committees in the New York Assembly, a number that increased to 29 by 1830 as committees were given the authority to introduce legislation. In Pennsylvania standing committees were in existence by 1813 and institutionalized in the rules by 1827 (Dodds 1918, 37). Examining the South Atlantic states during the first decade of the nineteenth century, Broussard (1977, 48) found a flourishing committee system, noting that, "Then, as now, much of the work of the legislature was done in committee, where petitions, claims, and executive messages were considered and bills first drafted."

The experience in New Jersey may have been typical. By 1830, the New Jersey Assembly operated with five standing committees: Incidental Expenses, Rules, Support, Taxes, and Unfinished Business. Within ten years additional standing committees were created to handle legislative matters on agriculture, corporations, education, elections, judicial proceedings, the militia, military pensions, and ways and means. The majority party almost always held a majority on the standing committees, and the committee's chair was usually a veteran member of the Assembly. Such experience was necessary, because committees played an important role in the legislative process. Although they did not have gate-keeping powers—all bills were brought to the floor—every piece of legislation had to first go to a committee and, once brought to the full chamber, committee members were given the opportunity to report on their findings (Levine 1977, 46–50).

State legislatures created after the revolutionary period appear to have developed standing committee system either from their inception or shortly thereafter. In Illinois, for example, standing committees appear from the second assembly on (Davis 1988, 104), and in Indiana they also are in evidence from very early in the institution's history (Walsh 1987, 93). State legislatures created in the middle of the nineteenth century instituted standing committee systems from the start. In Iowa, there were 15 standing committees in the House and 16 standing committees in the Senate during the legislature's first session in 1846 (Briggs 1916, 88–89, Horack 1916). Their immediate existence is not a surprise because it was a continuation of the practice of the territorial legislature (Briggs 1916, 36–37). Standing committees were also part of the California legislature's initial session in 1849 (Bancroft 1888, 315–17; Goodwin 1914, 262), as well as the first session of the Texas state Senate in 1845 (Spaw 1990, 170). Committee systems apparently had become standard operating procedure in American legislatures by the 1840s. Indeed, when the founders of the Confederacy created the Confederate Congress, standing committees were part of the original organization of both the House and Senate (Jenkins 1999, 1149).

Committee systems did, however, evolve in different ways across the states. On occasion, the number of committees in some state legislative chambers has been remarkably large. Between 1948 and 1956, for example, the 49-member Mississippi state Senate had 46 committees, with the median senator having nine assignments (Fortenberry and Hobbs 1967, 82). In the late 1950s the Florida Senate had 38 members and 39 committees; every member but the president chaired one (Beth and Havard 1961, 67). And in 1961, the Arkansas House of Representatives, with 100 members, had 70 committees (Wells 1967, 4). With the adoption of Rule XIII in 1963, however, the Arkansas House drastically reduced the number of committees to 26, including 24 standing committees and 2 subcommittees (Wells 1967, 3). Dramatic structural changes like this offer scholars opportunities for examining the effects of committees on members and the legislative process.

Currently, most state legislatures operate with relatively smaller numbers of committees. But there is still considerable variation between and across chambers. In 2002, for example, Colorado operated with 8 committees in the upper house and 12 committees in the lower house. In contrast, each chamber in Mississippi had 35 committees. And several state legislatures, notably Connecticut, Maine, and Massachusetts, developed systems that operate almost exclusively with joint standing committees rather than chamber-based standing committees. How committee systems developed in the states and why the systems vary are questions that need to be answered.

Committee Importance

One potential pitfall for legislative scholars is to assume that committees have the same impact in all state legislatures that they have in Congress. While committees in every legislature are involved in lawmaking, we know their importance varies, both over time within a particular legislature, and across legislatures. How do we develop a metric that permits us to capture these differences? Van Der Slik and Redfield (1986, 139) give an excellent example of over-time change in committee power. They report that during the 1960s committees in the Illinois House favorably reported 81 percent of the bills referred to them. The corresponding figure for committees in the state Senate was even higher: 83 percent. By the early 1980s committees in both houses were exercising considerably more gatekeeping authority, with House committees recommending only 46 percent of bills, and Senate committees 65 percent of bills. In terms of cross-sectional analysis, the difficulty is collecting information on a sufficiently large number of legislative chambers at one point in time. Francis (1989) provided one of the few comprehensive evaluations. He asked legislators serving in the 1981 legislative session to select the three most important decision-making loci from a list of nine possible sources. In this discussion, we will focus on just three areas: committees, leadership, and party caucus. As shown in table 4–2, committees were deemed to be an important decision-making center in 81 of the 99 legislative chambers. In only three states (i.e., California, Illinois, and New Jersey) were committees deemed to be unimportant in both chambers. In almost two-thirds of the chambers committees shared power with the leadership, the party caucus, or both entities. In only about 15 percent of the chambers did committees hold sway without the assistance of either the leadership or caucuses. Somewhat surpris-

ORGANIZATIONAL CHARACTERISTICS

TABLE 4-2 The Importance of Committees in State Legislative Decision Making[a]

Decision-Making Centers	Number of Chambers
Committees	15
Committees and Leadership	29
Committees and Party Caucus	16
Committees, Leadership, and Party Caucus	21
Leadership and Party Caucus	12
Leadership	5
Total	99

Source: Francis (1989, 44).
[a]Fifty percent of the majority party respondents must have selected the survey item for it to be included.

ingly, the same pattern of decision making occurred in both houses in just 21 of the 49 states with bicameral legislatures. For example, committees and leadership were identified as being key in the Massachusetts Senate, while leadership, be it presiding officers or majority leaders, was the only power center chosen by members of the Massachusetts House.[8]

What implications do these varied responses have for those who wish to study legislative committees? First, it may be useful to envision the role that committees play in the legislative process as falling along a continuum from negligible to very important. Data on committee importance across legislative chambers could be used to test theories formulated to explain what variables are associated with strong committees. For example, Francis' (1989, 46) work suggests that a crucial variable is size of the majority party. As the size of the majority party increases, committees take on more responsibility. If this observation is correct, then is it the case that as state legislatures in the South have become more competitive, the role of committees in those chambers has diminished? A second implication is that research questions could be posed that take advantage of the variability in committee importance. For example, how does variation in committee importance influence a committee member's interest and participation in committee deliberations? Does Krehbiel's (1991) notion of capturing gains from specialization while minimizing deviation from majority-preferred outcomes apply across the continuum of state legislatures given variation in committee power?

An important concern facing scholars investigating state legislative committees is whether data from the Francis study, collected during the 1981 legislative session, can prove useful for studies focusing on recent legislative sessions. Can we simply assume that these institutions are operating in a steady-state environment, and thus should exhibit stable patterns over time? Data that permit us to assess the stability of decision-making centers over time are sorely lacking. To our knowledge, the only cross-time data covers a 16-year period (1971–1986) for

36 chambers (Hamm and Hedlund 1994). In that study, the general rankings of the key centers of decision-making were fairly consistent over time, but enough chambers exhibited sufficient changes from the 1970s to the 1980s to warrant careful consideration of the issue. More importantly, it could be argued that the legislative environment in some state legislatures has changed drastically over a 20-year period, thus potentially altering the loci of decision making. Without question the imposition of term limits is one such event.

Committee Jurisdiction

The jurisdictional prerogatives of congressional committees are fairly well understood. According to Oleszek (2001, 81), "Precedent, public laws, turf battles, and the jurisdictional mandates of the committees as set forth in the rules of the House and Senate determine which committees receive which kinds of bills." Thus, as Stewart (2001, 277) notes, "The rules of both chambers now delineate in fine detail which matters belong to which committees."

The legislative scholar who approaches state legislatures with the expectation of finding such detail will be sorely disappointed. For example, a recent study of constitutions, statutes, and formal rules (but not resolutions, precedents, or usages) governing the 1999 legislative session found that in only 21 percent of 71 chambers investigated were full jurisdictions listed, while jurisdictions for a limited number of committees (e.g., appropriations) were found in another 13 percent of the chambers. In other words, no information on committee jurisdictions could be ascertained from the relevant documents in almost two-thirds of the chambers studied (Martorano, Hamm, and Hedlund 2000).

What are the research consequences for the fact that several state legislative chambers do not have formal committee jurisdictions? One possibility is that it will force scholars to spend a fair amount of time documenting the jurisdictions in particular state legislatures relying on resolutions, precedents, and norms. Even this strategy may prove futile in some cases since in a survey of legislative clerks and secretaries, respondents from 19 of the 91 participating chambers, including those from such professional bodies as the Michigan House, Ohio House, and Wisconsin Assembly, indicated that they did not use any criteria to refer bills (American Society of Legislative Clerks and Secretaries and National Conference of State Legislatures, listed hereafter as ASLCS and NCSL, 1998, 3–17). A second consequence is that the absence of jurisdictions in some chambers calls into question the applicability of theories of committees that assume this condition to exist. Theories developed basically from a congressional model will have to be reformulated to account for this variation. One possibility is to incorporate the jurisdictional concept as a variable and see what impact it has on the policymaking process.

ORGANIZATIONAL CHARACTERISTICS

Committee Assignments

The general outlines of the role of parties and seniority in the congressional committee assignment process are quite well understood, although major committee reforms adopted by the One Hundred and Fourth Congress altered some of the longstanding procedures (Evans and Oleszek 1997). For those familiar with the congressional system, the procedures used in the states can be confusing. We suggest that legislative scholars who focus on committee assignments at the state legislative level should be wary of four potential pitfalls.

The first potential problem involves assuming that the majority party stacks committees with a greater percentage of its members than their representation in the chamber would warrant, as tends to happen in the U.S. Congress, particularly on the most powerful committees. At the state legislative level proportional representation occurs in a number of chambers. In 25 of 91 chambers an explicit rule mandates proportional representation, while in another 45 chambers the practice is usually followed even though it is not required by any legal dictate (ASLCS and NCSL 1998, 4-4). A recent empirical analysis supports this finding. In examining data for the 1977–78 and 1989–90 legislative sessions Hedlund and Hamm (1996, 391) find, "a fair share rule, plus or minus 5% on either side of absolute proportionality, applies in a majority of the committees from chambers in which the majority party had less than 90% of the chamber seats." If overrepresentation of the majority party occurs, it is more likely to be on chamber control and fiscal committees (Hedlund and Hamm 1996).

The second potential pitfall is in assuming that the number of committee assignments is somehow dictated by the formal rules. At the congressional level, a major rules change in the One Hundred and Fourth Congress limited members to two full committees and four subcommittees, and even further limited chairs and ranking minority members (Smith and Lawrence 1997, 173). In contrast, in roughly eight out of ten state legislative chambers examined in 1999 there were no formal limits on the number of committee assignments a member could receive (Martorano, Hamm, and Hedlund 2000).[9]

A third potential pitfall is assuming that the minority party controls the assignment of its members to committees. According to a 1998 study by the ASLCS and NCSL (1998, Table 96-4.8), the minority leader appointed minority party members in only 18 chambers while making recommendations in another 22 chambers. In most of the remaining chambers, the presiding officer, who is usually from the majority party, makes the decision. For example, in the 2001 legislative session in the Vermont House, Republican Speaker Walter Freed (Mackey 2001, 46), "appointed Democrats to committees who were strong advocates for the minority position, in order to allow full and free debate on issues within each committee."

The fourth potential problem relates to the idea of a seniority system. In most states the rules are silent on this issue, but exceptions exist. A recent study of the rules in place during the 1999 legislative session in 71 chambers found seniority mentioned in 6 chambers (Martorano, Hamm, and Hedlund 2000). At one end of the continuum, a Michigan House rule (1.105) simply says that the person with authority "shall also consider the preferences and seniority as well as the experiences of members in making appointments." In a few chambers the focus is on chamber seniority. For example, in the Texas House (Rules of the Texas House 1999, Rule 4, Section 2), "a maximum of one-half of the membership on each standing committee, exclusive of the chair and vice-chair shall be determined by seniority." The rules went on to state that seniority referred to time served in the house, and that the rule did not apply to procedural committees. A slightly more restrictive case emerges in the Mississippi House (Rule 60(4b)). Members who have served more than four years and who were not appointed to either the Appropriations or Ways and Means Committee have the right to serve on at least three of seven key committees. Those members with less than four years service have the right to serve on two of the seven committees. Until the GOP took control of the South Carolina Senate in 2001 committee positions were filled based upon seniority (Hoope 2001, 32–34). Members made four choices of unfilled positions in order of seniority and then went back and made one more choice. The key, however, was a rule (Rule 19–4) awarding committee property rights: "Any Senator who served on a Standing Committee in the session immediately past shall have the right to serve on such committee regardless of the Senator's seniority in the Senate."[10] Finally, in the Georgia House, except for the Committee on Rules and the Committee on Interstate Cooperation, Rule 6 holds, "a member shall remain on the committee to which he is appointed so long as he is member of the House," while in the Georgia Senate the same rule (Rule 185g) applies without exception.

A hypothetical example demonstrates the possible consequences of not paying attention to the potential pitfalls. An aspiring graduate student, after taking a course on Congress, decides to develop a model using Cox and McCubbins' (1993) work on parties as cartels, focusing on how both the majority and minority parties go about assigning members to committees to see if party loyalty matters. Do members who vote most frequently with the majority of their party receive the most important assignments? Are those who are less loyal not reappointed? A basic assumption of the model is the not unreasonable supposition that each party controls the appointment process. Having few resources, the student decides to select a sample of legislative chambers based upon the most accessible material. The result is an eight-chamber study including the lower houses in Colorado, Georgia, Illinois, Iowa, Maine, New York, Texas, and Wisconsin. The analysis confirms the loyalty argument in five chambers, but not for the minority party in Iowa, New York, and Texas. The author suggests that the findings from Texas may be attributable to the recent development of a strong second party in that state. The cases of Iowa and New York are listed as anomalies in need of further research. The article is submitted for review and rejected. The reviewers point out that the research design is faulty. First, the minority party does not control the assignment process, either formally or informally, in four of the chambers (Georgia, Maine, New York, and Texas). Thus, two of the findings are false positives (Georgia and Maine) while the contrary findings are at least due to the nature of the assignment process. A second criticism is that the formal power to make assignments is lodged in the minority party only in Colorado and Illinois, while informal recommending occurs in Iowa and Wisconsin. Thus, the Iowa case may not conform because the minority leader does not make the final decision. Finally, some type of formal seniority rule is operative in two chambers (Georgia and Texas), thus calling into question any conclusions regarding either party.

Subcommittees

Not long ago, Congressional subcommittees were a major focus of legislative research (e.g., Deering and Smith 1985; Davidson 1981; Haeberle 1978). Since the mid-1990s (Stewart 2001, 303), "with the ascendance of the Republican party in the House, this era of subcommittee government ended—or at least changed significantly." For those who want to test arguments for the development and action of subcommittees in Congress at the state legislative level we offer a word of caution. If one were to inquire as to whether subcommittees are used in state legislatures, the answer would be yes in over 90 percent of the chambers (ASLCS and NCSL 1998). This figure, however, would be misleading because the term subcommittee takes on many meanings across the states. To make the answer to the question more relevant, we need to know whether the committees are permanent for the session or are more transitory. In roughly 40 percent of the state legislative chambers subcommittees are created for an issue that exists only temporarily or they are created to deal with only a specific bill.[11] Subcommittees that last for the entire session exist in slightly more than 50 of the chambers, but even among this group there is variation. Standing subcommittees of the sort discussed in the congressional literature exist in roughly 40 percent of state legislative chambers, sometimes in combination with more transitory types of subcommittees.[12]

Conference Committees

Tsebelis and Money (1997) argue that to understand the behavior within a legislative chamber in a bicameral system it is necessary to understand the interaction between the chambers. Of particular importance for our discussion is the way formal policy disagreements between the chambers of a legislature are resolved. While the option exists to shuttle legislation between chambers until a resolution is reached, a fair amount of recent literature has dealt in detail with the conference committee solution at the congressional level (Smith 1989; Longley and Oleszek 1989; Krehbiel 1991).

Are conference committees at the state level similar to those in Congress? It is important to observe that conference committees are not necessarily a regular feature of American legislatures. The New York state legislature, for example, first instituted conference committees only in 1995 (Fisher 1995; Silber 1995) and it still employs them only infrequently (McKinley 2002).[13] Up until 1993 the Washington state legislature used a process involving written statements giving the reasons for different provisions passed between the conferees from the two chambers followed by the appointment of a free conference committee if the initial process failed to resolve the differences. The initial conferees were constrained to only consider the specific provisions contained in the bills passed by each chamber, while the free conference committee was virtually unconstrained (Seeberger 1997, 71). And even where conference committees have long been part of the legislative process, they may not be the main mechanism for resolving differences between the chambers. In Colorado, for example, only about one bill in six that passes both chambers of the state legislature goes to conference. Most chamber differences are resolved through other means (Straayer 1996). The use of conference committees also changes over time within particular chambers. Only 19 conference committees were used in Minnesota in 1963; during the 1987–88 session over 157 conference committees were instituted (Hanson 1989, 125).

Even where conference committees are a routine part of the process, there are still five notable differences between their use in Congress and in state legislatures. First, at the congressional level there is no requirement that the number of members appointed to the conference committee from the two houses be equal (Tsebelis and Money 1997, 198). In contrast, equality of membership is the norm in most state legislatures, typically ranging from three to five members per chamber (ASLCS and NCSL 1998, Table 96–4.16).[14]

Second, in terms of membership (Longley and Oleszek 1989, 109), "when the House and Senate go to conference, members of each chamber delegation are traditionally drawn almost entirely from a single substantive committee of that house." The situation in the states is quite different as a recent report summarized (ASLCS and NCSL 1998, 4–39):

> ... those frequently named to conference committees are the authors of bills, the chairs of standing committees, those with expertise or interest in the issue and those able to represent the body or caucus most capably. Seventeen chambers even make

ORGANIZATIONAL CHARACTERISTICS

sure that opposing views are represented by requiring at least one appointee to have originally voted against the bills.

That study goes on to report that in 13 chambers no specific criteria are used to appoint conferees.

Third, as Tsebelis and Money (1997, 200) contend, ". . . the rules of the [congressional] conference committee deliberations are nonexistent: no quorum rules, no proxy rules, no amendment rules, no voting procedure rules." In more than a majority of the state legislatures, however, the conference committee procedure is set by joint rule (ASLCS and NCSL 1998, 4–41), although more research is needed to determine the nature of those rules.

Conference committees at the congressional level are supposed to deal only with issues of disagreement between the two chambers, although the use of substitute amendments by the second chamber significantly enhances the conference committee's freedom (Tsebelis and Money 1997, 201). At the state level, the decision making scope of conference committees ranges from always being limited to always being unlimited (ASLCS and NCSL 1998, 4–53). More importantly, in nine states the lower house and senate respondent to the question on scope of consideration (i.e., scope is always open versus scope is always closed) gave significantly different answers. If a legislative scholar wanted to undertake a comparative analysis of conference committees, great care would have to be made in determining the actual degree of freedom the conference committee is permitted.[15]

Fifth and finally, and perhaps most importantly, the operative decision rule in congressional conference committees is concurrent majorities of the two delegations. While this rule is the norm in state legislatures, conference committees in several states operate under a majority vote of all conferees (e.g., Alaska, Illinois, Louisiana, Maryland, Missouri, Virginia, West Virginia) and a few even operate under a unanimous vote requirement of all conferees (e.g., Indiana, New Hampshire) (ASLCS and NCSL 1998, Table 96–4.21). Legislative scholars need to explore the theoretical and empirical effects of these different decision rules.

One interesting question that has been raised at the congressional level is which chamber wins in conference committee (Ferejohn 1975; Steiner 1951; Strom and Rundquist 1977; Vogler 1970). Generally, congressional level studies have concluded that the Senate wins more than it loses. Strom and Rundquist (1977) suggest this happens because the Senate usually acts second, forcing the House, which has already compromised within its chamber to move the bill, to compromise further to get the bill out of the conference committee. Gross (1980) tested the Strom and Rundquist (1977) theory using conference committee data from ten state legislatures, generally finding consistent results. Given the variety of rules used to structure conference committee decision making across the states, more work is needed to further test theories suggesting that sequence matters.

Legislative Procedures

American legislatures operate with extensive and complex sets of rules and procedures. For the most part, it appears that newly established American legislatures inherit them from their ancestral assemblies. The initial colonial assemblies, for example, relied heavily on the established procedures of the British Parliament (Greene 1969, 345–47; Johnson 1987, 350–51; Pargellis 1927a, 83; 1927b, 156). In turn, the original assemblies became models for newer assemblies. Greene (1961, 458), for example, notes, "Younger bodies such as the Georgia Commons and the Nova Scotia Assembly were particularly indebted to their more mature counterparts in South Carolina and Massachusetts Bay."

The lineage of procedures and rules becomes somewhat more complicated in legislatures established since the American Revolution.[16] McConachie (1898, 367) provides this speculative account of the way rules were developed in Illinois:

> In 1818, the backwoodsmen of French Kaskaskia had small store of experience, and maybe but one exemplar in the way of books, the journals and annals of Congress. Appended to the former they fortunately—or unfortunately—found the rules of the national House, from which both chambers clipped out blocks of regulations almost word for word.

A more systematic examination of the heritage of the rules in the Indiana state legislature provides a more complex, yet consistent, picture (Walsh 1987, 92):

> The first general assemblies drew their rules from those adopted by the House of Representatives during the first territorial assembly in Indiana in 1805. These were in turn based upon rules adopted by the first session of the House of Representatives of the Northwest Territory in 1799.

The rules of the Northwest Territory House were direct descendants of the rules developed during the first session of the U.S. House.

Thus, the rules and procedures employed by American legislatures today share common roots. Over time in each legislature and each chamber, however, they evolve in different and sometimes very distinctive ways. Thus, while in some ways American legislatures today appear to be very similar, once the surface is scratched interesting differences appear.

Lawmaking: An Assembly Line?

From a functional standpoint, lawmaking is often seen as the main reason for

ORGANIZATIONAL CHARACTERISTICS

TABLE 4-3 Work Productivity in American Legislatures, 1997-98

State	Total Bills Introduced	Total Enactments	Total Vetoes	Percentage of Bills Enacted	Vetoes per Enactment	Bills per Member	Enactments per Member
AK	851	255	18	30.0%	7.1%	14.2	4.3
ND	881	554	11	62.9%	2.0%	6.0	3.8
MT	1013	552	7	54.5%	1.3%	6.8	3.7
VT	1072	179	0	16.7%	0.0%	6.0	1.0
OH	1129	239	1	21.2%	0.4%	8.6	1.8
SD	1129	597	20	52.9%	3.4%	10.8	5.7
NV	1167	691	3	59.2%	0.4%	18.5	11.0
DE	1181	490	18	41.5%	3.7%	19.0	7.9
CO	1218	691	43	56.7%	6.2%	12.2	6.9
UT	1359	819	13	60.3%	1.6%	13.1	7.9
NE	1363	426	19	31.3%	4.5%	27.8	8.7
KY	1369	552	4	40.3%	0.7%	9.9	4.0
ID	1405	842	15	59.9%	1.8%	13.4	8.0
WI	1521	338	9	22.2%	2.7%	11.5	2.6
KS	1730	395	3	22.8%	0.8%	10.5	2.4
NH	1998	739	9	37.0%	1.2%	4.7	1.7
AR	2041	1362	9	66.7%	0.7%	15.1	10.1
IA	2270	442	29	19.5%	6.6%	15.1	2.9
OK	2636	606	40	23.0%	6.6%	17.7	4.1
OR	3091	871	43	28.2%	4.9%	34.3	9.7
NC	3370	758	0	22.5%	0.0%	19.8	4.5
NM	3500	515	129	14.7%	25.0%	31.3	4.6
GA	3632	1035	28	28.5%	2.7%	15.4	4.4
WA	3908	804	195	20.6%	24.3%	26.6	5.5
IL	4390	668	90	15.2%	13.5%	24.8	3.8
CA	5142	2034	548	39.6%	26.9%	42.9	17.0
TX	5561	1487	36	26.7%	2.4%	30.7	8.2
HI	6841	717	37	10.5%	5.2%	90.0	9.4
MN	7309	392	30	5.4%	7.7%	36.4	2.0
U.S.	7732	404	8	5.2%	2.0%	14.5	0.8

Sources: Congressional data were collected from Ornstein, Mann, and Malbin (2000, 154–57, 160, 162–63). State legislative data were collected from *The Book of the States 1998–99*, pages 105–7, and *The Book of the States 2000–2001*, pages 108–9.

studying legislative bodies, even though scholars have suggested that legislatures or representative assemblies serve other manifest and latent functions (e.g., Packenham 1970). The "new institutionalism" of the 1990s magnified our focus on lawmaking, sometimes to the exclusion of other activities. Our question here is whether the lawmaking process is the same in the U.S. Congress and state legislatures. What generalizations can we apply that cover both Congress and state legislatures? If differences exist, are they crucial or simply nuances without much impact?

The first observation is that the number of bills introduced and enacted varies greatly across legislatures. As shown in table 4–3, more bills were introduced in Congress than in any of the 29 state legislatures for which we have readily available data. The median number of bills introduced during any two-year period in the state legislatures was only 1,730, or roughly 22 percent of the number introduced in Congress. Perhaps more importantly, the number of introductions varies widely across state legislatures, from the relatively minuscule numbers found in Alaska and North Dakota to numbers that approach those found in Congress in Hawaii and Minnesota.

The real surprise is contained in the second and third columns of table 4–3. Here we see a major distinction between Congress and most state legislatures. In Congress (Stewart 2001, 337), "almost no bills become law." Total enactments in Congress are greater than those in only a handful of state legislatures. Indeed, the median number of enactments in state legislatures is over 70 percent higher than in Congress. As a result, the five percent of bills enacted in Congress is a strikingly low figure when seen in comparative context. In 23 of the 29 state legislatures examined, the percentage of bills enacted is at least 20 percent, and in eight chambers it is greater than 50 percent. Even in California, a state legislature often thought comparable to Congress (e.g., Squire 1992a), close to 40 percent of bill introductions become law.

If the focus shifts to individual member activity, some of the disparity between Congress and the state legislatures disappears. The median number of bills introduced per member in state legislatures closely approximates that for Congress (15.1 versus 14.5). The difficulty, however, is that the range among the state legislatures is quite wide, from 4.7 to 90.0. The variation narrows among the more professional bodies, but even those bodies still display a wide array of bill activity by the average legislator, ranging from a fairly anemic level in Ohio to a fairly robust level in California. If one purpose of introducing and passing legislation is credit claiming, then the average member of Congress has little to show for his or her efforts. Indeed, the mean number of enactments per member is higher in every state legislature examined, in some states even reaching double digits. California is the outlier in this regard with the number of enactments per legislator averaging 17.

Majoritarian or Supermajoritarian Requirements

At the outset, we think that a major issue, often ignored in the literature, is the ability of the majority of the legislature to work its will. Recent research suggests how important supermajority requirements are to the legislative process (Krehbiel 1998; Brady and Volden 1998). While these treatments have focused on the issue of veto override requirements, the use of supermajority requirements may extend to a number of different aspects of the legislative process. As a first cut at

ORGANIZATIONAL CHARACTERISTICS

TABLE 4-4 The Extent of Supermajoritarian Requirements in American Legislatures

Super Majoritarian Score		Senate	Lower House
High	8.0	AK, FL, KS, MI, OK	AL, FL
	7.5		MI
	7.0	CA, MD, MS, OH, SD, TX, WA	MS, OK
	6.5	UT	CA
	6.0	AR, GA, ME, NM, SC, **U.S.**, VT, VA, WV	KS, MD, OH, SC, SD, TX, WA
	5.5	IL, NE, NJ	IL, UT
	5.0	AZ, CO, DE, LA, MT, NV, NC, TN, WI, WY	AZ, AR, DE, ME, MT, VT
	4.5		
	4.0	IA, MA, MN, NY, ND, OR, PA, RI	CO, GA, ID, LA, MA, NM, NC, OR, RI, TN, **U.S.**, VA, WV, WI, WY
	3.5	HI, CT	HI, NJ
	3.0	AL, IN, KY, MO, NH	AL, IN, KY, MN, MO, NV, NH, NY, ND, PA
	2.5		CT
	2.0		IA

this question, we examine supermajority requirements in regard to ten legislative procedures:

- recommending constitutional amendments
- overriding a veto
- suspending chamber rules
- passing a budget or appropriation bill
- adopting tax bills
- enacting emergency legislation
- expelling a legislator
- impeaching an executive official
- removing a judge
- censuring a legislator

For each issue, we determined if a supermajority, defined here as being more than a constitutional majority, was necessary to accomplish the activity. As shown in table 4-4, the various legislative bodies differ in their use of supermajority requirements. The supermajoritarian requirement in the U.S. Senate exists for overriding a veto, suspending rules, adopting a constitutional amendment,

119

expelling a legislator, removing a judge, and impeaching a member of the executive branch, while in the U.S. House the larger majority is required for overriding a veto, adopting a constitutional amendment, adopting a tax increase, and expelling a legislator. In some states, other sorts of votes require supermajorities. Measures raising taxes, for example, require supermajority votes in eleven state legislatures (Minzner 1999, 56). Across the possible supermajoritarian votes we examine, the scores for American legislatures range from 2 to 8 out of a possible 10. Using this approach, the most majoritarian body is the Iowa House, while the senates in Alaska, Florida, Kansas, Michigan, and Oklahoma along with the lowers houses in Alaska and Florida appear to the most supermajoritarian. The unexplored question is, what are the policymaking consequences of these requirements? Can we detect any noticeable differences in behavior in these different institutions based on the use of supermajoritarian rules? What other supermajoritarian rules matter, if any?

Reference to Committee

The initial step in the legislative process involves the reference of bills to committee. One major distinction between the U.S. House and Senate is that in the former the speaker makes the determination with no right of appeal, whereas in the Senate the presiding officer's decision can be appealed. In the states, the situation is slightly more complicated. A major difference is that in roughly one-third of the chambers the presiding officer does not make the referral. In a majority of these chambers the decision is made by another legislative leader—president pro tem, speaker pro tem, or majority leader. In nine chambers a committee (e.g., rules or committee on committees) makes the decision, while the final decision is made by the clerk in the Virginia Senate and by the clerk with direction from the speaker in the Virginia House. Only in the Maine House and Senate do the entire membership vote on the initial referral (ASLCS and NCSL 1998, Table 96–3.5). Another major difference with the process in the U.S. House is that the legislative chamber may vote to change the referral in approximately 60 percent of the state legislatures involved in a recent survey, while the leadership, be it the presiding officer or someone else, can do it in 36 chambers. Only in a handful of state legislative chambers (e.g., Colorado House, Iowa Senate, and Pennsylvania House and Senate) is it not possible to alter the final referral (ASLCS and NCSL 1998, 3–17 and Table 98–3.8).

Floor Procedures

The various aspects of congressional floor procedure are well documented (e.g.,

Oleszek 2004; Stewart 2001). Similar extensive descriptive material for each of the 99 state legislative chambers is difficult to find, if it exists at all. Thus, the legislative scholar who seeks to conduct comparative research in this area must be willing to spend an enormous amount of time acquiring basic information. It may seem prudent for a legislative scholar to simply move on to a different topic given that so much basic work must be done in this area. There is, however, substantial value for our understanding of legislative procedures and their effects in examining them in a wider range of institutions. Thus, we suggest three possible solutions for the data problem.

One approach is to utilize a team of researchers, each of whom is familiar with a particular legislature. A recent case in point would be the work of Herbert Döring (1995) and his colleagues, who compiled a comprehensive, cross-national account of organizational features and procedural rules of Western European parliaments as they typically operated during the 1990s. While comparative case studies of parliaments abound, what sets this volume apart from others is not only its focus on the "new institutionalism," but also the decision to construct the book around key issues—veto players, parliamentary questioning, parliamentary committees, and the like—in which data for all 18 countries are analyzed at the same time. In other words, the scholars pooled the information from the several parliaments and then wrote truly comparative studies around key structural or procedural issues.

A second strategy is for a smaller team to engage in a long-term commitment to collecting information on various rules over several years, such as that undertaken by Hamm, Hedlund, and Martorano (e.g., Hamm, Hedlund, and Martorano 1999, 2001; Martorano, Hamm, and Hedlund 2000; Martorano 2001). In this project, the authors gathered information on as many as 71 legislative chambers for multiple years throughout the twentieth century and did extensive cross checking of coding decisions. This type of effort is typically beyond the reach of a single researcher operating without some type of financial support and sufficient time. The third option, therefore, is to undertake more studies with few cases, but care must be taken in case selection. The most troubling problem is that unless a scholar knows the procedural characteristics of the population of state legislatures, it is difficult to justify the choice of any particular subset of chambers.

Of course, the goal in any such undertaking is not to simply catalogue all of the nuances of legislative procedure, but to show which aspects, taken singly or together, have major effects on the legislative process. At this stage, we can only speculate on the exact effects, but we can suggest some potentially important differences.

At the outset, it is useful to remember that significant differences exist between the U.S. House and Senate in scheduling of legislation for floor consideration (Stewart 2001; Oleszek 2004, 190). The House is much more rule bound and structured than the Senate. The House has developed a fine set of procedures to move different types of legislation through that body, including a specialized calendar system for consideration of particular types of legislation, and a specialized committee—the Rules Committee—to facilitate legislative consideration. The Senate has developed a much simpler formal structure, overall, relying instead largely on consensus among its members to get bills onto the floor for consideration.

There are two points of comparison with the states worth noting. It appears from a study of the formal rules that in two-thirds of 71 state chambers some intermediary group or persons (e.g., a rules committee or leadership) has discretion as to how the floor calendar is constructed, while in roughly one-third of the chambers bills go on the calendar in the order introduced or in the order reported from committee. Second, while the U.S. House and Senate operate with multiple calendars, the rules in only two-thirds of these legislative chambers provide for more than one calendar, although consent calendars may exist in some others via simple resolution (Martorano, Hamm, and Hedlund, 2000).

Differences exist between the U.S. House and Senate in terms of the floor amending process. The U.S. House uses a strict germaneness rule, the Rules Committee limits amendment rights, and debate is limited to the five-minute rule. None of these restrictions exist in the U.S. Senate (Oleszek 2004, 229). At the state level there is a mix of procedures. Most legislative chambers have a germaneness rule, but do not limit amendment rights to the degree found in the U.S. House. Debate is limited in roughly two-thirds of the state legislative chambers (Martorano, Hamm, and Hedlund 2000). In addition, the criteria under which amendments can be offered differ considerably across state legislatures. The range appears to extend from no specific limits on floor amending to the requirement that unanimous consent be granted for any floor amendment to be considered or adopted (e.g., Oregon), thus giving significant powers to members of legislative committees. What are the impacts of these various amendment procedures? Variations in this area offer some of the more intriguing opportunities for research.

Procedural Variation One: Filibusters

One attractive research opportunity involves the effect of filibustering rights on the legislative process and outcomes. The effects of unlimited debate and the cloture rule in the U.S. Senate have been given considerable scholarly attention in recent years (Alter and McGranahan 2000; Binder and Smith 1997; Binder, Lawrence, and Smith 2002; Fisk and Chemerinsky 1997). But, of course, the U.S. Senate is just one chamber, which operates under one set of rules, and its rules on debate and cloture change only very rarely. As noted above, about one-third of state legislative chambers do not place limits on debates. And filibusters do occur in these chambers. Some are particularly noteworthy. Democrats in the Rhode Island state Senate, for example, engaged in a three-day continuous filibuster in 1924, trying to force a vote on a proposed constitutional convention. According to one account (Hubbard 1936, 538), "The filibuster was finally broken by a stink-bomb mysteriously set off in the chamber, and the Republican members fled from the state for the remainder of the year so as to produce a permanent no-quorum." A 36-hour, two-member tag-team filibuster in the Texas state Senate defeated most parts of a package of segregationist measures in 1957 (Camia 2000).[17] Bitter feelings about a redistricting bill in Alabama led to separate filibusters of 22 hours, 58 hours, and 96 hours in 1961 (Jewell and Patterson 1966, 265). Abortion opponents filibustered a pro-choice bill for eight days in the Maryland Senate in 1990 (Ayres 1990a; 1990b). So, as in the U.S. Senate, in some state legislative chambers filibusters can be employed for various strategic purposes.

The specific rules governing filibusters, however, vary across state legislative chambers, and this variation provides the legislative studies community opportunities to examine how different rules produce different strategies and different outcomes. The Texas Senate, for example, does not place limits on debate, but does have a mechanism for ending a filibuster. If a point of order is raised for a third time that a senator who has the floor is filibustering, all that is required to sustain the objection is a simple majority.[18] The rules in South Carolina make it a bit more difficult to end a filibuster. A member is allowed to speak on a measure for four hours before any action can be taken to limit the debate. Any senator can request that the debate be brought to a close. The motion is immediately brought to a vote, but is sustained only with a vote of 28 members, which is slightly more than 60 percent of the membership. If debate is cut off, each senator is still entitled to speak for one hour, meaning that a final vote might be postponed for as much as 46 hours.[19] The rules in Nebraska make it even easier to filibuster. Until 2002, a senator could talk for eight hours before any attempt to end the debate could be made. A rule change now allows a motion to end debate to be made at any point, as long as the presiding officer believes that a full and fair debate has occurred. The rest of the process remains unchanged. The motion must be made by at least five members. More importantly, debate can only be halted with the support of two-thirds of the members.[20] Thus, some cloture procedures in state legislative chambers are easier to invoke than in the U.S. Senate, while other are more difficult to put into effect. One difference between the U.S. Senate and most state legislative chambers is important to keep in mind when assessing the potential power of a filibuster. As noted in chapter 2, most state legislative chambers face strict session length limits. Such limits raise the cost of any filibuster because, of course, time becomes a precious commodity.

CHAPTER 4

Procedural Variation Two: Discharge Petitions

The availability of the discharge procedure in the U.S. House has come to play a prominent role in theories explaining party and committee power in the chamber (e.g. Krehbiel 1995; Schickler and Rich 1997; Shepsle and Weingast 1987). The discharge rule was adopted in the U.S. House in 1910, and revised in 1931 (Beth 2001). The procedure has changed significantly since then, most notably with the decisions in 1935 to increase the number of signatures on the petition from 145 (one-third) to 218 (a majority), and in 1993 to make public the signature-gathering process (Beth 2001). Under the current rules, after a bill has been referred to a committee for 30 legislative days, a discharge petition can be initiated to remove the bill from the committee's jurisdiction and bring it to the floor. Discharge petitions are rarely attempted, and those that are started are almost never successful because the majority party protects its committee chairs and pressures its members not to sign (Oleszek 2004, 141–43).[21] Under the rules in place since 1935, without some support from the majority party a discharge petition is doomed.

Discharge procedures also exist in many state legislative chambers and have for a long time. In 1918, for example, 13 states had some form of a discharge procedure (Smith 1918, 621).[22] By 1930, most legislative chambers had a parliamentary mechanism to pull a bill from a committee and bring it to the floor by majority vote. A small group of states even required that all measures be reported from committee (Winslow 1931, 22–25). Missouri's current constitution, adopted in 1945, actually enshrines a discharge procedure, "After it has been referred to a committee, one-third of the elected members of the respective houses shall have power to relieve a committee of further consideration of a bill and place it on the calendar for consideration."[23]

There is, of course, a question as to how useful these procedures are. An early scholar of state legislative committee procedures raised doubts about them, observing (Smith 1918, 621), "In attempting, however, to discharge a committee under a recall rule, the merits of the bill frequently become involved with extraneous considerations, such as 'The committee and its chair must be sustained.'"[24] But clearly, the utility of a discharge procedure depends on how stringent it is. Where discharge procedures are easier to invoke they are used, and their strategic importance is easily understood. In 1925, for example, the Pennsylvania House of Representatives changed its discharge procedure from one that permitted a bill to be recalled from a committee with an affirmative vote of just 30 percent of all members to one requiring a majority vote of all members. The change was momentous. Frequent use was made of the earlier recall provision, but the more stringent version was almost never invoked (Winslow 1931, 93–94).[25]

A selection of current discharge procedures in lower houses is presented in table 4–5. There is considerable variation in the rules. None of the states employs

ORGANIZATIONAL CHARACTERISTICS

TABLE 4–5 Discharge Procedures in Several Lower Houses

State	Who	How	When	By What Vote
AZ	Any member	Petition	None specified	Petition: simple majority of all members to discharge bill from Rules Committee, petition signed by three-fifths of all members for other committees
IL	Any member	Motion	None specified	Motion: affirmative vote of 60 members (simple majority of all members).
KS	Any member	Motion	At least 10 legislative days after referral	Motion: Affirmative vote of 70 members (56%); rules measures discharged from Rules Committee by affirmative vote of 60 members (simple majority).
KY	Any member	Petition signed by 25 members (25% of chamber)	Within a reasonable time after referral	Motion on question raised by petition: affirmative vote of a majority of all members (51 members).
LA	Any member	Motion or resolution	None specified	Motion or resolution: affirmative vote of majority of members
MN	Chief author	Written demand	After 20 legislative days, chief author may request committee action; committee then has 10 days. If still not reported, demand made within 5 days to chamber	Chief author's demand becomes demand of House, and bill is considered to be in Chamber's possession. Bill may be re-referred by a majority vote of all chamber members.
PA	Any member	Petition signed by 25 members (4% of chamber)	15 legislative days after referral; no petitions considered during final 6 legislative days of session.	Resolution on petition, affirmative vote of majority of all chamber members; if defeated, no further petitions on bill considered.
WI	Any member	Motion or petition	21 calendar days after referral	*Motion:* first attempt requires affirmative vote by majority of those present; subsequent attempts require affirmative vote by two-thirds majority of those present. *Petition:* signed by simple majority

Sources: Chamber rules: Arizona House Rule 37; Illinois House Rule 58; Kansas House Rule 1309; Kentucky House Rule 48; Louisiana House Rule 6.13; Minnesota House Rule 4.31; Pennsylvania House Rule 53; Wisconsin Assembly Rule 15.

a procedure exactly like the one in the U.S. House, Wisconsin's being the most similar. Arizona uses a petition like the U.S. House does, but requires the signatures of three-fifths of all members to pull most bills from committee. Both Kentucky and Pennsylvania use petitions with relatively low signature requirements to bring the recall effort to the floor, but in both chambers a majority of all members must support the measure to discharge a bill from committee. The other chambers rely on motions. Perhaps the most distinctive procedure is in Minnesota. Only the chief author of a measure can push to have it pulled from a committee. Should the committee ultimately refuse to send the measure to the floor, the chief author can force it on to the chamber's calendar. But the measure can be re-referred to the committee by a majority vote of the all of the chamber's members.

What difference do the variations in discharge procedures make? Certainly, they raise different strategic possibilities. In Pennsylvania in the 1950s, a discharge petition could again be brought to the floor with the express support of very few members. Such a process provides the minority party with significant political opportunities. In an examination of party voting in the Pennsylvania state legislature in 1951, Keefe (1954, 453) noted

> House Democrats—in the minority—sponsored a large number of resolutions to discharge bills from committee. In debate they contended that the vote to be taken in each instance was actually a vote on the bill itself, for it was only through this parliamentary procedure that it could be brought to the floor.

Thus, even though the discharge procedure almost always failed, the minority party's ability to force a vote on important issues provided them a chance to put their position and the majority party's position on important issues on the public record.[26]

Concluding Thoughts on the Importance of Variations in Legislative Rules

The rise of formal theory in legislative studies has brought the central importance of rules into stark relief. Almost all of these studies, however, have focused on a very limited set of rules, those of the U.S. House. Although examining these rules over time provides some variation, and studies that have done so have produced a raft of important work, our concern is that an exclusive focus on a single institution raises the possibility that theory is tailored to fit narrow circumstances. Broadening the range of institutions to be studied increases the prospects of devising theories that are more general in nature. As we have demonstrated in this chapter, the 101 American legislative chambers offer a wide array of rules and procedures to be studied. Supermajoritarian rules, for example, lead us to certain theoretically driven expectations about legislative organization and behavior. Examining these hypotheses across a range of legislative institutions and supermajoritarian rules offers legislative scholars the chance to determine which theories fit only one chamber and one set of rules and which are more generally applicable.

· 5 ·

Legislators and Legislative Careers

The first four chapters focused on the structures and organization of American legislatures, paying particular attention to how they change over time and how they compare across chambers. In this chapter we turn our attention to the members of American legislatures and their political careers. The study of legislative careers revolves around three related but distinct questions: who serve, why do they serve, and what difference does it make to the process and to policy outcomes that one sort of person serves rather than another sort of person? A great deal of scholarly effort has been directed at answering the question of who serve and why they serve, not only in American legislatures (Moncrief 1999) but also in legislatures elsewhere (Patzelt 1999). Comparative analysis of these two questions using the full range of American legislatures is, of course, of considerable interest because of the large numbers of legislators and contexts in which they serve that may be examined. Indeed, as pointed out in chapters 2 and 3, American legislatures provide substantial variance on member pay, time demands, facilities, and resources, all of which help account for who serves and why they serve.

But the last of the three questions—what difference does it make who serves—is, perhaps, the most important one. The question has two aspects. First, how do careers influence a legislature's policy outputs? We might anticipate, for example, that if the composition of a legislature changes over time through increasing the number of women or minorities or members from different occupational or social groups, there should be some noticeable change in the sort of legislation that gets proposed, debated, and adopted. As we will argue in this chapter, an exclusive focus on the U.S. Congress leaves social scientists in a weak position to answer these sorts of questions in a rigorous fashion. Only the number of cases and greater variance provided by examination of state legislative chambers allows for the appropriate analyses.

Answers to the second part of this question—how do career aspirations influence the sort of organizational structures and rules employed in legislative chambers—also require looking beyond Congress. Remember, as noted in chapters 1 and 2, the rules and procedures adopted by American legislatures are generally left to legislators to decide. This means that the organizational schemes adopted by each chamber to some degree reflect the desires of their members. And desires and schemes both can and do change over time. As we have pointed out in earlier chapters, the differences we see among Congress and state legislatures today have only emerged over time; they have evolved from institutions that once looked very similar to ones with noticeable differences today. But again, it is important to stress that the variations in organizational contexts offered by examination of some 8,000 legislators in 101 chambers provide considerably more analytical leverage for answering critical questions about legislative development than can the limited variation provided by studying 535 legislators in two chambers.

The Development of an Electoral Career Hierarchy in American Legislatures

Today, we are used to thinking of American electoral careers as following a well-established hierarchy, with lower level offices such as state legislatures serving as stepping-stones to higher level offices such as the U.S. House and Senate. Career movement is unidirectional: ambitious office holders move up the ladder; only rarely do they move back down it.

The current American political career hierarchy has been around for a long time, but not for forever. The establishment of the federal system with the ratification of the Constitution created two electoral levels: federal offices and state offices. Initially, federal level offices were not necessarily more highly valued than were state level offices. For example, although Jonathan Dayton was elected to serve as a member of the U.S. House of Representatives from New Jersey in 1788, he declined the post in order to serve instead as speaker of the New Jersey Assembly. Even into the early nineteenth century, it was not uncommon for a member of Congress to give up his seat to take a state level position. Speakers of the U.S. House often left their post to hold office back home, including as a state legislator (Polsby 1968, 149–51). The U.S. Senate was not immune from such defections. In 1792, for example, U.S. Senator Charles Carroll resigned his seat so that he could move to the Maryland state Senate (Riker 1955, 462).

The hierarchy with which we are familiar today became established in the second half of the nineteenth century. Riker (1955, 462) reported that, "from 1790 to 1849, 48 [U.S.] senators resigned to take state office; from 1850 to 1949 only eight." A similar tale is told in figure 5–1. Between 1790 and 1960, there was a

FIGURE 5–1 Career Movement between State Office and Congress, 1789–1960

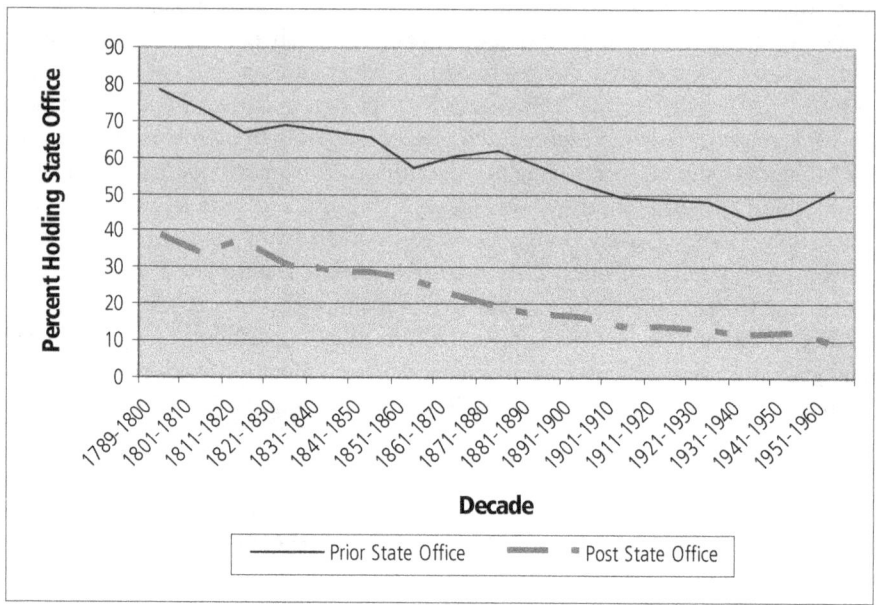

Source: Calculated from data in Bogue et al. (1976, pp. 289, 293).

steady decline in the percentage of U.S. representatives who held state office after leaving the House (Bogue, Clubb, McKibbin, and Traugott 1976, 293–94). The percentage of U.S. representatives who previously served in state office also decline over this time period (Bogue, Clubb, McKibbin, and Traugott 1976, 289–90). But at the end of the time series, almost no U.S. House members left to take a state office, while the percentage of them who held state office before moving to Washington remained fairly high.

We have two caveats to offer to our understanding of the current political career hierarchy in the United States. First, the universality of the unidirectional nature of the hierarchy has changed at the margins in those states that have term-limited state legislatures. In those states it is no longer uncommon for an upper house member to leave that chamber and move to the lower house. Second, although the unidirectional career movement from the state level to the federal level evolved to be the norm in the United States, it is not necessarily the accepted path in other democracies. Stolz (2003) identifies several federal systems where movement goes in the opposite direction—from the national to the subnational level—as well as other places where no discernible directionality emerges. Thus, it is important to keep in mind that the political career hierarchy that evolved in the United States was not the inevitable result of the adoption of a federal system.

Who Serves in American Legislatures?

Who serves is important for matters of symbolic representation and policy representation. But one potential problem is that (Jewell and Patterson 1986, 50) "one of the rather peculiar features of the American legislative systems [is] that . . . only those with relatively high occupational status have a good chance of achieving legislative membership." The question of who serves in American legislatures focuses primarily on two sorts of characteristics: occupation and membership in underrepresented groups.

Occupational Diversity

The study of state legislators' occupations by social scientists has a long history. Examinations of legislatures at the beginning of the twentieth century (Haynes 1900, 218–24; and Orth 1904) and a few decades later (Fox 1938; Hyneman 1940; Key 1956, 258–263; Lange 1938; McHenry 1938; and Zeller 1954, 71) revealed similar findings: lawyers and farmers were the dominant occupations, but legislators were drawn from many vocations. And, of course, there were substantial variations across the states. But the preponderance of lawyers has always merited special scrutiny. In 1900, for example, Haynes noted wryly (1900, 224),

> In some quarters the notion seems to be prevalent that lawyers constitute the most corrupting element in our legislatures. In view of this opinion it is of interest to note that in the Delaware legislature of 1899 there was not a single lawyer in either house;—and yet it has been suspected that in that legislature guile was not completely unknown.[1]

Farmers and Lawyers in the Legislature

Have lawyers and farmers always been relatively dominant in American legislatures? Tracking the occupations of legislators over time is difficult because of incomplete data, but from what we can gather, farmers once dominated, but over time lawyers became more prominent. Between 1635 and 1688, for example, 62 percent of Maryland Assembly members were planters, while only 7 percent were attorneys (Falb 1986, 101). Similar numbers were found in New Jersey. Between 1703 and 1776, 70 percent of Assembly members were planters, while lawyers constituted only 8 percent. But, underneath the surface in New Jersey, occupational changes were brewing. While the percentage of members who were planters was relatively constant between 1703 and 1776, the percentage of attorneys increased from just 4 percent before 1738, to 12 percent after that year (Purvis 1980, 595).

The Revolution produced significant changes in the sort of person elected to the new state legislatures. Before the war, the vast majority of those elected—planter and lawyer alike—were drawn from the wealthier strata of colonial society. According to an analysis by Main (1966, 404), following the war, "Voters were ceasing to elect only men of wealth and family. . . . Significantly, the people more and more often chose ordinary yeomen or artisans." Thus, while those whose main source of income was derived from agriculture continued to constitute a significant proportion of state legislators, there was an important shift away from the very wealthy planters to small farmers, albeit ones who were still reasonably well-to-do.

The available evidence from the decades just before the Civil War suggests that farmers still constituted the bulk of the membership of most state legislatures. In 1850, for example, farmers comprised 57 percent of legislators in 13 southern and border states, while lawyers were just 24 percent of the membership. A decade later the figures had barely changed for both groups. The percentage of attorneys stayed at 24 percent while the percentage of farmers barely dropped to 55 percent.[2] But, again, buried in these aggregate numbers were harbingers of the change to come. In Arkansas, for example, the state Senate, which was composed of 79 percent farmers in 1850, was only 57 percent farmers a decade later. Over that decade lawyers increased in the membership from 8 percent to 33 percent. And by 1860, 50 percent of Kentucky state senators were attorneys, while only 18 percent were farmers. But while relatively few lawyers served in state legislatures during this time period, they dominated the leadership ranks. From 1823 to 1878, 59 percent of all lower house speakers were lawyers, and only 8 percent were farmers (Ritter and Wakelyn 1989, xi–xii).

Toward the end of the nineteenth century the shift from farmer-legislators to lawyer-legislators became even more pronounced. Even in the agricultural heartland the trend was detectable. In the decade from the mid-1880s to the mid-1890s, farmers held from less than a third to just under half of the state legislative seats in Illinois, Iowa, and Wisconsin, while lawyers held between 10 percent to 24 percent of the seats (Campbell 1980, 38). But by the first two decades of the twentieth century the tide had shifted in Indiana. There, lawyers held 36 percent of the seats in the state legislature to only 23 percent for farmers (VanderMeer 1985). But the process took longer in Wisconsin; lawyers did not overtake farmers in the legislature until around 1950 (Jewell and Patterson 1966, 109).

A more comprehensive look over time at lawyers and farmers in a single state legislature is given in figure 5–2. In Massachusetts in 1780, 45 percent of state legislators were drawn from agriculture, while only 7 percent were from the legal field. Over the next 100 years, the percentage of lawyers increased slowly, if only in fits and starts. The percentage of legislators from the agricultural sector,

FIGURE 5-2 Occupations of Massachusetts Legislators, 1780–1950

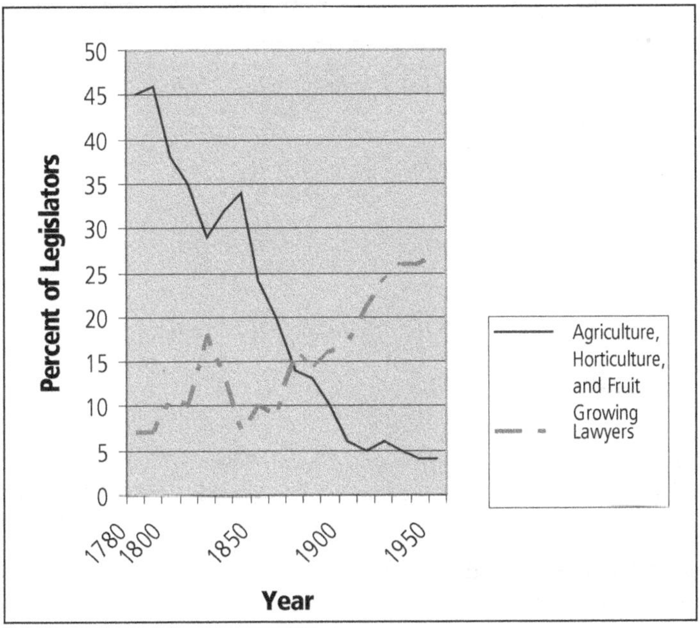

Source: Data from Davis (1951, pp. 94–95).

however, decreased with a fairly consistent rate. The two lines finally crossed in 1870. From that point on, the percentage of lawyers increased, to 27 percent by 1950, while the percentage of farmers dropped to only 4 percent.[3]

Interestingly, in contrast with state legislatures, law had always been the most dominant occupation in Congress. Even in the very first House of Representatives, over 40 percent of members were drawn from the legal field, while just over 10 percent made their living from agriculture. From that point farming supplied an increasingly smaller proportion of House members, while the percentage of attorneys continued to rise, comprising over 60 percent of the membership from 1830 to 1920 (Bogue, Clubb, McKibbin, and Traugott 1976, 284). Since then, law too has claimed a declining share of the House. By 2001, only 36 percent of representatives were attorneys. (The Senate still drew disproportionately from the legal field, with 59 of its members being lawyers.)

The Changes in Occupations among State Legislators across the Twentieth Century

By the early twentieth century, lawyers were overtaking farmers as the most common occupation found in state legislatures. The data presented in table 5–1

TABLE 5-1 Selected Occupations of State Legislators, 1909, 1949, and 1999, in Percent

Occupation	1909	1949	1999
Farming & Fishing	25	21	7
Law	20	18	15
Business and Services	22	26	27
Government (not legal)	4	4	17
Education	3	3	9
Retired	1	3	8
Housewife	0	2	1
Health Services	5	2	4
General Labor	1	2	1
No Occupation Listed	3	4	3
Number of Chambers	52	52	52
Number of Legislators	4,460	4,576	4,398

document that change as well as the increasing diversification of the occupations of state legislators across the last hundred years. In this table we present occupational data we gathered for 52 chambers at three points in time: 1909, 1949, and 1999.[4] The percentage of state legislators who were lawyers actually declined during this period, although not dramatically. Beneath these aggregate numbers there was, of course, considerable variation across the states in the percentage of legislators who were lawyers. In the most recent time period 53 percent of West Virginia state delegates were attorneys compared to only one percent of representatives in North Dakota. The percentage of farmers holding legislative office also declined over time, but much more severely to 7 percent in 1999 from 25 percent 90 years earlier. This drop is not surprising given the decrease in farmers as a percentage of the nation's population. But again there was substantial variation across the states. Most recently, almost 33 percent of lower house members in North Carolina and North Dakota were from the agricultural sector, while 14 chambers had no farmers at all among their members.

The number of members claiming full-time legislator as their occupation has increased substantially over the course of the century. Among the 52 chambers for which we have data at each point in time, only three had any members who claimed full-time status in 1909, with the Minnesota state senate leading with 5 percent of its members claiming legislator as their occupation. Only two chambers had any members listing themselves as legislators in 1949. But by 1999, most chambers had at least a few full-time legislators; some had significant proportions. The percentage of full-time legislators in the Pennsylvania House was 66 percent, and 52 percent in the state Senate called themselves full-time. It is likely, however, that our figures underestimate the number of full-time legislators, especially in the more professionalized bodies. In Michigan, for example, before term limits, observers believed that two-thirds of the members were really full-time legislators, but only one-third of them publicly admitted it because they feared negative electoral repercussions from being labeled career politicians (Rosenthal 1989, 72; Bazar 1987, 4). Overall, those who admit to being full-time legislators are concentrated in the more professionalized legislatures.[5] In a majority of states, however, relatively few members claim to make their living from public office.

These figures stand in great contrast to Congress. Members of the U.S. House and Senate are, by definition, professional legislators. Their prior occupations, however, have changed over time as well (Ornstein, Mann, and Malbin 2000, 20–21, 26–27). The percentage of lawyers in the House declined precipitously to 37 percent in 1999 from 57 percent in 1953. The drop in the Senate over that same time period was only from 59 percent to 55 percent. Similarly, the percentage of members from agriculture also dropped, to 5 percent from 12 percent in the House, and to 6 percent from 22 percent in the Senate. But other occupations have gained, and overall, there is greater occupational diversity in the House and Senate today than 50 years ago.

None of these changes are, of course, particularly surprising. Agriculture has been a declining part of the economy for many decades and there are far fewer farmers to run for office and far fewer farm families to vote for them. And the natural linkage between the study of law and interest and success in politics is well documented (Eulau and Sprague 1964; Schlesinger 1957), accounting for the prominent position of lawyers in American politics. But it is important to note that a wide range of occupations is represented in America's legislatures. Indeed, occupational diversity increased over the course of the twentieth century.

Member occupations matter because they have implications for the way legislatures organize and the way members behave. Occupations influence organization because they often influence structuring of the committee assignment process, where members get placed on particular committees which have jurisdiction over a subject on which the member has substantive expertise. They may impact behavior as legislators pursue policy interests motivated by their professions. Along these lines it may be useful to note that the most common prior experience of members of Congress is state legislative service. In 2001, for example, 41 percent of senators and 53 percent of representatives previously served in state legislatures.[6] The importance of state legislatures as a congressional farm team has long been noted (see, for example, Mason 1938, 178). Indeed, 39 of the original 65 members of the U.S. House in 1789 had previously served in a state legislature (Galloway 1958, 455). From our perspective, this strong link between the two institutions suggests that they are more similar than different because they have been populated by many of the same people.

CHAPTER 5

Traditionally Underrepresented Groups

For most of American legislative history women did not serve as legislators. Perhaps the first effort by a woman to hold legislative office was made by Margaret Brent, who in 1648 claimed without success that her work as an attorney for the proprietor entitled her to a seat in the Maryland Assembly (Clarke 1943, 151). Women waited a very long time to gain entrance to Congress with the first one serving in the U.S. House in 1917 and in the Senate in 1922.[7] The number of women serving in Congress has, of course, increased substantially since then. But their numbers are still relatively small. In 2003, 14 percent of senators and 14 percent of representatives were women.

Before a woman was first sent to Congress, a number of them had already served in state legislatures. The first women were elected to a state legislature in 1894, when Clara Cressingham, Carrie Clyde Holly, and Francis S. Klock all ran successfully as Republican candidates for the Colorado House of Representatives. The 1894 election was the first in which women were allowed to vote for the Colorado state legislature and although men outnumbered women in the state, women voters turned out at a much higher rate than did men, giving the three women candidates a significant boost at the polls.[8] Once in office the women had an immediate impact on the institution. Decorum reportedly improved with their arrival; male legislators cleaned up their language and smoking on the floor was banned (Cox 1996, 17). When Holly successfully pushed a bill she authored to raise the age of consent through the legislature and into law her feat gained national attention (Cox 1994, 18). And Klock became the first woman to hold a leadership position when she chaired the Indians and Veterans Affair Committee. The first woman elected to a state senate came soon afterward in 1896 when Dr. Martha Hughes Cannon won a seat in Utah. Cannon, a physician and a fourth wife in a polygamous marriage, won on a Democratic slate that defeated a Republican slate that included her husband (Cox 1994, 14).

By the time the first woman was elected to the U.S. House, women had already served in the state legislatures not only in Colorado and Utah, but also in Arizona, Idaho, Oregon, Washington, and Wyoming (Cox 1996, 329). As figure 5–3 shows, over the next several decades the number of women serving in state legislatures far outstripped the number elected to Congress. Indeed, by 1935, 139 women served as state legislators in 34 states. But clearly sexism still prevailed; contemporaneous observers noted that those numbers meant (State Government 1937, 213), "At the present, 14 states have no pretty parliamentarians among their legislators."

The number of female legislators in the states continued to grow through the twentieth century, reaching more than 600 in 1975 and over 1,000 in 1985. By 2003, 1,648 women were state legislators, a figure representing 22 percent of all state legislative seats. Several state legislatures had large percentages of

FIGURE 5-3 Women Serving in American Legislatures, 1895–2003

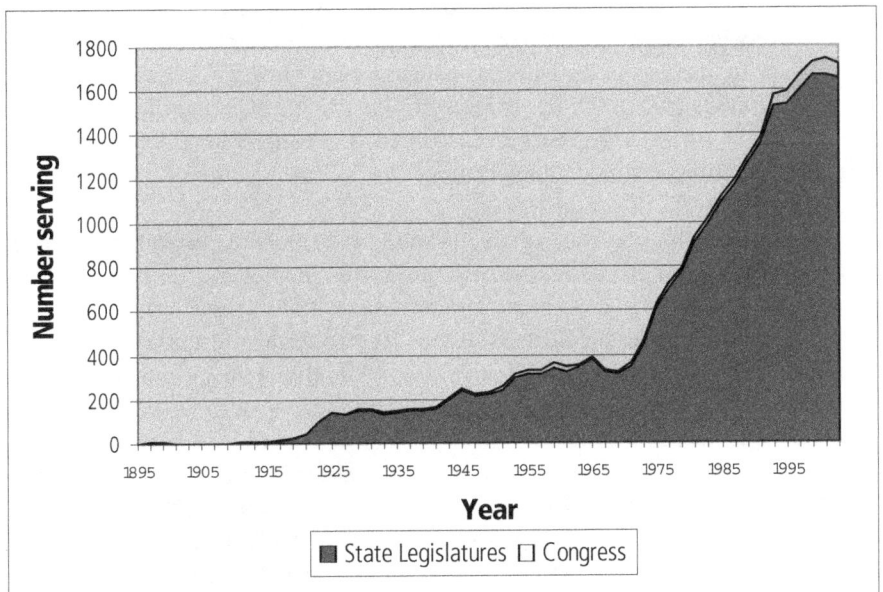

women—Washington had the most at 37 percent, with two other states having more than one-third women—while in only five state legislatures—South Carolina, Alabama, Kentucky, Oklahoma, Mississippi—did women constitute a smaller percentage of the membership than they did in Congress. A milestone was reached in 1999, when 67 percent of the majority party Democrats in the Washington state Senate was female, giving women effective control of a chamber for the first time.[9]

Overall, the percentage of women in the state legislature is negatively related to legislative professionalization (Squire 1992b). But, given their numbers, it is not surprising that women were far more likely to hold leadership positions in state legislatures than in Congress. Indeed, in 2003 women chaired only two congressional committees, both in the Senate and neither one of much importance. The situation in the states was far different, with women holding many of the highest positions and numerous committee chairs, and they held them in proportion to their numbers in the legislatures (Darcy 1996; Little, Dunn, and Dean 2001; Whistler and Ellickson 1999). The election of Nancy Pelosi as the U.S. House minority leader in 2003 was noteworthy because it was the first time a woman had held a major leadership post in Congress. In contrast, women have held important positions in state legislatures for many decades, albeit in limited numbers. The first woman minority leader in a lower state house was in Montana in 1921, followed shortly by the first woman speaker in North Dakota in 1933

(Cox 1996, 334). In 2003, five women were serving as speaker in their states.[10] Thus, scholars wanting to investigate the impact women have on the legislative process, or what difference it makes to have women legislators in leadership positions, have to study state legislatures, not Congress. Only the former provide the number of cases and variation necessary to investigate such questions rigorously. Indeed, the most convincing works on such questions have focused almost exclusively on women in state legislatures (e.g., Crowley 2004; Reingold, 2000; C. Rosenthal 1998b; Thomas 1994).

Similar problems confront scholars wanting to explore the impact members of various minority groups have made on legislatures and policies. The first African Americans entered the U.S House and Senate in 1870 as the result of Reconstruction politics. Over the next three decades two African Americans served in the Senate and twenty served in the House, all as Republicans and all from the South. But Jim Crow era electoral laws ended the opportunities for African Americans to serve in Congress. No African Americans held a seat in Congress after 1901 until 1935 when Oscar De Priest was elected to the House from Chicago. African Americans did not hold a second House seat until 1945.

A similar pattern is found in the state legislatures. The first African American to hold a state legislative seat appears to have been Alexander L. Twilight, who represented Burlington in the Vermont House of Representatives from 1836 to 1837 (Logan and Winston 1982, 613).[11] In 1866 two African Americans, Edward G. Walker and Charles L. Mitchell, were elected to the Massachusetts House of Representatives (Logan and Winston 1982, 623). Then, as in Congress, Reconstruction resulted in a large number of African Americans serving in southern state legislatures. Between 1868 and 1872, for example, 34 African Americans served in the South Carolina state legislature. Every legislative committee in that state during that time had at least one African American appointed to it and an African American even chaired a committee (Balanoff 1972). In Texas 46 African Americans served in the state legislature between 1871 and 1895 (Brewer 1935). But, again as with Congress, the end of Reconstruction and the rise of Jim Crow laws resulted in African Americans being shut out of service in southern state legislatures.

Outside of the South, African Americans entered state legislatures only gradually in the decades following the Civil War. The first African Americans were elected to the legislatures in Illinois and Ohio in the 1870s, Colorado and Rhode Island in the 1880s, and Michigan and Minnesota in the 1890s. But progress was slow and fitful. Oklahoma, for example, elected its first African American state legislator in 1909; another one was not elected until 1964. The first African American legislator in California was elected in 1918, but the legislature did not have two African Americans holding seats until 1948.

Over the last few decades the number of African Americans elected to American legislatures has grown substantially. But, although the numbers of African

Americans in the U.S. House has increased, there are still too few of them to make rigorous analysis of their influence or behavior easy. In 2003, for example, only 37 U.S. representatives were African Americans, constituting just 9 percent of the House. (There were, of course, no African Americans serving in the Senate.) In the states, 595 legislators were African American. Across state legislatures, however, the number of African American members varied substantially. In some states they made up substantial portions of the membership. More than a quarter of state legislators in Mississippi and Alabama were African American, and over 20 percent were in Georgia, Louisiana, and Maryland.[12] Having more legislatures with significant numbers of African American members and more African American legislators in total provides scholars more data and more variation on important variables with which to work. This can make a significant difference. State legislative scholars have been able, for example, to compare the backgrounds and attitudes of African American and white legislators (Button and Hedge 1996), and to explore the policy preferences of female African American legislators (Barrett 1995). Perhaps even more instructive for our purposes here, a study of African American legislators in five state legislatures by Haynie (2001) found that they are much more likely to introduce and push legislation of particular interest to the African American community than are other legislators, contrary to Swain's (1993) findings on the behavior of African Americans in Congress. The difference between the findings in the two studies may result from real differences between the two sorts of institutions, or it could be the result of one study having more and better data with which to test these important propositions.

The study of Hispanic legislators is similarly constrained by a focus on the congressional level. The first Hispanic American to serve in Congress was Romualdo Pacheco, a Republican from California who served in the U.S. House from 1877 to 1883. Only eight other Hispanics were elected to Congress over the next eight decades. Of those eight, six were sent to Washington from New Mexico, including the only two Hispanics to serve in the Senate. That Hispanics were well integrated into New Mexico's political system early on is demonstrated by their success in gaining entry to the state legislature. In 1912, over 40 percent of the lower house and 20 percent of the state senate were Hispanic, percentages that increased over the next two decades (Holmes 1967, 230).

Outside of New Mexico, Hispanics have only slowly won seats in American legislatures. In 2003, 22 Hispanics served in Congress, all in the House. At the state level the numbers were a bit more impressive: 59 Hispanic state senators and 158 lower house members (National Association of Latino Elected and Appointed Officials Education Fund 2002).[13] Thus, for the foreseeable future the rigorous study of Hispanics in American legislatures is likely to be limited to studies at the state level.

CHAPTER 5

How Long Do Members Serve?

Membership turnover over time in the U.S. House of Representative has received a fair amount of scholarly attention (e.g., Brady, Buckley, and Rivers 1999; Bullock 1972, 1295–96; Epstein, Brady, Kawato, and O'Halloran 1997, 973–74; Fiorina, Rohde, and Wissel 1975, 29–33; Gilmour and Rothstein 1996, 65; Swain, Borrelli, Reed, and Evans 2000, 439–40). Although it is not yet settled as to when and why the House became a careerist body, the contours of the House career are reasonably well established. We have, for example, a good idea when voluntary retirements peaked and when members began to seek reelection on a regular basis.

We know only interesting bits and pieces about the contours of state legislative careers from a historical perspective. Over time, turnover in the colonial assemblies generally declined. Most colonial assemblies experienced very high turnover rates at the end of the seventeenth century, but these figures were dramatically lower in most assemblies by the time of the Revolution (Greene 1981). In the most extreme case, turnover in Pennsylvania dropped to a mean of 18 percent in the decade from 1766 to 1775 from a mean of 62 percent in the decade from 1696 to 1705. Many members served for more than 15 terms, even though elections were annual events (Leonard 1948a, 238). In many respects, this increasing level of membership stability is reminiscent of that experienced by the U.S. House of Representatives during the nineteenth century and may be evidence of the institutionalization of the colonial assemblies (cf. Polsby 1968). Unlike the experience in modern American legislatures, however, there is evidence that a nontrivial percentage of those elected to colonial assemblies declined the opportunity to serve (Corey 1929, 115–16; Gallay 1988, 257; Waterhouse 1986, 150–51; Weir 1969, 484).

The general career pattern revealed in the early state legislatures, however, is very different from that seen over the course of the colonial experience. As figures 5–4 and 5–5 show, in Connecticut (Deming 1889; Luce 1924, 355–56), Georgia (DeBats 1990, 430) and New York (Gunn 1980, 278) legislative turnover increased dramatically over the first half of the nineteenth century. Increasing instability prevailed in other state legislatures as well. According to Levine (1977, 76), 42 percent of all members of the New Jersey state legislature between 1829 and 1844 served for only one year. In most southern states turnover was even higher. In North Carolina between 1836 and 1850, 61 percent of lower house members served only a single term, while between 1849 and 1861 59 percent of lower house members in Virginia were in office only one term (Wooster 1975, 43). Remarkably, in Arkansas between 1836 and 1861, over 93 percent of lower house members served only a single term, a level approached in Kentucky where 89 percent of lower house members from 1849 to 1859 failed to serve more than one term (Wooster 1975, 43). During the 1850s, 61 percent of lower

LEGISLATURES AND LEGISLATIVE CAREERS

FIGURE 5-4 Mean Turnover Rate in Early New York and Georgia Legislatures by Decade, 1777–1867

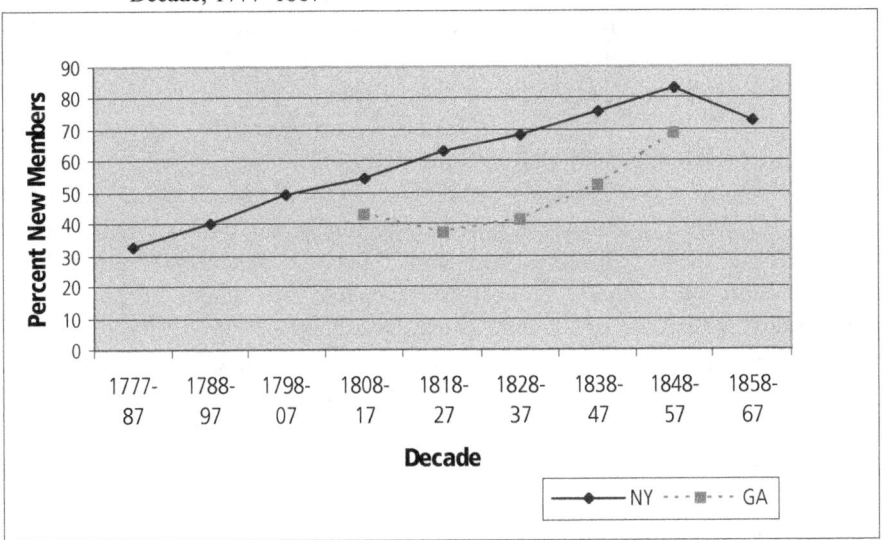

Source: Data for New York from Gunn (1980, p. 278); data for Georgia from DeBats (1990, p. 430).

FIGURE 5-5 Turnover Rate in Connecticut House of Representatives, 1790–1919

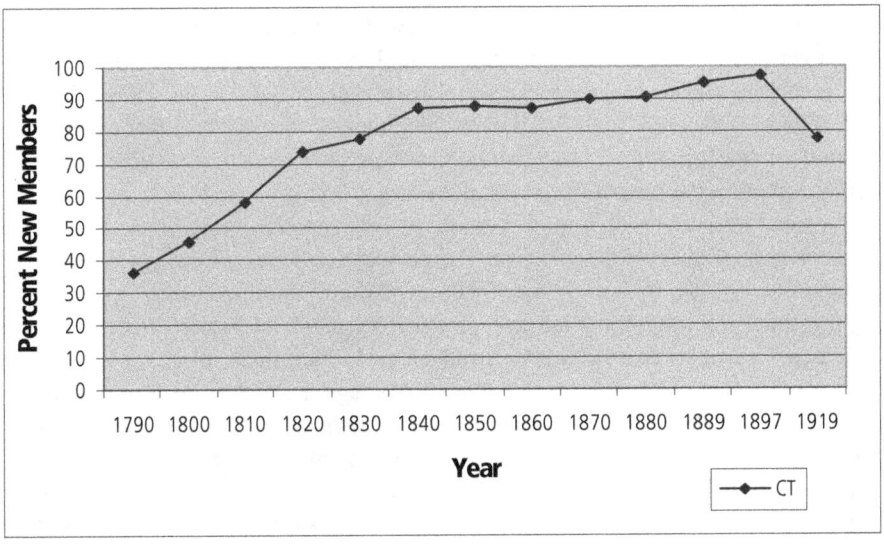

Source: Data from Deming (1889, p. 426) and Luce (1924, pp. 355–56).

house members in Mississippi served for only one term; in the lower house in Florida the percentage was even higher, around 80 percent (Wooster 1969, 41–42). Thus, state legislatures had relatively stable memberships at the end of the eighteenth century, but the trend changed rather quickly to very high levels of turnover by the middle of the nineteenth century.

Available evidence suggests that legislative turnover rates did not begin to decline in most states until well into the twentieth century, lagging behind the trend evidenced several decades earlier in the U.S. House. Between 1886 and 1895, for example, freshmen composed 68 percent of the lower house in Illinois, 62 percent of the lower house in Iowa, and 75 percent of the lower house in Wisconsin (Campbell 1980, 31–32, 228). At the turn of the century, turnover in California hovered around 70 percent (Fisher, Bell, and Price 1973, 12).

Membership turnover in state legislatures began to decline from very high levels starting at the beginning of the twentieth century. In Indiana, for example, first-term members constituted 81 percent of the lower house in 1881, 65 percent in 1901, and 55 percent in 1921 (VanderMeer 1985, 165). A similar pattern emerged in Michigan, where the percentage of first-term members in the lower house dropped to 38 percent in 1947 from 70 percent 60 years earlier (Shull and McGuinness 1951, 473–74).[14]

Studies of legislative turnover across different samples of states and time periods collectively reveal that state legislative memberships became considerably more stable during the twentieth century (Hyneman 1938; Moncrief, Niemi, and Powell 2004; Niemi and Winsky 1987; Ray 1974; 1976; Rosenthal 1974; Shin and Jackson 1979). As can be seen in table 5–2, membership stability continues to vary widely across state legislatures, with some chambers still exhibiting turnover rates of the sort experienced by the U.S. House in the nineteenth century. Generally, however, turnover rates fell substantially from the 1930s through the 1980s. And a few state legislative chambers have lower turnover rates today than does the U.S. House. In general, however, state legislatures still experience greater membership instability than does either house of the U.S. Congress.

It must be noted that from a comparative perspective, state legislatures have two sources of turnover that Congress does not experience. Some state legislative chambers qualify as springboard bodies, where members have exceptional opportunities to use their current position to move to higher elective office (Squire 1988a; 1988b; 1992a). Turnover is higher than might otherwise be expected in these chambers because members regularly seize the chance to move up. Being a springboard has consequences for legislative organization and member behavior. Members of springboard legislatures make different sorts of demands on their leaders (Squire 1988b; Clucas 2001), and they also tend to be more responsive to constituents on policy preferences than are legislators in other sorts of chambers (Maestas 2000).

The other distinct source of turnover is a more obvious one: term limits. As

TABLE 5-2 Turnover in U.S. House and State Legislatures by Chamber and Decade, 1930–2000, with Highest- and Lowest-Turnover Chambers, in Percent

Chamber	1931–40	1941–50	1951–60	1961–70	1971–80	1981–90	1991–2000
U.S. House	28	25	17	17	19	12	17
Upper House	51	43	40	37	29	22	23
Lower House	59	51	45	41	32	24	25
State Chamber with Highest Turnover	94 AL (S)[a] DE (H)	99 GA (S)	98 GA (S)	84 AL (S)	72 AL (S)	40 WV (H)	43 KS (S)
State Chamber with Lowest Turnover	24 NY (S)	14 VA (S)	17 PA (S)	18 MO (S)	13 AR (S)	10 DE (S)	10 DE (S) OK (S)

Sources: U.S. House data from Davidson and Oleszek (2002, 120) and Swain, Borrelli, Reed, and Evans (2000). State legislative data from Moncrief, Niemi, and Powell (2004); Niemi and Winsky (1987); and Shin and Jackson (1979).
[a] S stands for "state senate," H for state "lower house."

noted in chapter 2, limits on legislative service were in effect in 15 state legislatures in 2004.[15] In states that already experienced high turnover, term limits probably do not further increase it in the aggregate. But turnover in chambers which had relatively low turnover rates has increased as limits have kicked into effect. Indeed, part of the uptick in turnover rates in the 1990s found in table 5–2 is the result of term limits forcing out members in some states (Moncrief, Niemi, and Powell 2004). How term limits change legislative organization and membership behavior is still to be sorted out. According to Carey, Niemi, and Powell (1998) limits have not changed the sort of person who gets elected, but they may reorder member policy priorities, and they appear to increase the influence of the executive branch—the governor and the bureaucracy—in legislative decision making. Another major impact is that legislators in term-limited legislatures are less obliged to focus on their constituents and more attentive to concerns beyond their districts, thus creating a "Burkean shift" in representation (Carey, Moncrief, Niemi, and Powell 2003). Indeed, term limits may turn legislatures in which they are in effect into springboard bodies, chambers organized to meet the needs of ambitious politicians en route to other offices (Powell 2000). Thus, because turnover in some states is caused by different things than in Congress, its effects may have different consequences.

CHAPTER 5

Member Careers and the Internal Organization of American Legislatures

How do changes in career orientations effect changes in legislative organization? A prominent theory linking careers to internal organization is Polsby's (1968) notion of institutionalization. An institutionalized legislature (Polsby 1968, 145) is characterized by the establishment of well-defined boundaries, the growth of internal complexity, and the adoption of universalistic criteria and automated methods for internal decision making. The example used by Polsby is the modern U.S. House. Among the measures employed by Polsby to demonstrate aspects of institutionalization were mean years of member service and percentage of first-term members, years of service before becoming speaker and reason for leaving that office, the rise of a seniority rule in naming committee chairs, and expenditures for operation of the House. Although boundedness, complexity, and universalism may be manifested in other ways, clearly the focus of institutionalization is on how the body operates, particularly how it handles its work load and distributes positions of power.

The dynamic element leading to the development of an institutionalized legislature is closely related to the end result of professionalization. Polsby (1975, 297) notes that the state legislative professionalization movement was driven by the adoption of the modern U.S. House as the model to be emulated. A professionalized body is likely to be one where members look on their service as being their career; after all, service is full-time and the pay offered reflects that fact. Legislators who adopt this long-term or professional perspective mold the organization to meet their needs; that is, to institutionalize it. Discussing the changes begun in the late nineteenth century, for example, Kernell (1977, 671) observes, "Perhaps the prime reason for the transformation of the House can be found in the changing needs and incentives of congressmen." As turnover rates declined in the House and average member years of service increased, the organization evolved norms and rules, like seniority, and established a full-blown, powerful committee system (Polsby 1968; Polsby, Gallagher, and Rundquist 1969; Price 1975). Similarly, changing member career goals are important in explaining more recent organizational reform in Congress (Dodd 1986). The House restructures as the career orientation of its membership changes.

Institutionalization's general theoretical tenets have long been criticized (e.g., Cooper and Brady 1981b; Hibbing 1988; 1999; Judge 2003; Rosenthal 1996; Sisson 1973). And alternative perspectives to explain legislative evolution have surfaced. Some, such as those offered by Binder (1995; 1996) and Schickler (2001) focus on the changing needs of the majority party as the driving force behind transformations in legislative rules and procedures. Krehbiel (1991) takes a different perspective, maintaining that legislative evolution is driven by asymmetries in legislators' talents that produce asymmetries in their information.

Asymmetries in information across legislators result in the adoption of different rules and procedures that take these informational discrepancies into account. This suggests that over time legislatures become more complex organizations as resources are allocated and parliamentary rights are assigned differentially. Krehbiel's approach is compatible with organization-theory-based perspectives that focus on the explanatory roles of external stresses and internal demands in explaining legislative evolution (Cooper 1977; Cooper and Brady 1981b; Davidson and Oleszek 1976; Moncrief and Jewell 1980).

Like institutionalization, most of the competing theories offered to explain legislative evolution have been developed with the U.S. House in mind and their tests confined to that chamber. Only on rare occasion have theories attempting to explain the over-time change in legislatures been motivated by attention to other chambers, Swift's (1989) study of the transformation of the early U.S. Senate being a notable example. Thus, as is often the case, we are confronted with theories that are intended to be generalizable but are really fixated on Congress, or more specifically, the U.S. House.

A theory that holds for more than one legislature must, of course, be tested in more than one chamber. In the American context, institutionalization has been tested in several state legislatures, where evidence of solidifying institutional boundaries and increasing internal complexity has been found (Berry, Berkman, and Schneiderman 2000; Squire 1992a). But universalistic standards and automatic methods of the sort Polsby found in the House are rare in state legislative chambers (Chaffey 1970; Chaffey and Jewell 1972; Squire 1992a), as also noted in chapter 4. And, as we pointed out in chapter 1, the manner in which the colonial assemblies unfolded as organizations was remarkably similar to how the U.S. House evolved more than a century later.

These findings are, however, just hints. As we have extolled at numerous points in the text, the methodological virtues of examining 101 legislative bodies rather than just one need to be exploited. Does institutionalization unfold in different ways at different points in time in different legislatures? Are the ways that rules and procedures developed in the U.S. House similar to the ways they evolved in other chambers? Do information advantages accrue the same sorts of benefits and procedures across American legislatures? Exploring these questions across a greater range of institutions offers us the promise of generalizable theories instead of those that are constructed to fit the particulars of a single chamber.

· 6 ·

Concluding Thoughts on American Legislatures in Comparison

Almost all of the best and most interesting theories about legislative organization and behavior in recent years were developed with Congress in mind (really, the House of Representatives) and tested with congressional data (meaning, again, the House). Although these theories are couched in general terms, the generic legislators about whom they theorize almost always exist in legislatures that take on the peculiar characteristics of Congress. In our view, this is too limiting and in the end sells the potential power of the theories too short. We think that these theories need to be tested beyond the confines of the U.S. House. If they are truly general, then they ought to be able to account for organization or behavior in other legislatures, particularly the ones in the states that in most fundamental respects look like Congress. If these theories fail to work outside of Congress, then they need to be reformulated to better account for the phenomena they wish to explain.

Our goal, obviously, is to encourage legislative scholars to exploit the fascinating variety of legislative organizations and behaviors found in the states. We have tried to highlight the opportunities we think the study of state legislatures present, while also noting potential problems and complications. In the end, we think our understanding of legislative organization, legislator behavior, and legislative processes will be greatly improved if we accept the challenges of expanding our scope of inquiry.

Lessons from Taking a Comparative Perspective: Ruminations on the Evolution of American Legislatures

We have, throughout the book, emphasized how American legislatures have changed over time. We observed that American legislatures germinated from the same colonial seeds and that by the end of the eighteenth century those chambers that existed bore great similarities. Over the next two centuries, however, significant differences emerged. How and why the American legislatures evolved in different ways is a critical question to answer. Although a full answer is beyond the scope of this effort, our analysis does raise some interesting ideas.

Looking simply at the organizational evolution of the colonial assemblies a century before a similar evolutionary process started in the U.S. House implies that legislative development—the rise of leadership structures, increasingly complicated procedures and rules, the creation of standing committees and the like—is less about modernization and more about the adoption of internal structures and procedures that function to make the organizations more efficient and more responsive to the needs of members and constituents. This view is consistent with Krehbiel's (1991, 248) observation that over time legislatures evolve into more complicated organizations. An important finding of our study is that this process is not time bound to the modern era.

Beyond describing familiar evolutionary processes, does the development of the colonial assemblies and their offspring offer any insights into the forces driving the changes? The machinations of political parties cannot, of course, explain what happened; they did not exist in the colonial assemblies, yet those bodies evolved in familiar ways. Polsby (1968, 164–65) proposes two alternative explanations for the evolutionary process, each focused on a changing organizational environment: increased workload and increased membership size. We might also hypothesize that a legislature becomes more organizationally developed as its membership becomes more stable.

Increased Workload

Workloads in the colonial assemblies increased over time. As we pointed out in chapter 1, between the second and sixth decades of the eighteenth century, the number of petitions grew substantially in seven of the nine assemblies for which we have data. The importance of petitions in the legislative process increased as well. Olson (1992, 556) estimates that approximately half of all laws passed by the colonial assemblies during the eighteenth century originated as petitions, a conclusion supported by data on assemblies in New Jersey (Purvis 1986, 178), Pennsylvania (Tully 1977, 99), and Virginia (Bailey 1979, 64). Another piece of evidence suggesting that colonial assemblies experienced greater workloads over time is the amount of legislation they produced. Data gathered by Olson (1992, 562–63) documents a substantial increase in law production in most colonies between the 1730s and the 1760s. The increase in bill production is tied to a dramatic swelling of the agenda placed before the colonial assemblies. Problems such as defense, Indian relations, and transportation that had been resolved at the local government level in the early years proved to require colony wide solutions in later years (Olson 1992, 552).

Thus it seems reasonable to claim that the colonial assemblies became more complex organizations at the same time they were also experiencing increasing workloads. These data are, of course, only suggestive. They cannot sort out whether workload drove organization, or organization drove workload. More complete data might allow us to tease out the relationship. But it may also be the case that they happened together with an increase in one leading to an increase in the other in a series of feedback loops. Indeed, a cursory glance at the evolution of American legislatures across the last two centuries would suggest that increasing workloads—or demands made on legislatures by the external environment—are likely to play a significant part in explaining the evolutionary process.

Membership Size

The colonial assemblies began as relatively small bodies, as table 1-1 showed. By the time of the Revolution, most were larger, some considerably. There were, however, substantial differences in their sizes. The memberships varied from small chambers of 18 to 36 assemblymen in Delaware, Georgia, New Hampshire, New Jersey, New York, and Pennsylvania, to much larger chambers with 118 to 138 assemblymen in Connecticut, Massachusetts, and Virginia (Corey 1929, 112; Greene 1981, 461; Harlow 1917, 63; Main 1966; Lutz 1999, 65–66). Assemblies in Maryland, North Carolina, Rhode Island, and South Carolina were of moderate size, with between 51 and 81 members (Greene 1981, 461). It must be noted, however, that membership sizes within each chamber fluctuated over time. In Georgia, for example, the first assembly had 19 members, the second 14 members, and the fourth 25 members (Corey 1929, 112). Because representation was based on geography, membership growth was driven by increases in the numbers of towns and counties. In 1752 the Virginia House of Burgesses had 94 members—two from each of the 45 counties and one from each of the four boroughs. In 1774 the number of counties had grown to 61, increasing the House's membership to 126 (Griffith 1970, 18).

Do these data suggest membership size is related to institutionalization? On the one hand, colonial assemblies increased in membership over time. On the other hand, while probably the most developed assembly, Virginia's, was among the largest bodies, so was the much less developed assembly in Massachusetts. In addition, evidence from the last two hundred years raises doubts about this relationship. The California state legislature, for example, has not changed one seat in size since 1879, yet it has evolved to become a much more complicated institution. And, of course, as noted in chapter 2 several state legislative chambers have reduced their membership sizes over the last several decades—most notably the Illinois House and the Massachusetts House—without any discernible change in their evolutionary paths.

Membership Stability

Using membership turnover rates to explain the evolutionary process creates something of a problem because Polsby (1968) used turnover as an indicator of institutionalization or development in the U.S. House during the nineteenth century. In and of itself, increased membership stability may not necessarily produce more complex organizations. But increasing membership stability rates are likely to be associated with increasing levels of development for several reasons. As members serve longer it seems likely that they will adopt rules that place greater value on serving apprenticeships prior to being awarded leadership positions. Complexity in structure increases as longer serving members seek to exploit asymmetries of information and talent (Krehbiel 1991, 248). Longer serving members also have greater incentive to seek to influence legislative decision making (Squire 1988; 1992), thus forcing the adoption of universalistic rules and automatic methods of the sort Polsby (1968) found. Thus greater membership stability should increase the probability that legislators will adopt increasingly complex rules and procedures, and more universalistic norms.

Over time, colonial assemblies enjoyed increasingly stable memberships. From 1696 to 1775, turnover dropped in every assembly save New Jersey, and the decline was almost always impressive (Greene 1981). In the most extreme case, turnover in Pennsylvania dropped to a mean of 18 percent in the decade from 1766 to 1775 from a mean of 62 percent in the decade from 1696 to 1705. And well over half of the "new" members in later decades were actually former legislators returning to the institution (Tully 1977, 181–82). Many Pennsylvania members served for more than 15 terms, even though elections were annual events (Leonard 1948a, 238). Similarly, members of the Connecticut Assembly came to average around nine terms in office, even with semi-annual elections (Daniels 1986, 40). Thus, the evidence shows that colonial assemblies evolved into more complex organizations at the same time their memberships were stabilizing.

Legislative Evolution and Path Dependency

An important issue raised by our examination of American legislatures involves the directionality of legislative evolution. The possibility that legislatures can travel both directions on the evolutionary path has been suggested by Hibbing

(1999, 156). Indeed, as noted in chapter 3, recent analyses of American state legislatures provide evidence of deprofessionalization over the last two decades (Brace and Ward 1999; Rosenthal 1996; 1998). The evolutionary story of the colonial assemblies and early state legislatures offers an interesting twist on the question of directionality. If the colonial assemblies evolved as the evidence provided in chapter 1 suggests, why did modern state legislatures, their direct descendants, have to retrace much of the same ground a century or two later? This is a compelling question because of the remarkable organizational continuity between the colonial assemblies and the state legislatures that succeeded them. With little more than a few name changes and increases in number of seats the assemblies became lower houses in bicameral legislatures (Lutz 1999, 49; Morey 1893–1894, 220). The universal inclination at the time of the American Revolution was to simply maintain the existing assemblies more or less as they were. Colvin (1913, 31), for example, writes of New York's 1777 constitution, "This tendency to keep existing forms is shown in preserving the legislative system practically as it was established in 1691." Similarly, Beeman (1972, 44) observes that in Virginia, "The structure of the new House of Delegates differed little from that of the colonial House of Burgesses." This remarkable continuity across a revolutionary regime change may actually constitute the strongest possible evidence of the assemblies' institutionalization.

Why, then, did legislative institutions that became highly developed in the eighteenth century and which survived intact during the transition from the colonial period through independence start regressing in the nineteenth century? Changing workloads is probably not a good explanation. Most important policy decisions at this time were made at the state level, and state legislatures were the dominant governmental institution; thus if workloads changed at all they grew bigger over time. And legislative membership sizes tended to grow, not decline. Thus it is hard to believe that changing workloads or memberships explain organizational deterioration. Membership turnover is a more likely culprit. As demonstrated in chapter 5, the colonial assemblies and new state legislatures enjoyed low turnover during the last decades of the eighteenth century, but they came to suffer extraordinary turnover rates during the first half of the nineteenth century, typically averaging between 70 to 90 percent by the 1850s (Davis 1988, 98–99; DeBats 1990, 430; Deming 1889, 426; Gunn 1980, 278; Wooster 1969, 41–42; 1975, 43). More suggestively, as membership stability declined dramatically over time, on at least one critical dimension the legislatures' organizational boundaries disintegrated. In both Georgia (DeBats 1990, 438) and New York (Gunn 1980, 282–83)—the two state legislatures for which such data have been collected—by the time of the Civil War speakers had considerably less experience in the chamber before taking the post and served much shorter tenures once ensconced than they had in the late eighteenth century and early nineteenth century.

CONCLUDING THOUGHTS ON AMERICAN LEGISLATURES IN COMPARISON

Overall, organizational development in the colonial assemblies, state legislatures, and U.S. House tracks well with increasing membership stability. Indeed, the more recent concerns with deprofessionalization and perhaps even deinstitutionalization in state legislatures are again tied to increasingly unstable memberships, this time largely precipitated by the imposition of term limits. Thus, legislative evolution appears to emphasize the importance of stable memberships. But, as Hibbing (1999, 157–59) points out, legislatures could be highly developed even with substantial membership turnover. Indeed, it seems easy to argue that while some American state legislatures with term limits have much higher turnover rates than before the reform was imposed, most of the indices of their development levels have not changed much at all. Leaders are still typically drawn from the more experienced (if now truncated) ranks, and the ways these chambers organize and make decisions are overwhelmingly the same. Committee systems, for example, continue as before, and the same rules and precedents are still observed.

What, then, is the relationship between membership stability and legislative evolution? It may be that the linkage is determined by when in a legislature's history it is assessed. The relationship may be very pronounced in newly established legislatures, such as the colonial assemblies. Once highly developed, organizational inertia or "stickiness" (Pierson and Skocpol 2002, 700) may exert a strong enough pull on a legislature that it does not organizationally regress, at least very quickly, even in the face of very high turnover rates.

Another observation can be made about the relationship between evolution and the time at which a legislature is established. The creation of new legislatures does not occur in a vacuum. Over time, the experience of existing legislatures is incorporated into the structures and organization of new bodies. As noted in chapter 4, during the colonial period younger assemblies created in Georgia and Nova Scotia imported the procedural precedents and arrangements developed by the well-established assemblies in South Carolina and Massachusetts (Greene 1961, 458). Standing committee systems developed slowly but surely in the new state legislatures in the decades following independence (Dodds 1918, 36–37; Harlow 1917, 66; Jameson 1894, 267). By the second decade of the nineteenth century such systems developed within a session or two in the new legislatures in Illinois (Davis 1988, 104) and Indiana (Walsh 1987, 93). By the 1840s, state legislatures created in California (Bancroft 1888, 315–17; Goodwin 1914, 262), Iowa (Briggs 1916, 88–89), and Texas (Spaw 1990, 170), immediately had full blown standing committee systems, emulating the schemes then in place in existing American legislatures. Thus, while later generations of legislatures may not be created fully evolved in organizational terms, they are likely to start farther along in that process than did their predecessors.

The experience of the colonial assemblies and early state legislatures generates two new insights into the process of legislative evolution. First, institutional regression in legislatures occurs slowly. Because of organizational inertia, we might allow for a considerable time lag between increased membership turnover and its manifestations in changed rules, norms, and operating procedures. Second, as the early state legislatures suffered organizational declines, they did not return to their original, primitive states. Important aspects of development remained in the form of rules and norms, committee systems, and the like. Thus, the state legislatures maintained some degree of boundedness, internal complexity, and universalistic norms. Their later upswings in the characteristics associated with development during the second half of the twentieth century track very well with their increases in membership stability (Hyneman 1938; Moncrief, Niemi, and Powell 2004; Ray 1974; Shin and Jackson 1979). Increased membership stability did not produce organizational development directly, but members who serve longer had the incentive to push their institutions to evolve.

More importantly, understanding the evolution of American legislatures, with all the ebbs and flows, requires us to take full account of their almost 400 year history. And this leads to the argument at the foundation of our effort in this book. Studying a single institution in isolation, whether it is the U.S. House or the California Assembly, can provide numerous insights into many aspects of legislative behavior. But only by examining those insights in a broader context, only by testing them comparatively, can a more complete understanding be approached.

NOTES

Notes to Introduction

1. The 10 journals consulted were *American Journal of Political Science, American Political Science Review, British Journal of Political Science, Comparative Political Studies, Comparative Politics, Journal of Legislative Studies, Journal of Politics, Legislative Studies Quarterly, Political Research Quarterly,* and *World Politics.*

2. Among the non-state legislative articles, roughly three in four articles examine behavior or processes in a single institution.

3. Kiewiet, Loewenberg, and Squire (2002) argue for the necessity and plausibility of cross-national testing of congressional based theories.

Notes to Chapter 1

1. By American colonies we mean the 13 future American states and the colonies incorporated into them. Representative assemblies were, of course, established in other North American British colonies (in chronological order of establishment: Bermuda, Barbados, St. Kitts, Antigua, Montserrat, Nevis, Jamaica, the Bahamas, Nova Scotia, and Prince Edward Island). See Kammen (1969).

2. It is important to note, however, that their institutional survival was not inevitable. The federal assembly created in the Leeward Islands in 1682, for example, disappeared from the political scene by early in the eighteenth century (Higham 1926).

3. In East Jersey the initiative for moving to a bicameral system appears to have come from the seven councilors who feared during their first meeting in 1668 that they would be outvoted by the ten representatives (Moran 1895, 27–28).

4. Kukla (1985, 289) suggests that Virginia's legislature became bicameral in 1643, "At the next meeting of the assembly in March 1643, the elected members organized themselves, for the first time in any English colonial assembly, as a lower house meeting separately from the governor and the councilors."

5. Kammen (1969, 22) observes that a "silly dispute over a stray sow produced a permanent separation and bicameralism." The conflict arose over the question of control over local affairs and involved a law passed in 1631 (Morey 1893–1894, 207), "that all swine found in any man's corn shall be forfeited to the public . . ." and another law passed in 1633, "that it shall be lawful for any man to kill any swine that comes into his corn." Thus, as Pole (1969, 68) notes wryly regarding the advent of bicameralism in America, "The process . . . began as early as 1644 in Massachusetts after the deputies and the assistants differed over the celebrated case of Widow Sherman's sow, a beast which surely deserves to rank with [General Robert E. Lee's horse] Traveller in the animal contributions to American history." See also the discussions in Moran (1895, 11–12); Moschos and Katsky (1965, 255–59); and Wright (1933, 172–73).

6. Because the development of bicameral systems is somewhat nebulous, different sources will suggest different paths. Thus, according to Barnett (1915, 451), "over half of

the American colonies began the representative system with single legislative chambers. ... Although the single chambers persisted in some of the colonies longer than in others, only one such legislature, that of Pennsylvania, was left at the end of the seventeenth century." He goes on to claim that Georgia and Vermont had reverted back to unicameral legislatures by the time the constitutional convention met. Luce (1924, 24–25) argues that unicameral legislatures were less common during the colonial period than Barnett suggests. In a sense, both claims can be argued to be true.

7. By the mid-1750s, the South Carolina Council's lack of political independence led to a substantial decline in its political power and public standing. Indeed, notable South Carolinians refused to accept appointment to the body. As the Council's reputation declined, the House's reputation climbed (Sirmans 1961, 390–91; Weir 1969, 491).

8. Of the legislative bodies established in the other British colonies in North America during the seventeenth century, Antigua, Montserrat, Nevis, and St. Kitts evolved into bicameral bodies from unicameral origins, and Barbados and Jamaica were initially created as bicameral legislatures. Only the legislature in Bermuda stayed unicameral. See Kammen (1969, 11–12).

9. The number of constituents per assembly member was, however, rising in many of the colonies, particularly in Maryland, New Jersey, New York, and Pennsylvania, as the growth in assembly membership size failed to keep up with population increases (Greene 1981, 461; 1994, 28).

10. A history of the right to petition in America is given in Higginson (1986).

11. We calculated the average number of days in session for the New York Assembly using data in Bonomi (1971, 295–311).

12. It should be noted that one Pennsylvania speaker, John Kinsey (1739–49), clearly took seniority into account in making committee assignments (Ryerson 1986, 119).

13. The committee was empowered to initiate investigations (Miller 1907, 72). In 1742 and 1756 the House of Burgesses further standardized procedures to be followed in resolving disputed elections (Pargellis 1927a, 143, 145).

14. According to Hitchcock and Seale (1976, 7), providing separate assembly and council chambers on opposing sides of a central hall was a standard feature of colonial statehouses.

15. Hitchcock and Seale (1976) say the Assembly first met in the new facilities in 1746.

16. In the 1730s committees in South Carolina also met in taverns and private homes (Frakes 1970, 66).

17. Not all assemblies were fortunate to have their own facilities. The Georgia Assembly, for example, met in houses in Savannah; the Assembly met downstairs while the Council met upstairs (Corey 1929, 111). The governor of North Carolina built a large government building in the early 1770s, but he only used it to house the governor and the Council. The Commons House was left out (Hitchcock and Seale 1976). Cook (1931, 258) says the Assembly got to use a room in one wing of the building.

18. Assemblies in Maryland, North Carolina, Rhode Island, and South Carolina were of moderate size, with between 51 and 81 members (Greene 1981, 461). It should also be pointed out that membership sizes within each chamber fluctuated over time. In Georgia, for example, the first assembly had 19 members, the second 14 members, and the fourth 25 members (Corey 1929, 112). Growth in the Virginia House of Burgesses was driven by population growth. In 1752, for example, the House had 94 members—two from each of

NOTES

the 45 counties and one from each of the four boroughs. In 1774 the number of counties had increased to 61, increasing the House's total number of members to 126 (Griffith 1970, 18).

19. Both colonies were content with their existing governmental structures and the charters that created them (Wright 1933, 178–79). Connecticut added a new preamble to its charter declaring its independence, and Rhode Island simply substituted the phrase, "The Governour and Company of the English Colony of Rhode Island and Providence Plantations" wherever the name of the king appeared in oaths and appointment powers in the charter (Adams 1980, 66–67, see also Morey 1893–1894, 219). Connecticut did not write a state constitution until 1818, Rhode Island not until 1842.

20. Biographical data on the signers of the Constitution were gathered from the National Archives and Records Administration webpage (http://www.nara.gov/education/teaching/constitution/signers.html). The signers who had served in colonial assemblies were: George Washington (VA), John Blair (VA), George Mason, George Wythe (VA), Benjamin Franklin (PA), Thomas Mifflin (PA), James Wilson (PA), Charles Cotesworth Pinckney (SC), John Rutledge (SC), Roger Sherman (CT, both houses), William Samuel Johnson (CT, both houses), Daniel of St Thomas Jenifer (MD, Council), John Dickinson (DE and PA), George Read (DE), Alexander Martin (NC), Elbridge Gerry (MA), Nathaniel Gorham (MA), William Livingston (NJ), and John Langdon (NH).

Signers of the Constitution with prior service in state legislatures were James Madison (VA), George Clymer (PA), Thomas Mifflin (PA), Gouverneur Morris (PA), Robert Morris (PA), Alexander Hamilton (NY), John Lansing, Jr. (NY), Charles Cotesworth Pinckney (SC, both houses), John Rutledge (SC), Daniel Carroll (MD Senate), Daniel of St Thomas Jenifer (MD, Senate), John Francis Mercer (VA, although MD convention delegate), Richard Bassett (DE, both houses), Gunning Bedford, Jr. (DE), Jacob Broom (DE), George Read (DE Legislative Council), William Blount (NC), William Richardson Davie (NC), Alexander Martin (NC, Senate), Richard Dobbs Spaight, Sr. (NC), Hugh Williamson (NC), Elbridge Gerry (MA), Nathaniel Gorham (MA, both houses), Rufus King (MA), Caleb Strong (MA), Jonathan Dayton (NJ), William C. Houston (NJ), William Patterson (NJ, Legislative Council), Abraham Baldwin (GA), William Few (GA), William Leigh Pierce (GA), and John Langdon (NH, both houses).

21. Scholars have long made this observation. Morey (1893–1894, 202) noted, "The chief historical significance which attaches to the first State constitutions rests in the fact that they were the connecting links between the previous organic law of the colonies and the subsequent organic law of the Federal Union. They grew out of colonial constitutions; and they formed the basis of the Federal Constitution, and furnished the chief materials from which that later instrument was derived." Similarly, Binkley (1962, 5) observed, "The framers of the Constitution did not have to cross the sea to find models for a plan of national government. These were close at hand in the governments of the thirteen states that has so recently made the transition from colonies. John Adams, who knew more about such matters than any of his contemporaries, even went so far as to say that it was from the constitutions of Massachusetts, New York, and Maryland that the Constitution of the United States was afterwards almost entirely drawn. Most of the others, of course, contributed something and none of them represented a sharp break with the government of the colony from which it had evolved."

22. An initial proposed constitution was rejected in 1778. A constitutional convention met in 1779 and 1780 and produced the document that was accepted. Authorship of the

constitution is credited to John Adams. Massachusetts was the first state to both use a special convention to draft the constitution and put the final product to the voters for their approval (Lutz 1980, 45).

23. According to Kenyon (1951, 1092), Franklin and Paine were the leading proponents of unicameralism at the time.

24. Luce (1924, 24) argues that Georgia's council played a significant role in the legislative process and thus the legislature was not really unicameral.

25. North Carolina did not change the name of its lower house to House of Representatives from House of Commons until its 1868 constitution (Luce 1924, 23).

26. Colvin (1913, 31) writes of New York's 1777 constitution, "This tendency to keep existing forms is shown in preserving the legislative system practically as it was established in 1691."

27. A few constitutions provided explicit membership sizes for their new legislative chambers, but most have to be calculated using the number of counties in each state at the time the particular constitution was adopted. Thus, the exact membership size in many chambers is subject to debate. The relative size is correct.

28. New Hampshire changed the name in 1784, Delaware in 1792, and New Jersey not until 1844. Rhode Island initially used the name "Upper House" and then tried to employ House of Magistrates. The latter name did not, however, take, and by 1799 it too was labeled the senate (Luce 1924, 21–22).

29. Religious qualifications could have powerful effects. In Maryland in the first decades of the eighteenth century, Richard Bennett never held legislative or other office, even though he was one of the richest men in the colonies and a member of a politically powerful family—his grandfather was a governor of Virginia, his father a Maryland assemblyman, his stepfather the speaker of the assembly, and his half brothers were members of the upper house. Bennett could not hold office because he was Catholic while the rest of his family was Protestant (Hardy 1994, 204).

30. Weir (1969, 477) supplies a similar answer in his analysis of South Carolina politics, "Economic independence promoted courage and material possessions fostered rationale behavior. In addition, a large stake in society tied a man's interest to the welfare of the whole. Wealth enabled him to acquire the education believed necessary for statecraft. Finally, the influence and prestige of a rich man helped to add stature and effectiveness to government."

31. Vestrymen, however, were not disqualified from legislative service, and many of them became legislators. In Virginia, for example, well over 60 percent of members of the House of Burgesses were vestrymen, giving the church considerable influence in legislative affairs (Spangenberg 1963).

32. Ministerial disqualification also appeared in constitutions in Florida, Kentucky, Louisiana, Mississippi, Missouri, Tennessee, and Texas (Swem 1917, 76–77).

33. A federal district court tossed out Maryland's disqualification clause in 1974 (*Kirkley v. Maryland,* 381 F. Supp. 327). The Supreme Court held Tennessee's disqualification to be unconstitutional four years later (*McDaniel v. Paty,* 435 U.S. 618). A discussion of the legal issues raised in the Maryland and Tennessee cases can be found in Wood (1977).

34. Madison uses that exact phrase at the beginning of *The Federalist No. 53*. In a 1776 letter to John Penn, John Adams used the phrase (Luce 1924, 110), "where annual elections end, there slavery begins." The latter version is mentioned in Adams (1980, 243).

35. This term limit was rooted in Pennsylvania history. Penn's Charter of Libertie of April 25, 1682, held in regard to members of the Provincial Council, "THAT-After the First Seven Years every one of the said Third parts that goeth yearly off shall be uncapable of being Chosen again for one whole year following that so all may be fitted for the Government and have Experience of the Care and burthen of it." These limits were discontinued in 1696 (Luce 1924, 346).

36. Benjamin Franklin, a proponent of unicameral legislatures, apparently said nothing in their favor at the Constitutional Convention (Galloway, 1961, 1). The Constitution implicitly accepts bicameralism as the norm in Article 1, section 2: "and the Electors in each State shall have the Qualifications requisite for Electors of the most numerous Branch of the State Legislature."

37. There is evidence that the electoral college system for selecting Maryland state senators was the inspiration for the similar system adopted for presidential selection in the federal Constitution (Slonim 1986, 38).

38. The constitutional clauses that provide that the legislature "shall" make its own rules may imply more freedom than those that say "may" make its own rules, although the importance of this difference probably hinges on the existence of a voter initiative process in the constitutional process (Castello 1986, 528). Constitutional provisions providing legislative rulemaking powers give legislatures considerable protection from judicial interference in their procedures (Miller 1990). In a 1905 decision, the California State Supreme Court went so far as to say (*French v. Senate of State of California*, 80 P. 1031, at 1032), "The Constitution provides that the Senate 'shall determine the rules of its proceedings . . .' If this provision were omitted, and there were no other constitutional limitations on the power, the power would nonetheless exist, and could be exercised by a majority." More recent court decisions along the same lines come from Rhode Island (*National Association of Social Workers v. Harwood*, 69 F.3d 622) and Arizona (*Davids v. Akers*, 549 F.2d. 122). In 2003, however, the Supreme Court of Nevada ruled during a severe budget impasse that the legislature's constitutional duty to balance the state budget and fund education overrode a voter imposed constitutional provision requiring tax increases to be passed by a two-thirds vote in each chamber. See *Governor Guinn v. Nevada State Legislature*, Supreme Court of Nevada Docket No. 41679 and Whaley and Vogel (2003a). A few days after the court's decision, however, both houses of the legislature passed the budget with two-thirds majorities (Whaley and Vogel 2003b).

39. According to Jennings (1957, 254–55), in practice the Parliament is governed by a rule first adopted in 1706 and made permanent in 1713 that requires taxation must be introduced by a minister on behalf of the Crown.

40. Only Vermont in 1793 and Illinois in 1818 created a shared veto power along the lines of the New York model. All three states later shifted to giving the governor the sole veto power, New York in 1821, Vermont in 1836, and Illinois in 1848 (Fairlie 1917, 477).

Notes to Chapter 2

1. That earlier state constitutions influenced later state constitutions needs to be emphasized so as to not give undue credit to the influence of the federal Constitution. The original Tennessee constitution of 1796, for example, was drawn largely from the North Carolina and Pennsylvania constitutions, with its provisions on the legislature

taken mainly from the latter (Barnhart 1943; 546–47). Along the same lines, Bancroft (1888, 296) noted that in drafting California's original constitution, "There was a good deal of 'slavish copying' of the constitutions of New York and Iowa."

2. The original Wisconsin state constitution adopted in 1848, for example, mandated that banking legislation had to be passed by referenda, not by the legislature (Stark 1997, 7).

3. Among the constitutional restrictions noted by Bryce (1906) were rules specifying the size of majorities required to pass appropriations bills, specified time intervals between various readings of bills, committee referral procedures, bill amendment limitations, and germaneness rules. See also Reinsch (1907, 134–47).

4. Note that direct voter influence on legislative organization and procedures is not a recent phenomenon. Among the measures adopted by voters in 1917 and 1918, for example, were (Kettleborough 1919, 431–32), "An amendment proposed in Colorado, and ratified by an overwhelming majority, [that] . . . reduce the period during which bills may be introduced from the first 30 to the first 15 days of the session. . . . A Massachusetts amendment authoriz[ing] the recess of the legislature during the first 60 days of the session; [and] another [that] restricts the appointment of legislators to office, and their compensation for service upon recess committees."

5. The Rhode Island Supreme Court makes this point in its decision, *In re: Advisory Opinion to the Governor,* 732 A.2d 55 (1999). Analyses of the Court's advisory opinion are given in Kogan and Robertson (2001) and Topf (2000). Rhode Island is one of eight states with constitutional provisions providing for advisory opinions (Topf 2000, 389), another indication of the complexity of determining the separation of powers across the states.

6. Alabama, Colorado, Delaware, Idaho, Indiana, Kentucky, Minnesota, New Jersey, Oklahoma, Oregon, Pennsylvania, South Carolina, Texas, and Wyoming are states using "bills for revenue raising" language. A slightly different phrase, "bills for raising a revenue" is used in Maine, while "money bills" is found in Massachusetts and New Hampshire, and "all revenue bills" is employed in Vermont. The relevant origination language in Georgia and Louisiana covers revenue and appropriations measures. Montana had an origination clause in its 1889 constitution but did not include one in its 1972 constitution (Medina 1987, 208).

7. Other formal theories lend themselves to empirical testing using American legislatures. Notions about the relationship between bicameralism and stable and undominated outcomes (a core), for example, could also be tested with empirical evidence from 50 different American bicameral legislatures to supplement the experimental studies done by Miller, Hammond, and Kile (1996) and Bottom, Eavey, Miller, and Victor (2000).

8. Among U.S. territories and possessions, Guam and the U.S. Virgin Islands have unicameral legislatures; American Samoa, Northern Mariana Islands, and Puerto Rico have bicameral legislatures.

9. Carroll (1933) conducted analysis of this sort, using the Vermont experience. He compared the performance of the Vermont legislature ten years prior to and ten years after the switch to a bicameral system. He also compared the Vermont legislature over the last ten years under unicameralism to the performance of its neighboring legislature in New Hampshire over the same time period.

10. Vermont is claimed to have abandoned joint committees in 1917 because they were thought to invalidate bicameral principles (Luce 1922, 137). The suggestion that the existence of joint committees and other joint actions raises questions about bicameralism as a discrete concept was noted by a roundtable of legislative scholars in the early 1920s

NOTES

(see Dodds 1924). As far as we know, the question has yet to be fully investigated.

11. Perhaps the classic analysis along these lines is Froman (1967, 7–15).

12. While political scientists may well see the range of sizes of American legislatures as impressive, economists see the differences as relatively small (Stigler 1976, 19).

13. Membership size in state legislatures is generally established in each state constitution. Some constitutions, such as Alaska's (Article 2, section 1) are very specific: "The legislative power of the State is vested in a legislature consisting of a senate with a membership of twenty and a house of representatives with a membership of forty." Other state constitutions allow somewhat more flexibility. The New Hampshire Constitution (Part Second, article 9), for example, states, "The whole number of representatives to be chosen from the towns, wards, places, and representative districts thereof established hereunder, shall be not less than three hundred seventy-five or more than four hundred." The state senate, however, is given a definite size (Part Second, article 25), "The senate shall consist of twenty-four members." The Wisconsin constitution (Article IV, section 2) provides the legislature great flexibility in establishing the size of the lower house: "The number of the members of the assembly shall never be less than fifty-four nor more than one hundred." The size of the upper house, however, is tied to the size of the lower house: "The senate shall consist of a number not more than one-third nor less than one-fourth of the number of members of the assembly." Perhaps the most flexible limitation on size is Montana, which allows the legislature to establish its own size within a limited range by statute (Montana Constitution, Article 5, section 2), "The size of the legislature shall be provided by law, but the senate shall not have more than 50 or fewer than 40 members and the house shall not have more than 100 or fewer than 80 members." Occasionally legislative size is set outside the state constitution. For example, the current configuration of the Alabama state legislature with 35 upper house seats and 105 lower house seats was selected by a three-judge panel of the United States District Court for the Middle District of Alabama, Northern Division in 1972. Previously the lower house had 106 seats. See *Sims v. Amos,* 336 F. Supp. 924 (1972), affirmed by the Supreme Court, *Amos v. Sims,* 409 U.S. 942 (1972).

14. Luce (1924, 86–97) provides an interesting historical discussion of membership size in a number of different legislatures.

15. In 1911 Congress fixed the number of seats in the House at 435 following admission of Arizona and New Mexico as states in 1912. The number of seats was not frozen at 435, however, until an act of Congress in 1929 (Kromkowski and Kromkowski 1991, 133). The House was 437 members from 1959 to 1963.

16. Towns could be fined for not sending their delegates, but it appears few fines were actually imposed. Some towns elected representatives but barred them from attending the session because their cost had to be borne by the town. In addition, men from outlying areas were reluctant to serve because of the difficulty of travel and the fact that many of them did not enjoy Boston. Finally, some towns had a great deal of difficulty identifying candidates for office who met the property and wealth requirements (Banner 1969, 281).

17. Madison (Madison, Hamilton, and Jay 1961, 342) anticipated such problems in the *Federalist 55,* "In all very numerous assemblies, of whatever characters composed, passion never fails to wrest the scepter from reason. Had every Athenian citizen been a Socrates, every Athenian assembly would still have been a mob."

18. Massachusetts was not alone in experiencing wild swings in legislative membership size. The size of the Nevada state legislature, for example, changed 16 times between

1864 and 1919. The range in membership sizes was substantial, from 45 legislators (15 senators and 30 assembly members from 1893 to 1899) to 75 legislators (25 senators and 50 assembly members from 1875–1879, and 22 senators and 53 assembly members from 1913 and 1915). See Davie (2003).

19. As required by Article 7, section 1 and Article 8, section 1 of the Rhode Island Constitution, the House of Representatives was reduced to 75 seats from 100 seats, and the Senate to 38 seats from 50 seats. The chair of the commission that recommended creating a smaller, better paid legislature in Rhode Island stated (Fitzpatrick 2002), "The goal of the downsizing was to increase responsibility and give individual legislators an opportunity to influence decisions and be more effective in representing their constituents."

20. Cost savings to the state were the rationale behind the reduction in the number of seats. It appears that a majority of legislators actually favored a plan to increase the number of seats, arguing that it would better enable rural areas to be represented. But the Republican leadership in both houses and the Republican governor backed the reductions and were able to push their redistricting bill through the legislature. See Cole (2001) and Heitkamp (2001).

21. Adding a seat allowed the GOP majority to avoid eliminating a seat upstate and to draw districts in New York City that gave their party a competitive chance (Perez-Pena 2002).

22. The representative was Joseph Underwood, a Whig from Kentucky.

23. The constitutional qualifications for federal office may be more ambiguous than they appear. There are, for example, credible arguments that the three qualifications establish minimum standards and that states may, as they did at earlier points in time, add to them, such as by creating a district residency requirement. See the discussions in Eastman (1995) and Price (1996).

24. *Stiles v. Blunt,* 912 F.2d 260 (8th Cir. 1990), page 266, *cert. denied,* .499 U.S. 919 (1991).

25. See *The Oregonian* (2002). The groups actively opposed to the measure were the Parents Education Association Political Action Committee, and the Oregon Family Council.

26. We can offer two examples from the 2002 election cycle and another from 2003. The first case is from Wyoming in 2002 (*Casper Star-Tribune* 2002). A retiring state senator recommended that Dr. Sigsbee Duck be nominated to run as his replacement. Dr. Duck's candidacy, however, was declared invalid when it was learned that his home was 150 feet outside the district. The doctor promised to become a candidate sometime in the future, "when I figure out where I live." The second 2002 case is from West Virginia (*Charleston Gazette* 2002). A House of Delegates candidate learned that he did not live in the district in which he was running—as required by state law—when his opponent raised the issue during a debate. The opponent worked for the candidate's mother, prompting the unlawful candidate to observe, "so he knew exactly what part of the county I lived in more than me." Like his counterpart in Wyoming, this candidate also promised to run again in the future, noting, "as a first-time candidate, I've learned a political lesson . . . research." The 2003 case was a candidate for the Mississippi state Senate who was found to be living outside the district in which she was running after she was arrested and had to give police her current address (*Clarion-Ledger* 2003).

27. Interestingly, formal residency requirements were first instituted in England by an act passed during the reign of Henry V. The expectation that representatives would be closely tied to those they represented continued through the Elizabethan period, but slow-

NOTES

ly withered away thereafter. Parliament removed the residency requirement in 1774 (Huntington 1968, 106–7).

28. *Reynolds v. Sims,* 377 U.S. 533 (1964).

29. This represents some change over time. New Hampshire's first House of Representatives had 87 members, each representing 100 families.

30. Research along these lines has typically been conducted at the local government level.

31. Jacobson (2001, 15) notes briefly that, "The purely physical problems of campaigning in or representing constituencies differ greatly and can be quite severe." We agree and think studies need to be conducted to document the representational and policy consequences.

32. The following gives the year the lower house of the state legislature changed from a one-year to two-year term after the end of the Civil War (Luce 1924, 113, Zimmerman 1981, 124): Michigan (1868), Vermont (1870), Pennsylvania (1873), New Hampshire (1877), Maine (1880), Wisconsin (1881), Connecticut (1884), Rhode Island (1911), Massachusetts (1918), New York (1938), and New Jersey (1947).

33. North Dakota extended its term of office for the lower house to four years in 1996. Four-year terms were adopted by Louisiana in 1879, in Mississippi in 1890, in Alabama in 1901, and in Maryland in 1922 (Luce 1924, 113). Among states with four-year terms for both houses, North Dakota is the only one that staggers its elections, with half of the seats in each house up for election every two years. In Alabama, Maryland, Mississippi, and Louisiana, all seats are up for election on the same four-year cycle. State legislative elections are held in odd-numbered years in both Mississippi and Louisiana, as well as in New Jersey and Virginia. Currently, every state but Louisiana elects its legislators following the national election calendar, the first Tuesday following the first Monday in November. Louisiana holds its legislative elections on the fourth Saturday after the primary, which is held on the second to last Saturday in October. Such uniformity has not always been the case. In 1930, for example, Louisiana held its legislative elections on the first Tuesday following the third Monday in April, and Maine held its legislative elections on the second Monday in September (Toll 1930, 5). It may be, of course, that elections held at odd times are more likely to focus on state and local issues than elections all held on the same day which may give a more national flavor to the proceedings.

34. We are grateful to Tim Storey of the National Conference of State Legislatures for providing us with information and examples on how four-year terms in state legislatures are handled following the decennial redistricting.

35. More recently rotation agreements were used in some state legislatures, particularly in the one-party South, when legislative districts covered more than one county. The occupant of the seat would rotate among the counties in the district. The series of reapportionment decisions handed down by the Supreme Court in the early 1960s effectively ended such agreements. See Cobb (1970) and Jewell (1964, 181–82).

36. The exception is Utah, where legislators imposed term limits on themselves only to beat the voters, who had a more stringent limitation proposal before them, to the punch.

37. The case was *U.S. Term Limits, Inc. v. Thornton,* 514 U.S. 779 (1995).

38. See *Bates v. Jones,* 131 F.3d 843 (9th Cir. 1997), cert. denied, 118 S.Ct. 1302 (1998).

39. State courts in Massachusetts, Oregon, Washington, and Wyoming tossed out term limit measures passed by the voters.

Notes to Chapter 3

1. See, for example, the essays in Zeller (1954).
2. Alabama did not change to biennial sessions until 1939 (Powell 1948, 356).
3. In 2000 Kentucky voters passed an amendment allowing for annual sessions and in 2001 the state legislature instituted the new schedule, making it the 44th state to meet every year. The states still employing biennial sessions are Arkansas, Montana, Nevada, North Dakota, Oregon, and Texas. Among the annual session legislatures, six—Connecticut, Louisiana, Maine, New Mexico, North Carolina, and Wyoming—have sessions of limited scope in one of the years. The sessions are limited to budget matters to varying degrees of strictness. The limited-scope session occurs in the even year in each limited session state except for Louisiana, which moved to the odd year starting in 2004.
4. A similar situation had unfolded a decade earlier in Nevada. In 1958, 59 percent of the voters approved a constitutional amendment to move to annual legislative sessions. The regularly scheduled session in 1959 was productive, but the 1960 session—the first annual session—produced little in the way of legislation. News reports on the lackluster session swayed public opinion against annual meetings and later that year 58 percent of Nevada voters approved an amendment to revert to biennial sessions (Diggs and Goodall 1996, 79–80.)
5. These data are tabulated from *The Book of the States 2003 Edition,* pages 109–12, and the National Conference of State Legislatures, "Legislative Sessions" (http://www.ncsl.org/Programs/Legman/about/sesslimits.htm).
6. Alaska's constitution originally allowed for annual sessions of unlimited length, but in 1984 voters imposed a 120 day limit because (McBeath and Morehouse 1994, 121), "They were frustrated by the amount of time legislators were taking to divvy up oil revenues."
7. Campbell (1980, 45–46) notes that in the late nineteenth century, even though Iowa, Illinois, and Wisconsin had no formal limits placed on the length of their legislative sessions, informal norms forced them to keep sessions short. The power of per diem limitations to curb session lengths is suggested by the experience in Arkansas. During the first decade of the twentieth century the legislature was always in sessions for more than 100 days. In 1912 a constitutional amendment passed at the polls limiting the payment of per diems to no more than 60 days. For the next couple of decades the legislature rarely met for longer than 60 days. Only after the Constitution was amended again in 1958 to require legislators to be paid for each day in regular session did the legislature again regularly meet for more than 60 days (Kellams 2003).
8. In these states voters imposed split sessions and later abolished them. Zeller (1954, 92) reports that Alabama, Georgia, New Jersey, and Wisconsin used variants of the split session and that Massachusetts was constitutionally authorized to employ it. The variation employed in Alabama allowed the legislature to meet for a ten-day organization session in the January following a November election. This brief session was held to judge member qualifications, settle disputed elections, select leaders, and make committee appointments. The regular session where legislative business could be conducted was convened in May (Powell 1948, 356).
9. The following information on pay practices is drawn from *The Book of the States 2003 Edition,* pages 125–26.
10. See the New Hampshire Constitution, Part Second, article 15, as amended in 1889:

NOTES

"The presiding officers of both houses of the legislature, shall severally receive out of the state treasury as compensation in full for their services for the term elected the sum of $250, and all other members thereof, seasonably attending and not departing without license, the sum of $200," and the Texas Constitution, Article 3, section 24(a), "Members of the Legislature shall receive from the Public Treasury a salary of Six Hundred Dollars ($600) per month, unless a greater amount is recommended by the Texas Ethics Commission and approved by the voters of this State in which case the salary is that amount." The procedure involving the Ethics Commission recommendation followed by a public vote has never been used.

11. Rhode Island Constitution, Article 6, section 3: "Commencing in January 1995, senators and representatives shall be compensated at an annual rate of ten thousand dollars ($10,000). Commencing in 1996, the rate of compensation shall be adjusted annually to reflect changes in the cost of living, as determined by the United States government, during a twelve (12) month period ending in the immediately preceding year."

12. See Part the Second, Art. CXVIII: "The base compensation as of January first, nineteen hundred and ninety-six, of members of the general court shall not be changed except as provided in this article. As of the first Wednesday in January of the year two thousand and one and every second year thereafter, such base compensation shall be increased or decreased at the same rate as increases or decreases in the median household income for the commonwealth for the preceding two year period, as ascertained by the governor."

13. In nine of those states there are some relevant constitutional provisions.

14. A penalty for being absent was imposed in many colonies. In a few colonies tardiness was also fined (Cook 1931, 266–67; Clarke 1943, 181–82). Unexcused absences in Georgia brought a formal rebuke by the speaker in front of the assembly (Corey 1929, 118).

15. The following examination of salaries in California is drawn from Driscoll (1986, 79–80).

16. Legislative salaries in New York also fluctuated a great deal over time. According to Zimmerman (1981, 125) "The 1777 constitution was silent relative to legislative salaries, and the 1821 constitution allowed the legislature to determine the salaries of members. Reflecting the distrust of the legislature, the 1846 constitution restricted the compensation of members to a maximum of $3 a day up to a maximum of $300 . . . The 1894 constitution was the first one to specify an amount—$1,500—as compensation for legislators. Voters in 1911, 1919, and 1921 rejected a proposed constitutional amendment raising the salary of legislators but approved a 1927 amendment increasing the salary to $2,500. A proposed 1947 amendment . . . providing the salary of legislators would be 'fixed by law' was ratified by the electorate. From that time on New York legislators have remained among the best paid in the country."

17. The six states without per diems are Connecticut, Delaware, New Hampshire, New Jersey, Ohio, and Rhode Island. In 2001, a large number of members of the U.S. House of Representatives unsuccessfully pushed to establish a per diem to supplement their salary, citing the example of such pay schemes in state legislatures. See Bresnahan (2001) and Eilperin (2001).

18. Data on current state legislative retirement plans are drawn from *The Book of the States 2003 Edition,* pages 136–39, and National Conference of State Legislators, "2001 Retirement Benefits for Legislators Monthly Retirement Benefits & Formula," (http://www.ncsl.org/programs/legman/About/Table9b01.htm).

19. The initiative placed the following language in Article 4, section 1.5 of the California Constitution, "To restore a free and democratic system of fair elections, and to encourage qualified candidates to seek public office, the people find and declare that the powers of incumbency must be limited. Retirement benefits must be restricted, state-financed incumbent staff and support services limited, and limitations placed upon the number of terms which may be served." (These directives were actually carried out in more detailed language inserted elsewhere in the constitution.) For Rhode Island, see Rhode Island History, chapter IX: The Era of Reform, 1984–2000 (http://www.rilin.state.ri.us/studteaguide/RhodeIslandHistory/chapt9.html).

20. See *The Book of the States 2003 Edition,* pages 156–59.

21. It is important to note that most state legislators leave on their own, rather than through defeat at polls (e.g., Jewell and Breaux 1988).

22. A table with recent data on salary, sessions lengths, staff by state along with the Squire and Kurtz professionalization rankings is provided in Hamm and Moncrief (2004, 158).

23. Data on congressional days in session are drawn from Congressional Quarterly (1993, 483–87) and Ornstein, Mann, and Malbin (2000, 154–57).

24. Note that this time frame is consistent with Price's (1975) argument that the professionalization process in the U.S. House began in the late nineteenth century.

25. State legislative salaries were collected from several different sources. The 1910 data were calculated from information in the *Official Manual of Kentucky,* 1910, page 147. The 1931 data were calculated from Schumacker (1931, 10). Salary data for 1960, 1981, and 1999 were calculated from data in *The Book of the States* for the appropriate years. Note that data for Alaska and Hawaii are not included in our analyses. Data on congressional pay are taken from the Dirksen Congressional Center's CongressLink webpage: http://www.congresslink.org/sources/salaries.html.

26. Data on days in session were collected from various sources. Keith Hamm and Ronald D. Hedlund gathered the data for 1909 as part of a larger project on state legislative committees funded by the National Science Foundation (SBR-9511518). The data for 1926 to 1929 were reported in Christensen (1931, 6). The data for the later years were taken from the appropriate volumes of *The Book of the States.* Data on congressional days in session are drawn from Congressional Quarterly (1993, 483–87) and Ornstein, Mann, and Malbin (2000, 154–57).

27. The numbers used to produce Figure 3–4 do not include those for New Jersey's state legislature, because it reported being in session every day in 1958 and 1959.

28. The election pairs we used were 1904–08, 1924–28, 1952–56, 1972–76, and 1992–96.

29. We also tested a measure using Mayhew's (1986) traditional party organization score, with the expectation that more highly organized states would be more supportive of professionalized legislatures. The measure performed very poorly both statistically and substantively in almost every equation. We do not report those results in this work.

30. In the 1910 equations, state population is substituted for total state income because the data for the latter are not available before 1929. This creates little problem, however, because as noted above, the two variables are highly correlated. State population in 1930, for example, correlates with total state income in 1931 at .95; state population in 1910 correlates with state income in 1931 at .91. Substituting one variable for the other does not change our findings, either statistically or substantively.

NOTES

31. During the earlier time periods, the correlations between Democratic party support level variable and both the South dummy variable and the Traditionalistic dummy variable are very high. This raises the strong possibility of collinearity problems. Dropping the political culture variables from the equations does not, however, boost the Democratic party support variables to statistically significant levels.

32. It must be noted that early studies of professionalization split on the question of its impact on policy outcomes. Some studies found little relationship with the policy content of legislation, notably Karnig and Sigelman (1975), LeLoup (1978), and Ritt (1973). Others found stronger effects, among them Carmines (1974) and Roeder (1979).

Notes to Chapter 4

1. Impeachment provisions appeared in Delaware, Georgia, Massachusetts, New Hampshire, New York, North Carolina, Pennsylvania, and South Carolina (Hoffer and Hull 1979, 75).

2. See *The Book of the States 2003 Edition,* pages 197–98.

3. The numbers are taken from Davidson and Oleszek (2002, 162, 174). The positions in the House include the speaker, majority and minority leaders and whips, campaign committee chairs, conference and caucus chairs and vice chairs, and the steering and policy committee chairs. In the Senate the positions include president pro tempore, majority and minority leaders and whips, campaign committee chairs, conference chairs, GOP committee on committees chair and policy committee chair, and the Democratic policy committee chair and steering committee chair.

4. The following data are drawn from *The Book of the States 2003 Edition,* pages 121–23, and state legislative web pages. See also Rosenthal (1998, 247–48).

5. The leadership positions are president pro tem, majority leader, chief deputy president pro tempore and majority caucus chair, two deputy presidents pro tempore, chief deputy majority leader, two deputy majority leaders, majority caucus whip, chief assistant president pro tempore and federal relations liaison, assistant president pro tempore, chief assistant majority leader, assistant majority leader, minority leader, minority leader pro tempore, two chief deputy minority leaders, deputy minority leader-at-large, four deputy minority leaders, four assistant minority leaders, and two minority whips. All 15 members of the minority party held leadership positions.

6. Galloway (1958, 459–60) reports that one standing committee—the Committee of Elections—was created in the First Congress.

7. Galloway (1958, 460) gives an example of the state legislative experience with legislative committees informing the behavior of members of the First Congress.

8. A more discursive examination of the relative powers of committees, caucuses, and party leaders in four state legislatures in the 1950s that documents similar diversity can be found in Wahlke, Eulau, Buchanan, and Ferguson (1962, 52–66).

9. Note that with no limits, as the number of committees in a legislature changes over time, the average number of committee assignments per member also changes, sometimes dramatically. In the Illinois House, for example, members had an average of three committee assignments in 1877. As committee numbers burgeoned, the average number of committee assignments ballooned to seven by 1897, and twelve by 1911 before declining again to five assignments in 1915 (Reinsch 1907, 162–63; Smith 1918, 610–11).

10. A thorough discussion of the committee appointment procedures formally used in the South Carolina Senate can be found in Graham and Moore (1994, 128–29).

11. Calculated from ASLCS and NCSL (1998: Table 96–4.13).

12. Calculated from ASLCS and NCSL (1998: Table 96–4.13).

13. Many legislators expressed reservations about the introduction of conference committees in New York. One of the first chairs of a conference committee in New York complained (Fisher 1995), "We're following the example of the Federal government, which is notorious for not getting anything done. We don't need this process."

14. This practice is of long standing. At the beginning of the twentieth century Reinsch (1907, 179–80) reported that both houses sent equal numbers of members—typically three—to conference committees. A couple of decades later, Winslow (1931, 26) reported some variation across the states, but with three members from each chamber composing the most common conference committee.

15. There may even be another layer of complexity to confuse scholars. Winslow (1931, 27) found that in Nevada and, as noted earlier, Washington, the first conference committee on a measure was limited to the points in contention between the two houses, but if they failed to resolve the differences any subsequent conference committee would be unlimited.

16. Some are easier to trace. The rules for both houses of the Confederate Congress, for example, were lifted almost completely from the rules governing the U.S. Congress (Jenkins 1999, 1149–1150).

17. One of the filibusterers was Henry B. Gonzalez, then a first-term state senator. He went on to serve in the U.S. House for 38 years.

18. See 77th Session Rules, article IV, rule 4.03 and editorial notes.

19. See Rules of the Senate, Rule 15. The ability to filibuster in South Carolina was not reduced when the GOP took control of the Senate in 2001, even though they worked to impose party rule by abolishing the seniority rule for committee chairs (Hoope 2001).

20. See Rules of the Nebraska Unicameral, Rule 7, section 10, cloture. See also Hambleton (2002). Note that, as in the Nebraska case, rules governing the filibuster within a chamber can change over time. In 2004, for example, the Democratic party majority in the Maryland state Senate passed a rule reducing the cloture requirement to a three-fifths majority (29 of 47 members) from a two-thirds majority (32 members). See Craig (2003) and Penn (2004).

21. Beth (2001) reports that from 1931 to 2000, discharge petitions were filed on 551 measures. The House adopted only 26 discharge motions (5 percent), although 41 other measures made their way onto the House floor through alternative means.

22. The thirteen states were Alabama, Colorado, Idaho, Illinois, Indiana, Kentucky, Maryland, Michigan, Missouri, New Jersey, Ohio, Pennsylvania, and Tennessee.

23. See Article III, section 22.

24. Such arguments still resonate with legislators. In 2003, the Kentucky House of Representatives failed to get a bill to redefine the legal status of fetuses pulled from a committee, falling four votes short of the required majority. The House majority leader had encouraged a no vote on the discharge petition by asking members to respect the committee system (Lexington *Herald-Leader* 2003).

25. No doubt strategic considerations are at the heart of the decision to make discharge procedures more difficult to invoke. In 2004, the Mississippi House voted largely on party lines to change the required vote for discharging a bill to two-thirds of those present and

voting from the long-standing majority of those present and voting (House Resolution 39 as adopted by House, March 3, 2004). Although the discharge procedure had rarely been used, the majority Democrats feared the minority Republicans would successfully pull two controversial bills out of committee, thus prompting the desire to change the rule. See Kanengiser (2004).

26. A more recent example of this occurred in the Kentucky House of Representatives early in 2004. A discharge petition signed by 26 members of the minority party Republicans was submitted to pull a proposed constitutional amendment banning gay marriages out of a committee that was refusing to report the measure. The GOP whip stated (Loftus 2004a), "I believe the vote on the discharge petition will give everyone a pretty good idea of how the whole body will vote [on the amendment]." The Democrats managed to avoid a vote on the discharge petition through a parliamentary procedure withdrawing the proposed amendment from consideration on the floor (Loftus 2004b).

Notes to Chapter 5

1. Curiously, just as in 1899, not a single lawyer served in the Delaware General Assembly in 1986 (Bazar 1987; Hirsch 1996).

2. These numbers were calculated by the authors from data in Wooster (1969; 1975).

3. By 1901 lawyers already outnumbered farmers in the Pennsylvania state legislature (Farmerie 1967, 34).

4. Occupation data were collected by Keith Hamm and Ronald D. Hedlund as part of their study of the development of state legislative committee systems throughout the twentieth century. The project was funded by the National Science Foundation (SBR-9511518). Rice University provided some funding for collecting the 1999 data. Including data we have for additional chambers for 1949 and 1999 changes the numbers presented in table 5–1 remarkably little. Moreover, the numbers reported for 1999 in table 5–1 are entirely consistent with the results of a survey of state legislators that asked their occupations conducted by the The Pew Center on the States in 2003.

5. The highest percentages of self-identified legislators in 1995 were found in Pennsylvania (82 percent), New York (76 percent), Massachusetts (55 percent), and Wisconsin (51 percent).

6. These data are drawn from National Conference of State Legislatures, "Former State Legislators in the 107th Congress."

7. The first woman in the Senate, Rebecca L. Felton, a Georgia Democrat, was in office for only a single day. The first woman to serve in the Senate in a substantial way was Hattie W. Caraway, a Democrat from Arkansas who took her late husband's seat in 1931 and served until 1945.

8. Cox (1994, 12) reports that 78 percent of women turned out compared to 56 percent of men.

9. Once in the majority the first power play pursued by the women was to commandeer the biggest bathroom off the chamber floor from the men (Ammons 1999, 23).

10. Women speakers were found in Colorado, Connecticut, Missouri, North Dakota, and Oregon.

11. The first African American to serve in a legislative body in America might have been Mathias de Sousa, who served in the Maryland Assembly in 1642 (Bogen 2001). But

de Sousa's heritage is remarkably unclear. Different sources refer to him as Portuguese, African, Jewish, and Catholic. See King, Chaney, and Ford (2001).

12. These data are from the National Conference of State Legislatures, updated as of 29 December 2003. See also Bositis (2002, 18).

13. Data from the National Conference of State Legislatures, updated as of 29 December 2003, reveal three fewer Hispanics in lower houses.

14. Over the same time period the percentage of first-term members in the state senate dropped to 50 percent from 84 percent (Shull and McGuinness 1951, 473–74).

15. State courts in Oregon, Massachusetts, Washington, and Wyoming tossed out voter passed term limits. Legislators in Idaho and Utah repealed term limits.

REFERENCES

Abernathy, Byron R. 1959. *Constitutional Limitations on the Legislature.* Lawrence, KS: University of Kansas, Governmental Research Center.

Adams, Greg D. 1996. "Legislative Effects of Single-Member vs. Multi-Member Districts." *American Journal of Political Science* 40:129–44.

Adams, Willi Paul. 1980. *The First American Constitutions.* Chapel Hill, NC: University of North Carolina Press.

Alter, Alison B., and Leslie Moscow McGranahan. 2000. "Reexamining the Filibuster and Proposal Powers in the Senate." *Legislative Studies Quarterly* 25:259–84.

American Society of Legislative Clerks and Secretaries in cooperation with the National Conference of State Legislatures. 1998. *Inside the Legislative Process.* Denver, CO: National Conference of State Legislatures.

Ammons, David. 1999. "Washington's First in Women." *State Legislatures* 25 (May):22–25.

Andrews, Charles M. 1926. "The American Revolution: An Interpretation." *American Historical Review* 31:219–32.

Andrews, Charles McLean. 1944. "On the Writing of Colonial History." *William and Mary Quarterly* 1:27–48.

Ayres, B. Drummond, Jr. 1990a. "Filibuster on Abortion Drones On in Maryland." *New York Times,* 22 March.

Ayres, B. Drummond, Jr. 1990b. "Maryland Legislature Halts an Abortion Move." *New York Times,* 23 March.

Bailey, Raymond C. 1977. "Popular Petitions and Religion in Eighteenth-Century Colonial Virginia." *Historical Magazine of the Protestant Episcopal Church* 46:419–28.

Bailey, Raymond C. 1979. *Popular Influence upon Public Policy: Petitioning in Eighteenth-Century Virginia.* Westport, CT: Greenwood.

Baker, Ross K. 2001. *House and Senate,* 3rd ed. New York: Norton.

Balanoff, Elizabeth. 1972. "Negro Legislators in the North Carolina General Assembly; July, 1868–February, 1872." *North Carolina Historical Review* 49:22–55.

Bancroft, Hubert Howe. 1888. *History of California,* vol. VI. San Francisco: The History Company.

Banner, James M., Jr. 1969. *To the Hartford Convention: The Federalists and the Origins of Party Politics in Massachusetts, 1789–1815.* New York: Knopf.

Barclay, Thomas S. 1931. "The Split Session of the California Legislature." *California Law Review* 20:42–58.

Barnett, James D. 1915. "The Bicameral System in State Legislation." *American Political Science Review* 9:449–66.

Barnhart, John D. 1943. "The Tennessee Constitution of 1796: A Product of the Old West." *Journal of Southern History* 9:532–48.

Barrett, Edith J. 1995. "The Policy Priorities of African American Women in State Legislatures." *Legislative Studies Quarterly* 20:223–47.

Bassett, John Spencer. 1894. *The Constitutional Beginnings of North Carolina (1663–1729).* Baltimore, MD: Johns Hopkins University Press.

REFERENCES

Battista, James S. Coleman. 2000. "Institutional Choice in State Legislatures." Ph.D. diss. Duke University.

Bazar, Beth. 1987. *State Legislators' Occupations: A Decade of Change.* Denver: National Conference of State Legislatures.

Beeman, Richard R. 1972. *The Old Dominion and the New Nation, 1788–1801.* Lexington, KY: University Press of Kentucky.

Berkman, Michael B. 2001. "Legislative Professionalism and the Demand for Groups: The Institutional Context of Interest Population Density." *Legislative Studies Quarterly* 26:661–79.

Berry, William D., Michael B. Berkman, and Stuart Schneiderman. 2000. "Legislative Professionalism and Incumbent Reelection: The Development of Institutional Boundaries." *American Political Science Review* 94:859–74.

Beth, Loren P., and William C. Havard. 1961. "Committee Stacking and Political Power in Florida." *Journal of Politics* 23:57–83.

Beth, Richard S. 2001. "The Discharge Rule in the House: Recent Use in Historical Context," updated. Congressional Research Service 97–856 GOV.

Bianco, William, David B. Spence, and John D. Wilkerson. 1996. "The Electoral Connection in the Early Congress: The Case of the Compensation Act of 1816." *American Journal of Political Science* 40:145–71.

Billings, Warren M. 1974. "The Growth of Political Institutions in Virginia, 1634–1676." *William and Mary Quarterly* 31:225–42.

Binder, Sarah A. 1995. "Partisanship and Procedural Choice: Institutional Change in the Early Congress, 1789–1823." *Journal of Politics* 57:1093–1118.

Binder, Sarah A. 1996. "The Partisan Basis of Procedural Choice: Allocating Parliamentary Rights in the House, 1789–1990." *American Political Science Review* 90:8–20.

Binder, Sarah A., Eric D. Lawrence, and Forrest Maltzman. 1999. "Uncovering the Hidden Effect of Party." *Journal of Politics* 61:815–31.

Binder, Sarah A., Eric D. Lawrence, and Steven S. Smith. 2002. "Tracking the Filibuster, 1917 to 1996." *American Politics Research* 30:406–22.

Binder, Sarah A., and Steven S. Smith. 1997. *Politics or Principle? Filibustering in the United States Senate.* Washington, DC: The Brookings Institution.

Binder, Sarah A., and Steven S. Smith. 1998. "Political Goals and Procedural Choice in the Senate." *Journal of Politics* 60:398–416.

Binkley, Wilfred E. 1962. *President and Congress,* 3rd ed. New York: Vintage.

Bogen, David S. 2001. "Mathius de Sousa; Maryland's First Colonist of African Descent." *Maryland Historical Magazine* 96:68–85.

Bogue, Allan G., Jerome M. Clubb, Carroll R. McKibben, and Santa A. Traugott. 1976. "Members of the House of Representatives and the Process of Modernization, 1789–1960." *Journal of American History* 63:275–302.

Bolles, Albert S. 1890. *Pennsylvania: Province and State,* vol. VI. New York: Burt Franklin.

Bonomi, Patricia U. 1971. *A Factious People: Politics and Society in Colonial New York.* New York: Columbia University Press.

Bosher, Kate Langley. 1907. "The First House of Burgesses." *North American Review* 184:733–39.

Bositis, David A. 2002. *Black Elected Officials: A Statistical Summary 2000.* Washington, DC: Joint Center for Political and Economic Studies.

REFERENCES

Bottom, William P., Cheryl L. Eavey, Gary J. Miller, and Jennifer Nicoll Victor. "The Institutional Effect on Majority Rule Instability: Bicameralism in Spatial Policy Decisions." *American Journal of Political Science,* 44:523–40.

Bowman, Ann O'M., and Richard C. Kearney. 1988. "Dimensions of State Government Capability." *Western Political Quarterly* 41:341–62.

Brace, Paul, and Daniel S. Ward. 1999. "The Institutionalized Legislature and the Rise of the Antipolitics Era." In *American State and Local Politics,* ed., Ronald E. Weber and Paul Brace. New York: Chatham House.

Brady, David, Kara Buckley, and Douglas Rivers. 1999. "The Roots of Careerism in the U.S. House of Representatives." *Legislative Studies Quarterly* 24:489–510.

Brady, David W., and Craig Volden. 1998. *Revolving Gridlock: Politics and Policy from Carter to Clinton.* Boulder, CO: Westview.

Bresnahan, John. 2001. "Hastert, Gephardt Torpedo Per Diem." *Roll Call,* 19 February.

Brewer, John Mason. 1935. *Negro Legislators of Texas and Their Descendants, a History of the Negro in Texas Politics.* Dallas, TX: Mathis.

Briggs, John E. 1916. "History and Organization of the Legislature in Iowa." In *Statute Law-making in Iowa,* ed. Benjamin F. Shambaugh. Iowa City, IA: State Historical Society of Iowa.

Broussard, James H. 1977. "Party and Partisanship in American Legislatures: The South Atlantic States, 1800–1812." *Journal of Southern History* 43:39–58.

Bryce, James. 1906. *The American Commonwealth,* abridged and revised ed. New York: Macmillan.

Buchanan, James M., and Gordon Tullock. 1962. *The Calculus of Consent.* Ann Arbor, MI: The University of Michigan Press.

Bullock, Charles S. 1972. "House Careerists: Changing Patterns of Longevity and Attrition." *American Political Science Review* 66:1295–1300.

Bushman, Claudia L., Harold B. Hancock, and Elizabeth Moyne Homsey. 1986. *Proceedings of the Assembly of the Lower Counties on the Delaware, 1770–1776, the Constitutional Convention of 1776, and of the House of Assembly of the Delaware State, 1776–1781.* Newark, DE: University of Delaware Press.

Butler, David, and Bruce Cain. 1992. *Congressional Redistricting: Comparative and Theoretical Perspectives.* New York: Macmillan.

Button, James, and David Hedge. 1996. "Legislative Life in the 1990s: A Comparison of Black and White State Legislators." *Legislative Studies Quarterly* 21:199–218.

Calabrese, Stephen. 2000. "Multimember District Congressional Elections." *Legislative Studies Quarterly* 25:611–43.

Camia, Catalina. 2000. "Democratic Lawmaker was a Trailblazer in Texas." *Dallas Morning News,* 29 November.

Campbell, Ballard C. 1980. *Representative Democracy.* Cambridge: Harvard University Press.

Carey, John M., Gary F. Moncrief, Richard G. Niemi, and Lynda W. Powell. 2003. "Term Limits in the State Legislatures: Results from a New Survey of the 50 States." Paper presented at the annual meeting of the American Political Science Association.

Carey, John M., Richard G. Niemi, and Lynda W. Powell. 1998. "The Effects of Term Limits on State Legislatures." *Legislative Studies Quarterly* 23:271–300.

Carey, John M., Richard G. Niemi, and Lynda W. Powell. 2000. "Incumbency and the Probability of Reelection in State Legislative Elections." *Journal of Politics* 62:671–700.

Carmines, Edward G. 1974. "The Mediating Influence of State Legislatures on the Linkage Between Interparty Competition and Welfare Policies." *American Political Science Review* 68:1118–1124.

Carroll, Daniel B. 1932. *The Unicameral Legislature of Vermont.* Montpelier, VT: Vermont Historical Society.

Casper Star-Tribune. 2001. "Lawmaker Urges Downsizing of Mammoth District." 19 June.

Casper Star-Tribune. 2002. "Would-be Candidate Lives Just Shy of Senate District." 4 April.

Castello, James E. 1986. "Comment: The Limits of Popular Sovereignty: Using the Initiative Power to Control Legislative Procedure." *California Law Review* 74:491–563.

Chadha, Anita, and Robert A. Bernstein. 1996. "Why Incumbents are Treated So Harshly: Term Limits for State Legislators." *American Politics Quarterly* 24:363–76.

Chaffey, Douglas Camp. 1970. "The Institutionalization of State Legislatures: A Comparative Study." *Western Political Quarterly* 23:180–96.

Chaffey, Douglas Camp, and Malcolm E. Jewell. 1972. "Selection and Tenure of State Legislative Party Leaders: A Comparative Analysis." *Journal of Politics* 34:1278–86.

Chambers, William Seal. 1928. "The Separation of Powers in the Eighteenth Century." *American Political Science Review* 22:32–44.

Charleston Gazette. 2002. "Candidate Files for House But in the Wrong District." 26 April.

Christensen, Asher N. 1931. "Days to Days." *State Government* 4(7):6–9.

Citizens Conference on State Legislatures. 1971. *State Legislatures: An Evaluation of Their Effectiveness.* New York: Praeger.

Citizen's Guide to the Wyoming Legislature. 2001. (http://legisweb.state.wy.us/leginfo/webfaq.htm)

Clarion-Ledger. 2003. "Address Disqualifies Senate Candidate." 11 June.

Clarke, Mary Patterson. 1943. *Parliamentary Privilege in the American Colonies.* New Haven, CT: Yale University Press.

Cleland, Ethel. 1914. "Bill Drafting." *American Political Science Review* 8:244–51.

Cloner, Alexander, and Richard W. Gable. 1959. "The California Legislator and the Problem of Compensation." *Western Political Quarterly* 12:712–26.

Clucas, Richard A. 2001. "Principal-Agent Theory and the Power of State House Speakers." *Legislative Studies Quarterly* 26:319–38.

Cobb Edwin L. 1970. "Representation and the Rotation Agreement: The Case of Tennessee." *Western Political Quarterly* 23516–29.

Cole, Janet. 2001. "N.D. Legislative Districts Set, But Not Without Problems." *The Forum* (Fargo), 1 December.

Colvin, David Leigh. 1913. "The Bicameral Principle in the New York Legislature." Ph.D. diss. Columbia University

Congressional Quarterly. 1993. *Congress A to Z.* Washington, D.C.: Congressional Quarterly.

Conrad, Henry C. 1908. *History of the State of Delaware,* vol. I. Wilmington, DE: Henry C. Conrad.

Cook, Florence. 1931. "Procedure in the North Carolina Colonial Assembly, 1731–1770." *North Carolina Historical Review* 8:258–83.

Cooper, Joseph. 1977. "Congress in Organizational Perspective." In *Congress Reconsidered,* ed. Lawrence C. Dodd and Bruce I. Oppenheimer. New York: Praeger.

REFERENCES

Cooper, Joseph, and David W. Brady. 1981a. "Institutional Context and Leadership Style: The House from Cannon to Rayburn." *American Political Science Review* 75:411–25.

Cooper, Joseph, and David W. Brady. 1981b. "Toward a Diachronic Analysis of Congress." *American Political Science Review* 75:988–1006.

Corey, John Pitts. 1929. "Procedure in the Commons House of Assembly in Georgia." *Georgia Historical Quarterly* 13:110–27.

Cox, Elizabeth M. 1994. "The Three Who Came First." *State Legislatures* 20 (November):12–19.

Cox, Elizabeth M. 1996. *Women, State and Territorial Legislatures, 1895–1995: A State-by-State Analysis, with Rosters of 6,000 Women.* Jefferson, NC: McFarland.

Cox, Gary W. 2000. "On the Effects of Legislative Rules." *Legislative Studies Quarterly* 25:169–92.

Cox, Gary W., and Mathew D. McCubbins. 1993. *Legislative Leviathan: Party Government in the House.* Berkeley, CA: University of California Press.

Craig, Tim. 2003. "Democrats in Md. Try to Deflate Filibuster." *Washington Post*, 30 December.

Crain, W. Mark, and Robert D. Tollison. 1982. "Team Production in Political Majorities." *Micropolitics* 2:111–21.

Crane, Wilder, Jr., and Meredith W. Watts, Jr. 1968. *State Legislative Systems.* Englewood Cliffs, NJ: Prentice-Hall.

Crowley, Jocelyn Elise. 2004. "When Tokens Matter." *Legislative Studies Quarterly* 29:109–36.

Daniel, Jean Houston, and Price Daniel. 1969. *Executive Mansions and Capitols of America.* Waukesha, WI: Country Beautiful.

Daniels, Bruce C. 1986. "Diversity and Democracy: Officeholding Patterns among Selectmen in Eighteenth-Century Connecticut." In *Power and Status*, ed. Bruce C. Daniels. Middletown, CT: Wesleyan University Press.

Darcy, R. 1996. "Women in the State Legislative Power Structure: Committee Chairs." *Social Science Quarterly* 77:888–911.

Davidson, Roger H. 1981. "Subcommittee Government: New Channels for Policy Making." In *The New Congress*, ed. Thomas E. Mann and Norman J. Ornstein. Washington, DC: American Enterprise Institute.

Davidson, Roger H. 1990. "The Advent of the Modern Congress: The Legislative Reorganization Act of 1946." *Legislative Studies Quarterly* 15:357–73.

Davidson, Roger H., and Walter J. Oleszek. 1976. "Adaptation and Consolidation: Structural Innovation in the U.S. House of Representatives." *Legislative Studies Quarterly* 1:37–65.

Davidson, Roger H., and Walter J. Oleszek. 2002. *Congress and Its Members*, 8th ed. Washington, DC: CQ Press.

Davie, Brian L. 2003. "Legislative Redistricting." Nevada State Library and Archives (http://dmla.clan.lib.nv.us/docs/nsla/archives/political/legis/legis1.htm#0)

Davis, Horace B. 1951. "The Occupations of Massachusetts Legislators, 1790–1950." *New England Quarterly* 24, 89–100.

Davis, Rodney O. 1988. "'The People in Miniature': The Illinois General Assembly, 1818–1848." *Illinois Historical Journal* 81:95–108.

DeBats, Donald A. 1990. "An Uncertain Arena: The Georgia House of Representatives, 1808–1861." *Journal of Southern History* 56:423–56.

Deering, Christopher J., and Steven S. Smith. 1985. "Subcommittees in Congress." In *Congress Reconsidered*, 3rd ed., ed. Lawrence C. Dodd and Bruce I. Oppenheimer. Washington, DC: CQ Press.

Deming, Clarence. 1889. "Town Rule in Connecticut." *Political Science Quarterly* 4:408–32.

Diermeier, Daniel, and Roger B. Myerson. 1999. "Bicameralism and Its Consequences for the Internal Organization of Legislatures." *American Economic Review* 89:1182–1196.

Diggs, Don W., and Leonard E. Goodall. 1996. *Nevada Government and Politics*. Lincoln, NE: University of Nebraska Press.

Dippel, Horst. 1996. "The Changing Idea of Popular Sovereignty in Early America Constitutionalism: Breaking Away from European Patterns." *Journal of the Early Republic* 16:21–45.

Dodd, Lawrence C. 1986. "A Theory of Congressional Cycles: Solving the Puzzle of Change." In *Congress and Policy Change*, ed. Gerald C. Wright, Leroy N. Rieselbach, and Lawrence C. Dodd. New York: Agathon.

Dodds, H. W. 1918. "Procedure in State Legislatures." *Annals of the American Academy of Political and Social Science*, May supplement.

Dodds, H. W. 1924. "Round Table IV. Legislation." *American Political Science Review* 18:140–46.

Donnelly, Thomas C. 1947. *The Government of New Mexico*. Albuquerque, NM: University of New Mexico Press.

Döring, Herbert. 1995. *Parliaments and Majority Rule in Western Europe*. New York: St. Martins Press.

Driscoll, James D. 1986. *California's Legislature*. Sacramento, CA: Center for California Studies.

Eastman, John C. 1995. "Open to Merit of Every Description? An Historical Assessment of the Constitution's Qualifications Clauses." *Denver University Law Review* 73:89–140.

Eilperin, Juliet. 2001. "House Members Seek a Daily Allowance of $165." *Washington Post*, 3 March.

Elazar, Daniel J. 1984. *American Federalism: A View from the States*, 3rd ed. New York: Harper & Row.

Epstein, David, David Brady, Sadafumi Kawato, and Sharyn O'Halloran. 1997. "A Comparative Approach to Legislative Organization: Careerism and Seniority in the United States and Japan." *American Journal of Political Science* 41:965–88.

Erickson, Brenda. 2001. "Sources of Parliamentary Procedures: A New Precedence for Legislatures." *Journal of the American Society of Legislative Clerks and Secretaries* 7.

Eulau, Heinz, and John D. Sprague. 1964. *Lawyers in Politics*. Indianapolis, IN: Bobbs-Merrill.

Evans, C. Lawrence, and Walter J. Oleszek. 1997. *Congress under Fire*. Boston: Houghton Mifflin.

Fairlie, John A. 1917. "The Veto Power of the State Governor." *American Political Science Review* 11:473–93.

Falb, Susan Rosenfeld. 1986. *Advice and Ascent: The Development of the Maryland Assembly 1635–1689*. New York: Garland.

Farmerie, Samual A. 1967. "Pennsylvania Legislators 1901–1963." *Pennsylvania History* 34:31–43.

REFERENCES

Faust, Martin L. 1928. "Results of the Split-Session System of the West Virginia Legislature." *American Political Science Review* 22:109–21.

Ferejohn, John. 1975. "Who Wins in Conference Committee?" *The Journal of Politics* 37:1033–1046.

Fiorina, Morris. 1994. "Divided Government in the American States: A Byproduct of Legislative Professionalism?" *American Political Science Review* 88:304–16.

Fiorina, Morris. 1997. "Professionalism, Realignment, and Representation." *American Political Science Review* 91:156–62.

Fiorina, Morris P., David W. Rohde, and Peter Wissel. 1975. "Historical Change in House Turnover." In *Congress in Change,* ed. Norman J. Ornstein. New York: Praeger.

Fisher, Joel M., Charles M. Price, and Charles G. Bell. 1973. *The Legislative Process in California.* Washington, DC: American Political Science Association.

Fisher, Ian. 1995. "In Open Panel, Albany Tries Democracy in Lawmaking." *New York Times,* 30 March.

Fisher, Louis. 1980. "History of Pay Adjustments for Members of Congress." In *The Rewards of Public Service,* ed. Robert W. Hartman and Arnold R. Weber. Washington DC: The Brookings Institution.

Fisher, Sydney George. 1897. *The Evolution of the Constitution of the United States.* Philadelphia: J. B. Lippincott.

Fisk, Catherine, and Erwin Chemerinsky. "The Filibuster." *Stanford Law Review* 49:181–254.

Fitzpatrick, Edward. 2002. "The Incredible Shrinking Legislature." *State Legislatures* 28 (July/August): 51–54.

Fortenberry, C. N., and Edward H. Hobbs. 1967. "The Mississippi Legislature." In *Power in American State Legislatures: Case Studies of the Arkansas, Louisiana, Mississippi, and Oklahoma Legislatures,* ed. Alex B. Lacy, Jr. New Orleans: Tulane University.

Fox, Harrison W., Jr., and Susan Webb Hammond. 1977. *Congressional Staffs.* New York: The Free Press.

Fox, William T. R. 1938. "Legislative Personnel in Pennsylvania." *Annals of the American Academy of Political and Social Science* 195:32–39.

Frakes, George Edward. 1970. *Laboratory for Liberty: The South Carolina Legislative Committee System 1719–1776.* Lexington, KY: University Press of Kentucky.

Francis, Wayne L. 1985. "Leadership, Party Caucuses, and Committees in U.S. State Legislatures." *Legislative Studies Quarterly* 10:243–57.

Francis, Wayne L. 1989. *The Legislative Committee Game: A Comparative Analysis of 50 States.* Columbus, OH: Ohio State University Press.

Freeman, Patricia K. 1995. "A Comparative-Analysis of Speaker Career Patterns in U.S. State Legislatures." *Legislative Studies Quarterly* 20:365–76.

Freeman, Patricia K., and Ronald D. Hedlund. 1993. "The Functions of Committee Change in State Legislatures." *Political Research Quarterly* 46:911–29.

Freeman, Patricia K., and Lilliard E. Richardson, Jr. 1994. "Casework in State Legislatures." *State and Local Government Review* 26:21–26.

Freeman, Patricia K., and Lilliard E. Richardson, Jr. 1996. "Explaining Variation in Casework among State Legislators." *Legislative Studies Quarterly* 21: 41–56.

Freund, Ernst, John A. Lapp, and Frank A. Updyke. 1913. "Report of Standing Committee on Legislative Methods." *Proceedings of the American Political Science Association* 10:271–80.

Friedman, Lawrence M. 1973. *A History of American Law.* New York: Simon and Schuster.

Froman, Lewis A., Jr. 1967. *The Congressional Process.* Boston: Little, Brown.

Frothingham, Richard. 1886. *The Rise of the Republic of the United States.* Boston: Little, Brown.

Gallay, Alan. 1988. "Jonathan Bryan's Plantation Empire: Land, Politics, and the Formation of a Ruling Class in Colonial Georgia." *William and Mary Quarterly* 45:253–79.

Galloway, George B. 1958. "Precedents Established in the First Congress." *Western Political Quarterly* 11:454–68.

Galloway, George B. 1959. "Development of the Committee System in the House of Representatives." *American Historical Review* 65:17–30.

Galloway, George B. 1961. *History of the House of Representatives.* New York: Thomas Y. Crowell.

Gamm, Gerald, and Kenneth A. Shepsle. 1989. "Emergence of Legislative Institutions: Standing Committees in the House and Senate, 1810–1825." *Legislative Studies Quarterly* 14:39–66.

Gierzynski, Anthony. 1992. *Legislative Party Campaign Committees in the American States.* Lexington, KY: The University Press of Kentucky.

Gilligan, Thomas W., and John G. Matsusaka. 1995. "Deviations from Constituent Interests: The Role of Legislative Structure and Political Parties in the States." *Economic Inquiry* 33:383–401.

Gilligan, Thomas W., and John G. Matsusaka. 2001. "Fiscal Policy, Legislature Size, and Political Parties: Evidence from State and Local Governments in the First Half of the 20th Century." *National Tax Journal* 54:57–82.

Gilmour, John B., and Paul Rothstein. 1996. "A Dynamic Model of Loss, Retirement, and Tenure." *Journal of Politics* 58:54–68.

Goodwin, Cardinal. 1914. *The Establishment of State Government in California 1846–1850.* New York: Macmillan.

Gosnell, Cullen B., and C. David Anderson. 1956. *The Government and Administration of Georgia.* New York: Thomas Y. Crowell.

Graham, Cole Blease, Jr., and William V. Moore. 1994. *South Carolina Government and Politics.* Lincoln, NE: University of Nebraska Press.

Green, Fletcher M. 1930. *Constitutional Development in the South Atlantic States, 1776–1860.* Chapel Hill, NC: University of North Carolina Press.

Greene, Jack P. 1959. "Foundations of Political Power in the Virginia House of Burgesses, 1720–1776. *William and Mary Quarterly* 16:485–506.

Greene, Jack P. 1961. "The Role of the Lower Houses of Assembly in Eighteenth-Century Politics." *Journal of Southern History* 27:451–74.

Greene, Jack P. 1963. *The Quest for Power: The Lower Houses of Assembly in the Southern Royal Colonies 1689–1776.* Chapel Hill, NC: University of North Carolina Press.

Greene, Jack P. 1969. "Political Mimesis: A Consideration of the Historical and Cultural Roots of Legislative Behavior in the British Colonies in the Eighteenth Century." *American Historical Review* 75:337–60.

Greene, Jack P. 1981. "Legislative Turnover in British America, 1696 to 1775: A Quantitative Analysis." *William and Mary Quarterly* 38:442–63.

Greene, Jack P. 1994. "Colonial Assemblies." In *The Encyclopedia of the American*

REFERENCES

Legislative Process, vol. I, ed. Joel H. Silbey. New York: Scribners.

Griffith, Lucille. 1970. *The Virginia House of Burgesses 1750–1774,* rev. ed. University, AL: University of Alabama Press.

Groseclose, Tim, and David C. King. 2001. "Committee Theories Reconsidered." In *Congress Reconsidered,* 7th ed., ed. Lawrence C. Dodd and Bruce I. Oppenheimer. Washington, DC: CQ Press.

Gross, Donald A. 1980. "House-Senate Conference Committees: A Comparative-State Perspective." *American Journal of Political Science* 24:769–78.

Grumm, John G. 1971. "The Effects of Legislative Structure on Legislative Performance." In *State and Urban Politics,* ed. Richard I Hofferbert and Ira Sharkansky. Boston: Little, Brown.

Gunn, L. Ray. 1980. "The New York State Legislature: A Developmental Perspective: 1777–1846." *Social Science History* 4:267–94.

Haeberle, Steven. 1978. "The Institutionalization of Subcommittees." *Journal of Politics* 40:1054–1065.

Halter, Gary M. 1997. *Government & Politics of Texas.* Madison, WI: Brown & Benchmark.

Hambleton, Ken. 2002. "Filibusters Targeted." *Lincoln Journal Star,* 15 January.

Hamilton, Howard D. 1967. "Legislative Constituencies: Single-Member Districts, Multi-Member Districts, and Floterial Districts." *Western Political Quarterly* 20:321–40.

Hamm, Keith E. 2001. "Comparative Legislative Research: An Observer's Perspective." Prepared for the Conference on the Comparative Study of Deputy "Hill Style" in Latin American Legislatures, Texas A&M University, College Station, Texas.

Hamm, Keith E., and Robert Harmel. 1993. "Legislative Party Development and the Speaker System: The Case of the Texas House." *Journal of Politics* 55:1140–51.

Hamm, Keith E., and Ronald D. Hedlund. 1994. "Committees in State Legislatures." In *The Encyclopedia of the American Legislative System,* ed. Joel J. Silbey. New York: Scribner's.

Hamm, Keith E., and Ronald D. Hedlund. 1994. "Political Parties in State Legislatures." In *The Encyclopedia of the American Legislative System,* ed. Joel J. Silbey. New York: Scribner's.

Hamm, Keith E., and Ronald D. Hedlund. 1995. "The Development of Committee Specialization in State Legislatures." Paper presented at the annual meeting of the American Political Science Association.

Hamm, Keith E., Ronald D. Hedlund, and Nancy Martorano. 1999. "The Evolution of Committee Structure, Powers and Procedures in Twentieth Century State Legislatures." Paper presented at the annual meeting of the American Political Science Association.

Hamm, Keith E., Ronald D. Hedlund, and Nancy Martorano. 2001. "Structuring Committee Decision Making: Rules and Procedures in U.S. State Houses and Senates." *Journal of Legislative Studies* 7: No. 2 (Summer).

Hamm, Keith E., and Gary F. Moncrief. 2004. "Legislative Politics in the States." In *Politics in the American States,* 8th ed., ed., Virginia Gray and Russell L. Hanson. Washington, DC: CQ Press.

Hansen, Karen. 1989. "Are Coalitions Really on the Rise?" *State Legislatures* 15(4):11–12.

Hanson, Royce. 1989. *Tribune of the People: The Minnesota Legislature and Its Leadership.* Minneapolis: University of Minnesota Press.

Hardy, Beatriz Betacourt. 1994. "A Papist in a Protestant Age: The Case of Richard Bennett, 1667–1749." *Journal of Southern History* 60:203–28.

Harlow, Ralph Volney. 1917. *The History of Legislative Methods in the Period Before 1825.* New Haven, CT: Yale University Press.

Harmel, Robert. 1986. "Minority Partisanship in One-Party Predominant Legislatures: A Five-State Study." *Journal of Politics* 48:729–40.

Harrison, Robert. 1979. "The Hornet's Nest at Harrisburg: A Study of the Pennsylvania Legislature in the Late 1870s." *Pennsylvania Magazine of History and Biography* 103:334–55.

Haynes, George H. 1894. *Representation and Suffrage in Massachusetts, 1620–1691.* Baltimore, MD: Johns Hopkins University Press.

Haynes, George H. 1900. "Representation in State Legislatures." *Annals of the American Academy of Political and Social Science* 15:204–35.

Haynie, Kerry L. 2001. *African American Legislators in the American States.* New York: Columbia University Press.

Hedlund, Ronald D., and Keith E. Hamm. 1996. "Political Parties as Vehicles for Organizing U.S. State Legislative Committees." *Legislative Studies Quarterly* 21:383–408.

Heitkamp, Joel. 2001. "Fewer Districts is the Right Way." *Bismarck Tribune* 19 December.

Hero, Rodney E., and Caroline J. Tolbert. 1996. "A Racial/Ethnic Diversity Interpretation of Politics and Policy in the States of the U.S." *American Journal of Political Science* 40:851–71.

Herzberg, Donald G., and Alan Rosenthal. 1971. *Strengthening the States: Essays on Legislative Reform.* Garden City, NY: Doubleday.

Hibbing, John R. 1982. "Voluntary Retirements from the House in the Twentieth Century." *Journal of Politics,* 44:1020–1034.

Hibbing, John R. 1988. "Legislative Institutionalization with Illustrations from the British House of Commons." *American Journal of Political Science* 32:681–712.

Hibbing, John R. 1999. "Legislative Careers: Why and How We Should Study Them." *Legislative Studies Quarterly* 24:149–71.

Hibbing, John R., and John R. Alford. 1990. "Constituency Population and Representation in the U.S. Senate." *Legislative Studies Quarterly* 15:581–98.

Hibbing, John R., and Sara L. Brandes. 1983. "State Population and the Electoral Success of U.S. Senators." *American Journal of Political Science* 27:808–20.

Higginson, Stephen A. 1986. "A Short History of the Right to Petition Government for the Redress of Grievances." *Yale Law Journal* 96:142–66.

Higham, C. S. S. 1926. "The General Assembly of the Leeward Islands." *English Historical Review* 41:190–209.

Hinds, Asher C. 1909. "The Speaker of the House of Representatives." *American Political Science Review* 3:155–66.

Hirsch, Eric. 1996. *State Legislators' Occupations 1993 and 1995.* Denver: National Conference of State Legislatures.

Hitchcock, Henry-Russell, and William Seale. 1976. *Temples of Democracy.* New York: Harcourt Brace Jovanovich.

Hoffer, Peter C., and N. E. H. Hull. 1978. "The First American Impeachments." *William and Mary Quarterly* 35:653–67.

Hoffer, Peter C., and N. E. H. Hull. 1979. "Power and Precedent in the Creation of an

REFERENCES

American Impeachment Tradition: The Eighteenth-Century Colonial Record." *William and Mary Quarterly* 36:51–77.

Hogarty, Richard A. 1998. "When Legislators Become Administrators: The Problem of Plural Office-Holding." *Roger Williams University Law Review* 4:133–57.

Holcombe, Arthur N. 1931. *State Government in the United States*, 3rd ed. New York: Macmillan.

Holmes, Jack E. 1967. *Politics in New Mexico*. Albuquerque, NM: University of New Mexico Press.

Hoope, Heather. 2001. "Shakeup in the South Carolina Senate." *State Legislatures* 27 (July/August):32–34.

Horack, Frank E. 1916. "The Committee System." In *Statute Law-making in Iowa*, ed. Benjamin F. Shambaugh. Iowa City, IA: State Historical Society of Iowa.

Hubbard, Clifford C. 1936. "The Issue of Constitutional Amendment in Rhode Island." *American Political Science Review* 30:537–40.

Huber, John D., and Charles R. Shipan. 2002. *Deliberate Discretion? The Institutional Foundations of Bureaucratic Autonomy*. New York: Cambridge University Press.

Huntington, Samuel P. 1968. *Political Order in Changing Societies*. New Haven: Yale University Press.

Hyneman, Charles S. 1938. "Turnover and Tenure of Legislative Personnel." *Annals of the American Academy of Political and Social Science* 195:21–31.

Hyneman, Charles S. 1940. "Who Makes Our Laws." *Political Science Quarterly* 55:556–81.

In re: Advisory Opinion to the Governor. 1999. 732 A.2d 55.

Jacklin, Michele. 1989. "Conservative Democrats are Victorious in Connecticut House." *State Legislatures* 15(4):13–15.

Jacobson, Gary C. 2001. *The Politics of Congressional Elections*, 5th ed. New York: Addison Wesley Longman.

Jameson, J. Franklin. 1894. "The Origin of the Standing-Committee System in American Legislative Bodies." *Political Science Quarterly* 9:246–67.

Jefferson City News Tribune. 2002. "Students Push for Lower Age Limit to be Lawmaker." 11 February.

Jenkins, Jeffrey A. 1998. "Property Rights and the Emergence of Standing Committee Dominance in the Nineteenth-Century House." *Legislative Studies Quarterly* 23:493–519.

Jenkins, Jeffrey A. 1999. "Examining the Bonding Effects of Party: A Comparative Analysis of Roll-Call Voting in the U.S. and Confederate Houses." *American Journal of Political Science* 43:1144–1165.

Jennings, W. Ivor. 1957. *Parliament*, 2nd ed. New York: Cambridge University Press.

Jewell, Malcolm E. 1964. "State Legislatures in Southern Politics." *Journal of Politics* 26:177–96.

Jewell, Malcolm E. 1982. *Representation in State Legislatures*. Lexington, KY: University Press of Kentucky.

Jewell, Malcolm E., and David Breaux. 1988. "The Effect of Incumbency on State Legislative Elections." *Legislative Studies Quarterly* 13:495–514.

Jewell, Malcolm E., and Sarah M. Morehouse. 2001. *Political Parties and Elections in American States*, 4th ed. Washington, DC: CQ Press.

Jewell, Malcolm E., and Samuel C. Patterson. 1966. *The Legislative Process in the United States*. New York: Random House.

REFERENCES

Jewell, Malcolm E., and Samuel C. Patterson. 1986. *The Legislative Process in the United States,* 4th ed. New York: Random House.

Jewett, Aubrey and Roger Handberg. 1999. "GOP Rules Changes in the Florida House." *Comparative State Politics* 20 (August):27–48.

Jillson, Calvin, and Rick K. Wilson. 1994. *Congressional Dynamics: Structure, Coordination, and Choice in the First American Congress, 1774–1789.* Stanford, CA: Stanford University Press.

Johnson, Alvin W. 1938. *The Unicameral Legislature.* Minneapolis, MN: University of Minnesota Press.

Johnson, Richard R. 1987. "'Parliamentary Egotisms': The Clash of Legislatures in the Making of the American Revolution." *Journal of American History* 74:338–62.

Jones, Charles C., Jr. 1883. *The History of Georgia,* vol. I. New York: Houghton, Mifflin.

Jones, Harry W. 1952. "Bill-Drafting Services in Congress and the State Legislatures." *Harvard Law Review* 65:441–51.

Jordan, David W. 1987. *Foundations of Representative Government in Maryland, 1632–1715.* New York: Cambridge University Press.

Judge, David. 2003. "Legislative Institutionalization: A Bent Analytical Arrow?" *Government and Opposition* 38:497–516.

Ka, Sangjoon, and Paul Teske. 2002. "Ideology and Professionalism—Electricity Regulation and Deregulation Over Time in the American States." *American Politics Research* 30:323–43.

Kammen, Michael. 1969. *Deputyes and Libertyes: The Origins of Representative Government in Colonial America.* New York: Knopf.

Kanengiser, Andy. 2004. "Tort, Voter ID Bills Appear Dead." *Clarion-Ledger,* 4 March.

Karnig, Albert K., and Lee Sigelman. 1975. "State Legislative Reform and Public Policy: Another Look." *Western Political Quarterly* 28:548–552.

Keefe, William J. 1954. "Parties, Partisanship, and Public Policy in the Pennsylvania Legislature." *American Political Science Review* 48:450–64.

Keefe, William J., and Morris S. Ogul. 2001. *The American Legislative Process: Congress and the States,* 10th ed. Upper Saddle River, NJ: Prentice Hall.

Kellams, Laura. 2003. "State Lawmakers Easing Back to Long Sessions of Yesteryear." *Arkansas Democrat-Gazette,* 27 May.

Keller, Clair W. 1993. "The Failure to Provide a Constitutional Guarantee on Representation." *Journal of the Early Republic* 13:23–54.

Kellough, J. E., and S. C. Selden. 2003. "The Reinvention of Public Personnel Administration: An Analysis of the Diffusion of Personnel Management Reforms in the States." *Public Administration Review* 63:165–76.

Kennedy, John J. 1999. *The Contemporary Pennsylvania Legislature.* Lanham, MD: University Press of America.

Kenyon, Cecelia M. 1951. "Where Paine Went Wrong." *American Political Science Review* 45:1086–1099.

Kernell, Samuel. 1977. "Toward Understanding 19th Century Congressional Careers: Ambition, Competition, and Rotation." *American Journal of Political Science* 21:669–93.

Kersh, Rogan, Suzanne B. Mettler, Grant D. Reeher, and Jeffrey M. Stonecash. 1998. "'More a Distinction of Words than Things': The Evolution of Separated Powers in the

REFERENCES

American States." *Roger Williams University Law Review* 4:5–49.

Kettleborough, Charles. 1919. "Amendments to State Constitutions." *American Political Science Review* 13:429–47.

Key, V. O., Jr. 1956. *American State Politics*. New York: Knopf.

Kiewiet, D. Roderick, Gerhard Loewenberg, and Peverill Squire. 2002. "The Implications of the Study of the U.S. Congress for Comparative Legislative Research." In *Legislatures: Comparative Perspectives on Representative Assemblies,* ed. Gerhard Loewenberg, Peverill Squire, and D. Roderick Kiewiet. Ann Arbor: University of Michigan Press.

King, James D. 2000. "Changes in Professionalism in U.S. State Legislatures." *Legislative Studies Quarterly* 25:327–43.

King, Julia A., Edward Chaney, and Iris Carter Ford. 2001. "Defining Race and Identity in Early Md." *Baltimore Sun,* 4 February.

Kirby, John B. 1970. "Early American Politics—The Search for Ideology: An Historiographical Analysis and Critique of the Concept of 'Deference.'" *Journal of Politics* 32:808–38.

Klain, Maurice. 1955. "A New Look at the Constituencies: The Need for a Recount and a Reappraisal." *American Political Science Review* 49:1105–19.

Kogan, Bruce I., and Cheryl L. Robertson. 2001. "Chief Justice Joseph R. Weisberger's Page of History." *Roger Williams University Law Review* 6:501–38.

Kolp, John G. 1992. "The Dynamics of Electoral Competition in Pre-Revolutionary Virginia." *William and Mary Quarterly* 49:652–74.

Krasno, Jonathon S. 1994. *Challengers, Competition, and Reelection: Comparing Senate and House Elections.* New Haven, CT: Yale University Press.

Krehbiel, Keith. 1991. *Information and Legislative Organization.* Ann Arbor, MI: University of Michigan Press.

Krehbiel, Keith. 1993. "Where's the Party?" *British Journal of Political Science* 23:235–66.

Krehbiel, Keith. 1995. "Cosponsors and Wafflers from A to Z." *American Journal of Political Science* 39:906–23

Krehbiel, Keith. 1998. *Pivotal Politics: A Theory of U.S. Lawmaking.* Chicago: University of Chicago Press.

Krehbiel, Keith. 1999a. "Paradoxes of Parties in Congress." *Legislative Studies Quarterly* 24:31–64.

Krehbiel, Keith. 1999b. "The Party Effect from A to Z and Beyond." *Journal of Politics* 61:832–40.

Kromkowski, Charles A., and John A. Kromkowski. 1991. "Why 435? A Question of Political Arithmetic." *Polity* 24:129–45.

Kukla, Jon. 1981. *Speakers and Clerks of the Virginia House of Burgesses, 1643–1776.* Richmond, VA: Virginia State Library.

Kukla, Jon. 1985. "Order and Chaos in Early America: Political and Social Stability in Pre-Restoration Virginia." *American Historical Review* 90:275–98.

Kurtz, Karl, T. 1992. "Understanding the Diversity of American State Legislatures." *Extension of Remarks* (June):2–5.

Lange, Howard B., Jr. 1938. "They Legislate for Missouri." *Annals of the American Academy of Political and Social Science* 195:40–44.

Leibowitz, Arleen, and Robert Tollison. 1980. "A Theory of Legislative Organization: Making the Most of Your Majority." *Quarterly Journal of Economics* 94:261–77.

LeLoup, Lance T. 1978. "Reassessing the Mediating Impact of Legislative Capability." *American Political Science Review* 72:616–21.

Leonard, Cynthia Miller. 1978. *The General Assembly of Virginia July 30, 1619—January 11, 1978*. Richmond, VA: Virginia State Library.

Leonard, Sister Joan de Lourdes. 1948a. "The Organization and Procedure of the Pennsylvania Assembly 1682–1776 I." *The Pennsylvania Magazine of History and Biography* 72:215–39.

Leonard, Sister Joan de Lourdes. 1948b. "The Organization and Procedure of the Pennsylvania Assembly 1682–1776 II." *The Pennsylvania Magazine of History and Biography* 72:376–412.

Levine, Peter D. 1977. *The Behavior of State Legislative Parties in the Jacksonian Era: New Jersey, 1829–1844*. Rutherford, NJ: Fairleigh Dickinson University Press.

Lexington Herald-Leader. 2003. "Bill to Redefine Fetuses Defeated." 11 March.

Little, Thomas H., Dana Dunn, and Rebecca E. Dean. 2001. A View from the Top: Gender Differences in Leadership Priorities among State Legislative Leaders." *Women and Politics* 22:29–50.

Loewenberg, Gerhard. 1995. "Legislatures and Parliaments." In *The Encyclopedia of Democracy,* vol. III, ed. Seymour Martin Lipset. Washington, DC: Congressional Quarterly.

Loewenberg, Gerhard, and Samuel C. Patterson. 1979. *Comparing Legislatures.* Boston: Little, Brown.

Loftus, Tom. 2004a. "Kentucky House GOP Tries to Force Voter on Gay-Marriage Ban." *Courier-Journal,* 25 February.

Loftus, Tom. 2004b "Vote on State Gay Marriage Bill Halted." *Courier-Journal,* 26 February.

Logan, Rayford W., and Michael R. Winston. 1982. *Dictionary of American Negro Biography.* New York: Norton.

Lokken, Roy N. 1959. "The Concept of Democracy in Colonial Political Thought." *William and Mary Quarterly* 16:568–80.

Longley, Lawrence D., and Walter J. Oleszek. 1989. *Bicameral Politics: Conference Committees in Congress.* New Haven, CT: Yale University Press.

Longley, Lawrence D., and David M. Olson. 1991. *Two into One: The Politics and Processes of National Legislative Cameral Change.* Boulder, CO: Westview.

Longmore, Paul K. 1996. "'All Matters and Things Relating to Religion and Morality': The Virginia House of Burgesses' Committee for Religion, 1769 to 1775." *Journal of Church and State* 38:775–97.

Lounsbury, Carl R. 2001. *From Statehouse to Courthouse: An Architectural History of South Carolina' Colonial Capitol and Charleston County Courthouse.* Columbia, SC: University of South Carolina Press.

Luce, Robert. 1922. *Legislative Procedure.* Boston: Houghton Mifflin.

Luce, Robert. 1924. *Legislative Assemblies.* Boston: Houghton Mifflin.

Luttbeg, Norman R. 1992. "Legislative Careers in Six States: Are Some Legislatures More Likely to Be Responsive?" *Legislative Studies Quarterly* 17:49–68.

Lutz, Donald S. 1980. *Popular Consent and Popular Control: Whig Political Theory in Early State Constitutions.* Baton Rouge, LA: Louisiana State University Press.

Lutz, Donald S. 1999. "The Colonial and Early State Legislative Process." In *Inventing Congress: Origins and Establishment of the First Federal Congress,* ed. Kenneth R. Bowling and Donald R. Kennon. Athens, OH: Ohio University Press.

REFERENCES

Macartney, John. 1987. "Congressional Staff: The View from the District." In *Congress and Public Policy,* 2nd ed., ed. David C. Kozak and John D. Macartney. Prospect Heights, IL: Waveland.

Mackey, Scott. 2001. "New Directions for Vermont." *State Legislatures* 27 (July/August):40–42.

Maestas, Cherie. 2000. "Professional Legislatures and Ambitious Politicians: Policy Responsiveness of State Institutions." *Legislative Studies Quarterly* 25:663–90.

Maestas, Cherie. 2003. "The Incentive to Listen: Progressive Ambition, Resources, and Opinion Monitoring among State Legislators." *Journal of Politics* 65:439–56.

Madison, James, Alexander Hamilton, and John Jay. 1961. *The Federalist Papers.* Ed. Clinton Rossiter. New York: New American Library.

Main, Jackson Turner. 1966. "Government by the People: The American Revolution and the Democratization of the Legislatures." *William and Mary Quarterly* 23:391–407.

Main, Jackson Turner. 1967. *The Upper House in Revolutionary America 1763–1788.* Madison, WI: University of Wisconsin Press.

Malbin, Michael J. 1980. *Unelected Representatives.* New York: Basic Books.

Martorano, Nancy. 2001. "Using State Legislative Rules of Procedure to Test Existing Theories of Legislative Organization." Paper presented at the annual meeting of the American Political Science Association.

Martorano, Nancy, R. Bruce Anderson, and Keith E. Hamm. 2000. "A Transforming South: Exploring Patterns of State House Contestation." *American Review of Politics.* 21:179–200.

Martorano, Nancy, Keith E. Hamm, and Ronald D. Hedlund. 2000. "Examining Committee Structures, Procedures, and Powers in U.S. State Legislatures." Paper presented at the annual meeting of the Midwest Political Science Association.

Mason, John Brown. 1938. "The State Legislature as Training for Further Public Service." *Annals of the American Academy of Political and Social Science* 195:176–82.

Mayhew, David R. 1986. *Placing Parties in American Politics.* Princeton, NJ: Princeton University Press.

McAllister, Bill. 2002. "Alaska Senate District Tests Candidates' Stamina." *Stateline.org,* 17 October.

McBeath, Gerald A., and Thomas A. Morehouse. 1994. *Alaska Politics and Government.* Lincoln, NE: University of Nebraska Press.

McCarthy, Charles. 1911. "Legislative Reference Department." In *Readings on American State Government,* ed. Paul S. Reinsch. Boston: Ginn.

McCarty, Nolan, Keith T. Poole, and Howard Rosenthal. 2001. "The Hunt for Party Discipline in Congress." *American Political Science Review* 95:673–87.

McConachie, Lauros G. 1898. *Congressional Committees.* New York: Thomas Y. Crowell.

McCormick, Richard P. 1964. *New Jersey from Colony to State.* Princeton, NJ: Van Nostrand.

McCormick, Robert E., and Robert D. Tollison. 1978. "Legislatures as Unions." *Journal of Political Economy* 86:63–78.

McHenry, Dean E. 1938. "Legislative Personnel in California." *Annals of the American Academy of Political and Social Science* 195:45–52.

McKinley, James C., Jr. 2002. "Before Bills Move in Albany, 3 Leaders Cut Deals." *New York Times,* 21 October.

Medina, J. Michael. 1987. "The Origination Clause in the American Constitution: A Comparative Survey." *Tulsa Law Journal* 23:165–234.

Merl, Jean. 2000. "Solis Prepares to Take Another Step Up." *Los Angeles Times,* 28 Dec.

Miller, Gary J., Thomas H. Hammond, and Charles Kile. 1996. "Bicameralism and the Core: An Experimental Test." *Legislative Studies Quarterly* 21:83–103.

Miller, Elmer I. 1907. *The Legislature of the Province of Virginia; Its Internal Development.* New York: Columbia University Press.

Miller, Michael B. 1990. "Comment: The Justiciability of Legislative Rules and the 'Political' Political Question Doctrine." *California Law Review* 78:1341–1374.

Minzner, Max. 1999. "Entrenching Interests: State Supermajority Requirements to Raise Taxes." *Akron Tax Journal* 14:43–89.

Moncrief, Gary F. 1988. "Dimensions of the Concept of Professionalism in State Legislatures: A Research Note." *State and Local Government Review* 20:128–32.

Moncrief, Gary F. 1999. "Recruitment and Retention in U.S. Legislatures." *Legislative Studies Quarterly* 24:173–208.

Moncrief, Gary, and Malcolm E. Jewell. 1980. "Legislators' Perceptions of Reform in Three States." *American Politics Quarterly* 8:106–27.

Moncrief, Gary, Richard G. Niemi, and Lynda W. Powell. 2004. "Time, Term Limits, and Turnover: Membership Stability in U.S. State Legislatures." *Legislative Studies Quarterly* 29:357–81.

Moncrief, Gary F., Peverill Squire, and Malcolm E. Jewell. 2001. *Who Runs for the Legislature?* Upper Saddle River, NJ: Prentice Hall.

Monroe, J. P. 2001. *The Political Party Matrix: The Persistence of Organization.* Albany, NY: State University Press of New York.

Mooney, Christopher Z. 1994. "Measuring U.S. State Legislative Professionalism: An Evaluation of Five Indices." *State and Local Government Review* 26:70–78.

Mooney, Christopher Z. 1995. "Citizens, Structures, and Sister States: Influences on State Legislative Professionalism." *Legislative Studies Quarterly* 20:47–67.

Moran, Thomas Francis. 1895. *The Rise and Development of the Bicameral System in America.* Baltimore: Johns Hopkins University Press.

Morey, William C. 1893–1894. "The First State Constitutions." *Annals of the American Academy of Political and Social Science* 4:201–32.

Morgan, David R., and Laura Ann Wilson. 1990. "Diversity in the American States: Updating the Sullivan Index." *Publius* 20:71–81.

Morehouse, Sarah McCally. 1983. *State Politics, Parties and Policy.* New York: Holt, Rinehart, and Winston.

Moschos, Demitrios M., and David L. Katsky. 1965. "Unicameralism and Bicameralism: History and Tradition." *Boston University Law Review* 45:250–70.

Munroe, John A. 1979. *History of Delaware.* Newark, DE: University of Delaware Press.

National Association of Latino Elected and Appointed Officials Educational Fund. 2002. "Latinos Gain New Ground in Congress and State Houses." 11 November.

National Association of State Budget Officers. 2002. *Budget Processes in the States.* Washington, DC.

Neustadt, Richard E. 1990. *Presidential Power and the Modern Presidents: The Politics of Leadership from Roosevelt to Reagan.* New York: Free Press.

REFERENCES

Nevin, Allan. 1924. *The American States During and After the Revolution, 1775–1789.* New York: Macmillan.

Niemi, Richard G., and Laura R. Winsky. 1987. "Membership Turnover in U.S. State Legislatures: Trends and Effects of Districting." *Legislative Studies Quarterly* 12:115–23.

Oleszek, Walter J. 2001. *Congressional Procedures and the Policy Process*, 5th ed. Washington, DC: CQ Press.

Oleszek, Walter J. 2004. *Congressional Procedures and the Policy Process*, 6th ed. Washington, DC: CQ Press.

Olson, Alison G. 1992. "Eighteenth-Century Colonial Legislatures and Their Constituents." *Journal of American History* 79:543–67.

Oregonian, The. 2002. "Measure 17: Legislators Minimum Age." 20 October.

Ornstein, Norman J., Thomas E. Mann, and Michael J. Malbin. 2000. *Vital Statistics on Congress, 1999–2000.* Washington, DC: AEI.

Orth, Samuel P. 1904. "Our State Legislatures." *Atlantic Monthly* 94:728–39.

Ostrogorski, M. 1910. *Democracy and the Party System.* New York: Macmillan.

Overby, L. Marvin, and Thomas A. Kazee. 2000. "Outlying Committees in the Statehouse: An Examination of the Prevalence of Committee Outliers in State Legislatures." *Journal of Politics* 62:701–28.

Overby, L. Marvin, Thomas A. Kazee, and David W. Prince. 2004. "Committee Outliers in State Legislatures." *Legislative Studies Quarterly* 29:81–107.

Owings, Stephanie, and Rainald Borck. 2000. "Legislative Professionalism and Government Spending: Do Citizen Legislators Really Spend Less?" *Public Finance Review* 28:210–25.

Packenham, Robert A. 1970. "Legislatures and Political Development." In *Legislatures in Developmental Perspective,* ed. Allan Kornberg and Lloyd D. Musolf. Durham, NC: Duke University Press.

Pargellis, S. M. 1927a. "The Procedure of the Virginia House of Burgesses I." *William and Mary College Quarterly Historical Magazine* 7:73–86.

Pargellis, S. M. 1927b. "The Procedure of the Virginia House of Burgesses II." *William and Mary College Quarterly Historical Magazine* 7:143–57.

Parker, Glenn R. 1992. *Institutional Change, Discretion, and the Making of Modern Congress.* Ann Arbor, MI: University of Michigan Press.

Patzelt, Werner J. 1999. "Recruitment and Retention in Western European Parliaments." *Legislative Studies Quarterly* 24:239–79.

Peabody, Robert L. 1985. "Leadership in Legislatures: Evolution, Selection, and Functions." In *Handbook of Legislative Research,* ed. Gerhard Loewenberg, Samuel C. Patterson, and Malcolm E. Jewell. Cambridge: Harvard University Press.

Perez-Pena, Richard. 2002. "Questions from Justice Department Delay Plan to Add District to New York Senate." *New York Times,* 4 June.

Penn, Ivan. 2004. "3 GOP Senators Protest Filibuster Rule; Lawmakers Walk Out; Majority Needed to end Debate is Changed; General Assembly." *Baltimore Sun,* 21 January.

Perkins, John A. 1946. "State Legislative Reorganization." *American Political Science Review* 40:510–21.

Peters, Ronald M. 1997. *The American Speakership,* 2nd ed. Baltimore: Johns Hopkins University Press.

Phillips, Hubert. 1921. *The Development of a Residential Qualification for Representatives in Colonial Legislatures.* Cincinnati, OH: Abington.

Pierson, Paul and Theda Skocpol. 2002. "Historical Institutionalism in Contemporary Political Science." In *Political Science: The State of The Discipline,* ed. Ira Katznelson and Helen V. Milner. New York: Norton.

Pindyck, Robert S., and Daniel L. Rubinfeld. 1991. *Econometric Models and Economic Forecasting.* New York: McGraw-Hill.

Pole, J. R. 1962. "Historians and the Problem of Early American History." *American Historical Review* 67:626–46.

Pole, J. R. 1969. 1969. *The Seventeenth Century; the Sources of Legislative Power.* Charlottesville, VA: University Press of Virginia.

Polsby, Nelson W. 1968. "The Institutionalization of the U.S. House of Representatives." *American Political Science Review* 62:144–68.

Polsby, Nelson W. 1975. "Legislatures." In *The Handbook of Political Science,* vol. 5, ed. Fred I. Greenstein and Nelson W. Polsby. Reading, MA: Addison-Wesley.

Polsby, Nelson W., Miriam Gallagher, and Barry Rundquist. 1969. "The Growth of the Seniority System in the U.S. House of Representatives." *American Political Science Review* 63:787–807.

Powell, Alden J. 1948. "Constitutional Growth and Revision in the South." *Journal of Politics* 10:354–84.

Powell, Richard J. 2000. "The Impact of Term Limits on the Candidacy Decisions of State Legislators in U.S. House Elections." *Legislative Studies Quarterly* 25:645–61.

Price, H. Douglas. 1975. "Congress and the Evolution of Legislative 'Professionalism.'" In *Congress in Change,* ed. Norman J. Ornstein. New York: Praeger.

Price, Polly J. 1996. "Term Limits on Original Intent? An Essay on Legal Debate and Historical Understanding." *Virginia Law Review* 82:493–533.

Purvis, Thomas L. 1980. "'High-Born, Long-Recorded Families': Social Origin of New Jersey Assemblymen, 1703–1776." *William and Mary Quarterly* 37:592–615.

Purvis, Thomas L. 1986. *Proprietors, Patronage, and Paper Money: Legislative Politics in New Jersey, 1703–1776.* New Brunswick, NJ: Rutgers University Press.

Rainbolt, John C. 1970. "The Alteration in the Relationship between Leadership and Constituents in Virginia, 1660 to 1720." *William and Mary Quarterly* 27:411–434.

Ray, David. 1974. "Membership Stability in Three State Legislatures: 1893–1969." *American Political Science Review* 68:106–12.

Ray, David. 1976. "Voluntary Retirement and Electoral Defeat in Eight State Legislatures." *Journal of Politics* 38:426–33.

Reingold, Beth. 2000. *Representing Women: Sex, Gender, and Legislative Behavior in Arizona and California.* Chapel Hill, NC: University of North Carolina Press.

Reinsch, Paul S. 1907. *American Legislatures and Legislative Methods.* New York: The Century Co.

Riker, William H. 1955. "The Senate and American Federalism." *American Political Science Review* 49:452–69.

Riker, William H. 1984. "The Heresthetics of Constitution-Making: The Presidency in 1787, with Comments on Determinism and Rational Choice." *American Political Science Review* 78:1–16.

Risjord, Norman K. 1992. "Partisanship and Power: House Committees and the Powers of the Speaker, 1789–1801." *William and Mary Quarterly* 49:628–51.

Ritt, Leonard G. 1973. "State Legislative Reform: Does It Matter?" *American Politics Quarterly* 1:499–511.

REFERENCES

Ritter, Charles F., and John L. Wakelyn. 1989. *American Legislative Leaders, 1850–1910.* New York: Greenwood.

Roeder, Phillip W. 1979. "State Legislative Reform: Determinants and Policy Consequences." *American Politics Quarterly* 7:51–70.

Rogers, James R. 1998. "Bicameral Sequence: Theory and State Legislative Evidence." *American Journal of Political Science* 42:1025–60.

Rogers, James R. 2001. "An Informational Rationale for Congruent Bicameralism." *Journal of Theoretical Politics* 13:123–52.

Rogers, James R. 2002. "Free Riding in State Legislatures." *Public Choice* 113:59–76.

Rogers, James R. 2003. "The Impact of Bicameralism on Legislative Production. *Legislative Studies Quarterly* 28:509–28.

Rogers, Lindsay. 1941. "The Staffing of Congress." *Political Science Quarterly* 56:1–22.

Rosenthal, Alan. 1974. "Turnover in State Legislatures." *American Journal of Political Science* 18:609–16.

Rosenthal, Alan. 1981. *Legislative Life.* New York: Harper & Row

Rosenthal, Alan. 1986. "The Legislature." In *The Political State of New Jersey,* ed. Gerald M. Pomper. New Brunswick, NJ: Rutgers University Press.

Rosenthal, Alan. 1989. "The Legislative Institution: Transformed and at Risk." In *The State of the States,* ed. Carl E. Van Horn. Washington DC: CQ Press.

Rosenthal, Alan. 1993. "The Legislative Institution: In Transition and at Risk." In *The State of the States,* 2nd ed., ed. Carl E. Van Horn. Washington DC: CQ Press.

Rosenthal, Alan. 1996. "State Legislative Development: Observations from Three Perspectives. *Legislative Studies Quarterly* 21:169–98.

Rosenthal, Alan. 1998. *The Decline of Representative Democracy: Process, Participation, and Power in State Legislatures.* Washington, DC: CQ Press.

Rosenthal, Cindy Simon. 1995. "New Party or Campaign Bank Account? Explaining the Rise of State Legislative Campaign Committees." *Legislative Studies Quarterly* 20:249–68.

Rosenthal, Cindy Simon. 1998a. "Determinants of Collaborative Leadership: Civic Engagement, Gender, or Organizational Norms?" *Political Research Quarterly* 51:847–68.

Rosenthal, Cindy Simon. 1998b. *When Women Lead: Integrative Leadership in State Legislatures.* New York: Oxford University Press.

Rossiter, Clinton. 1953. "Richard Bland: The Whig in America." *William and Mary Quarterly* 10:33–79.

Ryerson, Richard Alan. 1986. "Portrait of a Colonial Oligarchy: The Quaker Elite in the Pennsylvania Assembly, 1729–1776." In *Power and Status,* ed. Bruce C. Daniels. Middletown, CT: Wesleyan University Press.

Salisbury, Robert H. and Kenneth A. Shepsle. 1981. "U.S. Congressman as Enterprise." *Legislative Studies Quarterly* 6:559–76.

Scalia, Laura J. 1999. *America's Jeffersonian Experiment: Remaking State Constitutions, 1820–1850.* DeKalb, IL: Northern Illinois University Press.

Scharf, J. Thomas. 1879. *History of Maryland,* vol. II. Baltimore: John B. Piet.

Schickler, Eric. 2001. *Disjointed Pluralism: Institutional Innovation and the Development of the U.S. Congress.* Princeton, NJ: Princeton University Press.

Schickler Eric, and Andrew Rich. 1997. "Controlling the Floor: Parties as Procedural Coalitions in the House." *American Journal of Political Science* 41:1340–1375.

Schlesinger, Joseph A. 1957. "Lawyers and American Politics: A Clarified View." *Midwest Journal of Political Science* 1:26–39.

Schumacker, Waldo. 1931. "What Price Law-Makers?" *State Government* 4(6):10.

Seeberger, Edward D. 1997. *Sine Die: A Guide to the Washington State Legislative Process.* Seattle: University of Washington Press.

Selsam, J. Paul. 1936. *The Pennsylvania Constitution of 1776.* Philadelphia: University of Pennsylvania Press.

Serra, George, and Neil Pinney. 2001. "Casework, Issues, and Voting in State Elections: Bridging the Gap Between Congressional and State Legislative Research." Paper presented at the annual meeting of the American Political Science Association.

Shepsle, Kenneth A., and Barry R. Weingast. 1981. " Structurally-Induced Equilibrium and Legislative Choice." *Public Choice.* 37:503–519.

Shepsle, Kenneth A., and Barry R. Weingast. 1987. "The Institutional Foundations of Committee Power." *American Political Science Review* 81:85–104.

Shepsle, Kenneth A., and Barry R. Weingast. 1994. "Positive Theories of Congressional Institutions." *Legislative Studies Quarterly* 19:149–79.

Shields, Johanna Nicol. 1985. "Whigs Reform the 'Bear Garden': Representation and the Apportionment Act of 1842." *Journal of the Early Republic* 5:355–82.

Shin, Kwang S., and John S. Jackson III. 1979. "Membership Turnover in U.S. State Legislatures: 1931–1976. *Legislative Studies Quarterly* 4:95–114.

Shull, Charles W., and Louis J. McGinness. 1951. "The Changing Pattern of Personnel in the Michigan Legislature: 1887–1947." *Michigan History* 35:467–78.

Silbur, Kenneth. 1995. "New York's Nightmare Legislature." *City Journal* 5:46–55.

Sirmans, M. Eugene. 1961. "The South Carolina Royal Council, 1720–1763." *William and Mary Quarterly* 18:373–92.

Sisson, Richard. 1973. "Comparative Legislative Institutionalization: A Theoretical Exploration." In *Legislatures in Comparative Perspective,* ed. Allan Kornberg. New York: David McKay Company.

Skladony, Thomas W. 1985. "The House Goes to Work: Select and Standing Committees in the U.S. House of Representatives, 1789–1828." *Congress & the Presidency* 12:165–87.

Slonim, Shlomo. 1986. "The Electoral College at Philadelphia: The Evolution of an Ad Hoc Congress for the Selection of a President." *Journal of American History* 73:35–58.

Smith, C. Lysle. 1918. "The Committee System in State Legislatures." *American Political Science Review* 12:607–39.

Smith, Steven S. 1989. *Call to Order: Floor Politics in the House and Senate.* Washington, DC: Brookings Institution.

Smith, Steven S., and Eric D. Lawrence. 1997. "Party Control of Committees in the Republican Congress." In *Congress Reconsidered,* 6th ed., ed. Lawrence C. Dodd and Bruce I. Oppenheimer. Washington, DC: CQ Press.

Snyder, Steven B. 1988. "Let My People Run: The Rights of Voters and Candidates Under State Laws Barring Felons From Holding Elective Office." *Journal of Law & Politics* 4:543–77.

Spangenberg, Bradford. 1963. "Vestrymen in the House of Burgesses; Protection of Local Vestry Autonomy during James Blair's Term as Commissary (1690–1743)." *Historical Magazine of the Protestant Episcopal Church* 32:77–99.

Spaw, Patsy McDonald. 1990. *The Texas Senate,* vol. 1. College Station, TX: Texas A&M University Press.

REFERENCES

Squire, Peverill. 1988a. "Career Opportunities and Membership Stability in Legislatures." *Legislative Studies Quarterly* 13:65–82.

Squire, Peverill. 1988b. "Member Career Opportunities and the Internal Organization of Legislatures." *Journal of Politics* 50:726–744.

Squire, Peverill. 1992a. "The Theory of Legislative Institutionalization and the California Assembly." *Journal of Politics* 54:1026–1054.

Squire, Peverill. 1992b. "Legislative Professionalization and Membership Diversity in State Legislatures." *Legislative Studies Quarterly* 17:69–79.

Squire, Peverill. 1992c. "Changing State Legislative Leadership Careers." In *Changing Patterns in State Legislative Careers,* ed. Gary F. Moncrief and Joel A. Thompson. Ann Arbor: University of Michigan Press.

Squire, Peverill. 1993. "Professionalization and Public Opinion of State Legislatures." *Journal of Politics* 55:479–91.

Squire, Peverill. 1997. "Another Look at Legislative Professionalization and Divided Government in the States." *Legislative Studies Quarterly* 22:417–32.

Squire, Peverill. 1998. "Membership Turnover and the Efficient Processing of Legislation." *Legislative Studies Quarterly* 23:23–32.

Squire, Peverill. 2000. "Uncontested Seats in State Legislative Elections." *Legislative Studies Quarterly* 25:131–146.

Squire, Peverill, Keith E. Hamm, Ronald D. Hedlund, and Gary Moncrief. N.d. "Electoral Reforms, Membership Stability, and the Existence of Committee Property Rights in American State Legislatures." *British Journal of Political Science.*

Sullivan, John L. 1973. "Political Correlates of Social, Economic, and Religious Diversity in the American States." *Journal of Politics* 35:70–84.

Stark, Jack. 1997. *The Wisconsin State Constitution: A Reference Guide.* Westport, CT: Greenwood.

State Government. 1937. "Women in State Capitols." 10:213–15.

State of Rhode Island and Providence Plantations. 2000. *Journal of the House of Representatives,* 31 May.

Steiner, Gilbert Y. 1951. *The Congressional Conference Committee: Seventieth to Eightieth Congresses.* Urbana: University of Illinois Press.

Stewart, Charles III. 2001. *Analyzing Congress.* New York: Norton.

Stigler, George J. 1976. "The Sizes of Legislatures." *Journal of Legal Studies* 5:17–34.

Stokes, Anson Phelps. 1950. *Church and State in the United States,* vol. I. New York: Harper and Brothers.

Stolz, Klaus. 2003. "Moving Up, Moving Down: Political Careers Across Territorial Levels." *European Journal of Political Research* 42:223–48.

Stonecash, Jeffrey M. 1993. "The Pursuit & Retention of Legislative Office in New York: 1870–1990: Reconsidering Sources of Change." *Polity* 26:301–15.

Stourzh, Gerald. 1953. "Reason and Power in Benjamin Franklin's Political Thought." *American Political Science Review* 47:1092–1115.

Straayer, John A. 1996. "How Prevalent Are State Legislative Conference Committees." *Comparative State Politics* 17 (April):4–8.

Straayer, John A. 2000. *The Colorado General Assembly,* 2nd ed. Boulder, CO: University Press of Colorado.

Strom, Gerald S., and Barry S. Rundquist. 1977. "A Revised Theory of Winning in House-Senate Conferences." *American Political Science Review* 71:448–53.

Swain, Carol M. 1993. *Black Faces, Black Interests: The Representation of African Americans in Congress.* Cambridge: Harvard University Press.

Swain, John W., Stephen A. Borrelli, Brian C. Reed, and Sean F. Evans. 2000. "A New Look at Turnover in the U.S. House of Representatives, 1789–1998." *American Politics Quarterly* 28:435–57.

Swem, E. G. 1917. "The Disqualification of Ministers in State Constitutions." *William and Mary College Quarterly Historical Magazine* 26:73–78.

Swift, Elaine K. 1989. "Reconstitutive Change in the U.S. Congress: The Early Senate, 1789–1841." *Legislative Studies Quarterly* 14:175–203.

Taswell-Langmead, Thomas Pitt. 1946. *English Constitutional History,* 10th ed. Boston: Houghton Mifflin.

Teaford, Jon C. 2002. *The Rise of the States: Evolution of American State Government.* Baltimore: Johns Hopkins University Press.

Teicher, Stacy A. 1999. "Their First Job After College? Lawmaker." *Christian Science Monitor,* 5 April.

Thomas, Sue. 1994. *When Women Legislate.* New York: Oxford University Press.

Thompson, Joel A. 1986. "State Legislative Reform: Another Look, One More Time, Again." *Polity* 19:27–41.

Tocqueville, Alexis de. 1969. *Democracy in America.* Ed. J. P. Mayer. Garden City, NY: Anchor Books.

Toll, Henry W. 1930. "The 48." *State Government* 3:3–11.

Topf, Mel. A. 2000. "The Advisory Opinion on Separation of Powers: The Uncertain Contours of Advisory Opinion Jurisprudence in Rhode Island." *Roger Williams University Law Review* 5:385–416.

Tsebelis, George, and Jeannette Money. 1997. *Bicameralism.* New York: Cambridge University Press.

Tully, Alan. 1976. "Constituent-Representative Relationships in Early America: The Case of Pre-Revolutionary Pennsylvania." *Canadian Journal of History* 11:139–54.

Tully, Alan. 1977. *William Penn's Legacy: Politics and Social Structure in Provincial Pennsylvania, 1726–1755.* Baltimore, MD: Johns Hopkins University Press.

Unruh, Jesse. 1965. "Science in Law-Making." *National Civic Review* 54:466–72.

VanderMeer, Philip R. 1985. *The Hoosier Politician.* Urbana, IL: University of Illinois Press.

Van Der Slik, Jack R., and Kent D. Redfield. 1986. *Lawmaking in Illinois.* Springfield, IL: Office of Public Affairs Communication.

Vogel, David J. 1970. "Patterns of One-House Dominance in Congressional Conference Committees." *Midwest Journal of Political Science* 14:303–20.

Wahlke, John C., Heinz Eulau, William Buchanan, and LeRoy C. Ferguson. 1962. *The Legislative System.* New York: Wiley.

Walsh, Justin E. 1987. *The Centennial History of the Indiana General Assembly, 1816–1978.* Indianapolis, IN: The Select Committee on the Centennial History of the Indiana General Assembly.

Walthoe, N. 1910. "The Council and the Burgesses." *William and Mary College Quarterly Historical Magazine* 19:1–10.

Waterhouse, Richard. 1986. "Merchants, Planters, and Lawyers: Political Leadership in South Carolina, 1721–1775." In *Power and Status,* ed. Bruce C. Daniels. Middletown, CT: Wesleyan University Press.

REFERENCES

Watts, Irma A. 1936. "Why Pennsylvania Abandoned Unicameralism." *State Government* 9:54–55.

Weber, Ronald E. 1999. "The Quality of State Legislative Representation: A Critical Assessment." *Journal of Politics* 61:609–27.

Webster, William Clarence. 1897. "Comparative Study of the State Constitutions of the American Revolution." *Annals of the American Academy of Political and Social Science* 9:380–420.

Weir, Robert M. 1969. "'The Harmony We Were Famous For': An Interpretation of Pre-Revolutionary War South Carolina Politics." *William and Mary Quarterly* 26:473–501.

Wells, Donald T. 1967. "The Arkansas Legislature." In *Power in American State Legislatures: Case Studies of the Arkansas, Louisiana, Mississippi, and Oklahoma Legislatures,* ed. Alex B. Lacy, Jr. New Orleans: Tulane University.

Wendel, Thomas. 1986. "At the Pinnacle of Elective Success: The Speaker of the House in Colonial America." In *Power and Status,* ed. Bruce C. Daniels. Middletown, CT: Wesleyan University Press.

West, Victor J. 1923. "California—The Home of the Split Session." *National Municipal Review* 12:369–76.

Whaley, Sean, and Ed Vogel. 2003a. "Constitutional Ruling: Court Paves Way for New Taxes." *Las Vegas Review-Journal* 11 July.

Whaley, Sean, and Ed Vogel. 2003b. "State Legislature: Budget Approved." *Las Vegas Review-Journal* 22 July.

Wheare, K. C. 1963. *Legislatures.* New York: Oxford University Press.

Whistler, Donald E., and Mark C. Ellickson. 1999. "The Incorporation of Women in State Legislatures: A Description." *Women and Politics* 20:81–97.

White, Howard. 1927. "Can Legislatures Learn from City Councils?" *American Political Science Review* 21:95–100.

Wilson, Woodrow. 1908. *Constitutional Government in the United States.* New York: Columbia University Press.

Winslow, C. I. 1931. *State Legislative Committees.* Baltimore: Johns Hopkins Press.

Witmer, T. Richard. 1964. "The Aging of the House." *Political Science Quarterly* 79:526–41.

Wood, Gordon S. 1969. *Creation of the American Republic 1776–1787.* Chapel Hill, NC: University of North Carolina Press.

Wood, Margaret K. 1977. "Tennessee Constitutional Provision Barring Ministers and Priests from Serving in the State Legislature Offends neither the Free Exercise Clause nor the Establishment Clause of the First Amendment." *University of Cincinnati Law Review* 46:893–904.

Wooster, Ralph A. 1969. *The People in Power: Courthouse and Statehouse in the Lower South 1850–1860.* Knoxville, TN: University of Tennessee Press.

Wooster, Ralph A. 1975. *Politicians, Planters and Plain Folk: Courthouse and Statehouse in the Upper South 1850–1860.* Knoxville, TN: University of Tennessee Press.

Wright, Benjamin F., Jr. 1933. "The Origin of the Separation of Powers in America." *Economica* 40:169–85.

Wright, Gerald C., and Brian F. Schaffner. 2002. "The Influence of Party: Evidence from the State Legislatures." *American Political Science Review* 96:367–79.

Young, Chester Raymond. 1968. "The Evolution of the Pennsylvania Assembly, 1682–1748." *Pennsylvania History* 35:147–68.

Zagarii, Rosemarie. 1987. *The Politics of Size*. Ithaca, NY: Cornell University Press.

Zeller, Belle, ed. 1954. *American State Legislatures*. New York: Crowell.

Zemsky, Robert M. 1969. "Power, Influence, and Status: Leadership Patterns in the Massachusetts Assembly, 1740–1755." *William and Mary Quarterly* 26:502–20.

Zemsky, Robert M. 1971. *Merchants, Farmers, and River Gods*. Boston: Gambit.

Zimmerman, Joseph F. 1981. *The Government and Politics of New York State*. New York: New York University Press.

INDEX

Abernathy, Byron R., 37
Adams, Greg D., 59
Adams, John, 19, 155n21, 155n22; in favor of bicameralism, 20–21, 156n34
Adams, Samuel, 19
Adams, Willi Paul, 20, 21, 23, 25, 28, 155n19, 156n34
African American legislators, in state legislatures, 138–39; in U.S. Congress, 138
Alabama state legislature, filibuster in, 123; membership size of, 159n13; as one-party body, 104; pay in 1910, 82; quadrennial sessions in, 67, 162n2; session length limits, 69; split (or bifurcated) session in, 162n8; term of office, 161n33
Alaska state legislature, bipartisan coalition in, 103; impeachment procedure in, 99; large district and representation, 60; membership size, 45, 159n13; session length changes, 162n6; supermajoritarian rules in, 120
Alford, John R., 55
Alter, Alison B., 122
American Society of Legislative Clerks and Secretaries in cooperation with the National Conference of State Legislatures, 110, 111, 113, 114, 115, 120, 166n11, 166n12
Ammons, David, 167n9
Amos v. Sims, 159n13
Anderson, R. Bruce, 104
Anderson, C. David, 7
Andrews, Charles M., 8, 18
Arizona state legislature, discharge petitions in, 125, 126; session length limits, 69
Arkansas state legislature, farmers in, 132; large number of standing committees, 107–8; lawyers in, 132; membership turnover in, 140; as one party body,

104; session lengths and per diem limits, 162n7
Articles of Confederation, 23, 25, 28, 30
assemblies, colonial: Antigua, 153n1, 154n8; Bahamas, 153n1; Barbados, 153n1, 154n8; Bermuda, 153n1, 154n8; committees in, 12–13; constituency size of 11, 154n9; impeachments in, 99; Jamaica, 153n1, 154n8; Leeward Islands, 153n2; legislative power, 11; meeting places, 17–18, 154n14; member pay in, 71; membership sizes of, 18, 148, 154n18; membership turnover in, 140, 149; Montserrat, 153n1, 154n8; Nevis, 153n1, 154n8; Nova Scotia, 116, 151, 153n1; parliamentary rules and procedures in, 13–14; Prince Edward Island, 153n1; relationship to U.S. Congress and state legislatures 1; rise of, 6–8; rules governing member behavior in, 18; St. Kitts, 153n1, 154n8; source of rules and procedures, 116; taxation powers, 30–31; terms of office, 14. *See also* Connecticut Assembly; Delaware Assembly; Georgia Assembly; Maryland Assembly; Massachusetts (Bay) Assembly; New Hampshire; New Jersey (East and West) Assembly, New York Assembly; North Carolina Assembly; Pennsylvania Assembly, Rhode Island Assembly; South Carolina Assembly; Virginia, House of Burgesses
Ayres, B. Drummond, Jr., 123

Bailey, Raymond C., 7, 11, 12, 15, 147
Baker, Ross K., 45
Balanoff, Elizabeth, 138
Baldwin, Abraham, 155n20
Bancroft, Hubert Howe, 72, 107, 151, 157n1

193

INDEX

Banner, James M., Jr., 46, 159n16
Barclay, Thomas S., 69
Barnett, James D., 153n6
Barnhart, John D., 37, 157n1
Barrett, Edith J., 139
Bassett, John Spencer, 9
Bassett, Richard, 155n20
Bates v. Jones, 161n38
Battista, James S. Coleman, 106
Bazar, Beth, 135, 167n1
Bedford, Gunning, Jr., 155n20
Beeman, Richard R., 150
Bell, Charles G., 142
Bennett, Richard, 156n29
Berkman, Michael B., 79, 80, 95, 145
Bernstein, Robert A., 64
Berry, William D., 79, 95, 145
Beth, Loren P., 107
Beth, Richard S., 124, 166n21
Bianco, William, 70
bicameralism, 41–44, 153n6; in American Samoa, 158n8; in Antigua, 154n8; in Barbados, 154n8; in Connecticut 9; consequences for internal organization, 42–43; in Delaware, 21; differences between in American and Great Britain 10; in Georgia, 43; in Maryland, 9–10; in Jamaica, 154n8; and joint committees, 158n10; and Massachusetts, 8–9; and membership ratios, 41–42; in Montserrat, 154n8; in Nevis, 154n8; in North Carolina, 9; in Northern Mariana Islands, 158n8; in original state constitutions, 20; in Pennsylvania, 10, 43; in Puerto Rico, 158n8; in Rhode Island, 9; rise of in colonial legislatures, 8–10, 153n5; in South Carolina, 10; in St. Kitts, 154n8; Vermont, 43–44, 158n9; theories for and against, 20–21
bicameral rivalry theory, 42–43
Billings, Warren M., 7
Binder, Sarah A., 45, 104, 105, 122, 144
Binkley, Wilfred E., 155n21
Blair, John, 155n20
Bland, Richard, 12, 19
Blount, William, 155n20
Bogen, David S., 167n11

Bogue, Allan G., 130, 133
Bolles, Albert S., 23, 25
Bonomi, Patricia U., 154n11
Borck, Rainald, 96
Borrelli, Stephen A., 140, 143
Bosher, Kate Langley, 6, 12
Bositis, David A., 168n13
Bottom, William P., 158n7
Bowman, Ann O'M., 79
Brace, Paul, 67, 82, 150
Brandes, Sara L., 55
Brady, David, 70, 101, 118, 140, 144, 145
Breaux, David, 164n21
Brent, Margaret, 136
Bresnahan, John, 163n17
Brewer, John Mason, 138
Briggs, John E., 107, 151
Broom, Jacob, 155n20
Broussard, James H., 107
Brown, Willie, 101
Bryce, James, 26, 37, 38, 61, 68, 72, 158n3
Buchanan, James M., 35
Buchanan, William, 165n8
Buckley, Kara, 70, 140
Bullock, Charles S., 140
Bushman, Claudia L., 7, 12
Butler, David, 55
Button, James, 139

Cain, Bruce, 55
Calabrese, Stephen, 58
California Citizens Compensation Commission, 74
California state legislature, annual salary in, 74; bipartisan coalition in, 103; committees unimportant in, 108; constituency size compared to U.S. Congress, 55; end of pension plan in, 74, 164n19; facilities in, 78; first African American elected to, 138; member pay over time in, 72–73, 74; membership turnover in, 141; as professionalized body, 81; relationship of pay and turnover in 70; session length limits, 69; split (or bifurcated) session in, 69; as springboard legislature, 79; staff in

194

INDEX

nineteenth century in, 76; standing committees established, 107, 151; work productivity in compared to U.S. Congress, 118
Camia, Catalina, 123
Campbell, Ballard C., 76, 132, 142, 162n7
Cannon, Joe, 102–3
Cannon, Dr. Martha Hughes, 136
Caraway, Hattie W., 167n7
Carey, John M., 79, 143
Carmines, Edward G., 165n32
Carroll, Charles, 129
Carroll, Daniel, 155n20
Carroll, Daniel B, 158n9
Casper Star-Tribune, 60, 160n26
Castello, James E., 30, 157n38
caucuses. *See* legislative parties
Chadha, Anita, 64
Chaffey, Douglas Camp, 145
Chambers, William Seal, 39
Chaney, Edward, 167n11
Charleston Gazette, 160n26
Chemerinsky, Erwin, 122
Christensen, Asher N., 85, 164n26
Citizens Conference on State Legislatures, 67, 79, 98
Citizen's Guide to the Wyoming Legislature, 78
Clarion-Ledger, 160n25
Clarke, Mary Patterson, 11, 14, 16, 17, 18, 26, 27, 136, 163n14
Cleland, Ethel, 76
Cloner, Alexander, 73
Clubb, Jerome M., 130, 133
Clucas, Richard A., 102, 103, 142
Clymer, George, 155n20
Cobb Edwin L., 161n35
Cole, Janet, 160n20
colonial assemblies. *See* assemblies, colonial
colonial government, 8
Colorado state legislature, exogenous generation of rules and procedures, 158n4; first African American elected to, 138; first women elected to, 136; limited conference committee use in, 114; small number of standing committees,

108; terms of office, 62. *See also* GAVEL
Colvin, David Leigh, 19, 150, 156n26
committees. *See* legislative committees
Common Sense (Paine), 20
Confederate Congress, as non-partisan body, 105; established with standing committees, 107; rules and procedures in, 166n16
conference committees. *See* legislative committees
Congress, under Articles of Confederation, term limits in, 28, 63; committees in, 106
Congress, U.S., bill reference procedure differences with state legislatures, 120; career movement in over time, 129–30; change in membership size in over time, 45, 55, 159n15; committee jurisdictions, 110; Confederate Congress comparisons, 105; conference committee differences with state legislatures, 114–15; constituency size, 55; decorum relationship with membership size, 48; discharge petition differences with state legislatures, 124–26; district offices in, 76; facilities in, 76, 81; farmers in, 133, 135; filibusters in compared to state legislatures, 123; germaneness rule differences with state legislatures, 122; importance attached to differences in size between House and Senate, 44–45; importance attached to differences in office terms between House and Senate, 61; lawyers in, 133, 135; membership qualifications, 160n23; membership turnover in, 140; multimember districts in, 58; pay in, 70, 81; pay compared to state legislatures, 82–85; pension in, 70, 74; per diem in, 70, 163n17; professionalization in, 81, 164n24; relationship of pay with turnover in, 70; rise of standing committees in, 105–6, 165n6; similarities with original state legislatures, 29, 165n7; state legislatures as farm team for, 135; subcommittee use compared

195

INDEX

to state legislatures, 113; staff in, 75, 81; women in leadership positions, 137; work productivity compared to state legislatures, 116–18

Congressional Quarterly, 85

Congressional Research Service, 75, 76

Connecticut Assembly, 6, 7, 8, 18; membership size, 148; membership turnover in, 149

Connecticut state legislature, bipartisan coalition in, 103; joint committees in, 44, 108; leadership posts in, 101, 165n5; membership turnover in, 140; term of office, 28, 161n32

Conrad, Henry C., 7

constitutions, state, 19; Alabama, 37; Alabama (1901), 38; Alaska (1956), 36, 44, 159n12; California (1849), 157n1; California (1879), 72, 164n19; conditions under which revolutionary constitutions written, 19–20; Connecticut, 20, 23, 25, 155n19; Connecticut (1965), 36; Delaware (1776), 22, 24, 31, 32; Florida (1968), 36; Georgia (1777), 22, 24, 31; Hawaii (1950), 36; Illinois (1970), 36; and impeachment 99; on internal organization of legislatures, 30, 35–37; and legislator pay, 71–72, 162n10, 163n11, 163n12, 163n16; and limitations on legislatures, 37–38, 158n2, 158n3; Louisiana, 37–38; Louisiana (1974), 36; Maryland (1776), 22, 24, 31, 32, 155n21; Massachusetts (1780), 22, 24, 25, 30, 31, 32, 33, 39, 155n21, 155n22; and membership size, 159n13; Michigan (1963), 36; Mississippi (1890), 37, 38; Missouri (1945), 124, 166n23; Montana (1889), 158n6; Montana (1972), 36, 68, 158n6, 159n13; and multi-member districts, 58; New Hampshire (1776), 20, 22, 24, 31, 32; New Hampshire (1784), 70, 159n13, 162n10; New Jersey (1776), 22, 24, 31, 32; New York (1777), 22, 24, 31, 33, 34, 39, 150, 155n21, 156n26, 163n16; New York (1821), 163n16; New York (1846), 163n16; New York (1894), 163n16; North Carolina (1776), 22, 24, 31; origination clauses in, 30–32, 42, 158n6; Pennsylvania (1776), 22, 24, 71; Pennsylvania (1874), 61; replacement of original constitutions, 20; Rhode Island, 20, 23, 25, 40, 70, 155n19; Rhode Island (1843), 40, 160n19, 163n11, 164n19; routinely amended, 37; as source for U.S. Constitution, 19, 155n21; South Carolina (1776), 20, 23 25, 31, 32, 33, 34; South Carolina (1778), 20, 23, 25, 31, 32, 34; and veto powers, 32–34; Tennessee (1796), 157n1; Texas (1876), 70, 162n10; Virginia (1776), 23, 25, 30, 31, 32; Virginia (1970), 36; West Virginia (1863), 64; Wisconsin (1848), 158n2, 159n13; Wyoming, (1889), 69

Constitution, U.S., 19, 23, 25, 68, 157n36, 157n37; and impeachment, 99; on internal organization of Congress, 30, 35–37; on member pay, 70; origination clause in, 30–32; veto power in, 32–34

contested elections, procedures for considering in colonial assemblies, 16–17

Cook, Florence, 12, 14, 17, 154n17, 163n14

Cooper, Joseph, 101, 144, 145

Corey, John Pitts, 12, 14, 18, 26, 31, 71, 140, 148, 154n17, 163n14

council, the colonial, 8, 18; membership sizes of, 18; selection procedures, 9–10

Cox, Elizabeth M., 136, 138, 167n8

Cox, Gary W., 38, 106, 112

Craig, Tim, 166n20

Crain, W. Mark, 49

Crane, Wilder, Jr., 76

Cressingham, Clara, 136

Crowley, Jocelyn Elise, 138

Daniel, Jean Houston, 17

Daniel, Price, 17

Daniels, Bruce C., 149

Darcy, R., 137

Davidson, Roger H., 44, 49, 61, 75, 113, 143, 145, 165n3

Davie, Brian L., 159n18

INDEX

Davie, William Jefferson, 155n20
Davis, Horace B., 133
Davis, Rodney O., 107, 150, 151
Dayton, Jonathan, 129, 155n20
Dean, Rebecca E., 137
DeBats, Donald A., 140, 141, 150
Deering, Christopher J., 113
Delaware Assembly, 7, 14; membership size, 148; spun out from Pennsylvania Assembly, 8
Delaware state legislature, lawyers in, 131, 167n1; membership size, 21, 26, 148; membership qualifications, 27, 50; name changes, 26, 156n28; professionalization trends, 84; term of office, 28, 62
Deming, Clarence, 64, 140, 141, 150
De Priest, Oscar, 138
Dickinson, John, 19, 155n20
Diermeier, Daniel, 42, 43
Diggs, Don W., 162n4
Dippel, Horst, 40
discharge petitions, 124–26, 166n22; in Arizona, 125, 126; in Illinois, 125; in Kansas, 125; in Kentucky, 125, 126, 166n24, 167n26; in Louisiana, 125; in Minnesota, 125, 126; in Mississippi, 166n25; in Missouri, 124, 166n23; in Pennsylvania, 124, 125, 126; in the U.S. House, 124, 166n21; in Wisconsin, 125, 126
Dodd, Lawrence C., 144
Dodds, H. W., 106, 151, 158n10
Donnelly, Thomas C., 69
Döring, Herbert, 121
Driscoll, James D., 69, 72, 76, 101, 163n15
Duck, Dr. Sigsbee, 160n26
Dulany, Daniel (the younger), 19
Dunn, Dana, 137

Eastman, John C., 160n23
Eavey, Cheryl L., 158n7
Eilperin, Juliet, 163n17
Elazar, Daniel J., 87, 88
election calendar, 161n33
electoral college, as used for Maryland state senate, 26

Ellickson, Mark C., 137
Epstein, David, 70, 140
Erickson, Brenda, 36–37
Eulau, Heinz, 135, 165n8
Evans, C. Lawrence, 100, 111
Evans, Sean F., 140, 143

Fairlie, John A., 34, 43, 157n40
Falb, Susan Rosenfeld, 10, 14, 131
Farmerie, Samual A., 167n3
Faust, Martin L., 69
Federalist Papers (Madison, Hamilton, and Jay), 28, 39, 48, 156n34, 159n17
Felton, Rebecca L., 167n7
Ferejohn, John, 115
Ferguson, LeRoy C., 165n8
filibusters, 122–23; in Alabama, 123; in Maryland, 123; in Nebraska, 123; in Rhode Island, 123; rules governing in Maryland, 166n20; rules governing in Nebraska, 166n20; rules governing in South Carolina, 123; rules governing in Texas, 123, 166n18; and session length limits, 123; in Texas, 123, 166n17
Fiorina, Morris, 88, 140
Fisher, Ian, 114, 166n13
Fisher, Joel M., 142
Fisher, Louis, 72, 74
Fisher, Sydney George, 21, 31
Fisk, Catherine, 122
Fitzpatrick, Edward, 160n19
Florida state legislature, bank officer disqualification, 54; large number of standing committees, 107; membership qualifications in, 156n32; membership turnover in, 141; as one-party body, 104; rules and procedures changes in, 100; supermajoritarian rules in, 120
Ford, Iris Carter, 167n11
Fortenberry, C. N., 37, 107
Fox, Harrison W., Jr., 75
Fox, William T. R., 131
Frakes, George Edward, 12, 15, 154n16
Francis, Wayne L., 43, 49, 104, 106, 108, 109
Franklin, Benjamin, 19, 155n20; in favor of unicameralism, 21, 156n23, 157n36

197

Freed, Walter, 111
Freeman, Patricia K., 78, 95, 96
French v. Senate of State of California, 157n38
Freund, Ernst, 76
Friedman, Lawrence M., 37
Froman, Lewis A., Jr., 159n11
Frothingham, Richard, 7
Few, William, 155n20

Gable, Richard W., 73
Gadsden, Christopher, 19
Gallagher, Miriam, 144
Gallay, Alan, 140
Galloway, George B., 31, 81, 106, 135, 157n36, 165n6, 165n7
Gamm, Gerald, 106
GAVEL (Give a Vote to Every Legislator), 38
Georgia Assembly, 7, 14, 16, 18; meeting places, 154n17; member pay in, 71; membership qualifications, 26; membership size, 148, 154n18; source of original rules and procedures in, 116, 151; unexcused absence penalty, 163n14
Georgia state legislature, membership qualifications, 27; as one-party body, 104; role of lt. governor in state senate, 101; membership turnover in, 140; rise of standing committees in, 106; seniority used in, 112; and speaker tenure in nineteenth century, 150; split (or bifurcated) sessions in, 162n8; terms of office, 61
Gerry, Elbridge, 155n20
Gierzynski, Anthony, 104
Gilligan, Thomas W., 49
Gilmour, John B., 140
Gonzalez, Henry B., 166n17
Goodall, Leonard E., 162n4
Goodwin, Cardinal, 107, 151
Gorham, Nathaniel, 155n20
Gosnell, Cullen B., 7
Government Accountability Office, 75
Governor Guinn v. Nevada State Legislature, 157n38

governors, colonial, 8
Graham, Cole Blease, Jr., 166n10
Green, Fletcher M., 26
Greene, Jack P., 7, 8, 11, 12, 14, 15, 16, 18, 19, 26, 30, 31, 116, 140, 148, 149, 151, 154n9, 154n18
Griffith, Lucille, 148, 154n18
Groseclose, Tim, 42
Gross, Donald A., 115
Grumm, John G., 79
Gunn, L. Ray, 76, 140, 141, 150

Haeberle, Steven, 113
Halter, Gary M., 101
Hambleton, Ken, 166n20
Hamilton, Alexander, 19, 39, 48, 155n20, 159n17
Hamilton, Howard D., 59
Hamm, Keith E., 1, 104, 106, 110, 111, 112, 121, 122, 164n22, 164n26
Hammond, Thomas H., 158n7
Hammond, Susan Webb, 75
Hancock, Harold B., 7, 12
Handberg, Roger, 100
Hansen, Karen, 103
Hanson, Royce, 114
Hardy, Beatriz Betacourt, 156n29
Harlow, Ralph Volney, 12, 15, 18, 21, 106, 148, 151
Harmel, Robert, 104
Harrison, Robert, 64
Hastert, Dennis, 102–3
Havard, William C., 107
Haynes, George H., 8, 131
Haynie, Kerry L., 139
Hawaii state legislature, terms of office, 62
Hedge, David, 139
Hedlund, Ronald D, 95, 104, 106, 110, 111, 112, 121, 122, 164n26
Heitkamp, Joel, 160n20
Henry, Patrick, 19
Hero, Rodney E., 88
Herzberg, Donald G., 67
Hibbing, John R., 55, 70, 74, 98, 144, 149–50, 151
Higginson, Stephen A., 11, 154n10
Higham, C. S. S., 153n2

INDEX

Hinds, Asher C., 30
Hirsch, Eric, 167n1
Hispanic legislators, in New Mexico, 139; in state legislatures, 139; in U.S. Congress, 139
Hitchcock, Henry-Russell, 17, 154n14, 154n15, 154n17
Hobbs, Edward H., 37, 107
Hoffer, Peter C., 99, 165n1
Hogarty, Richard A., 40
Holcombe, Arthur N., 39
Holly, Carrie Clyde, 136
Holmes, Jack E., 139
Homsey, Elizabeth Moyne, 7, 12
Hoope, Heather, 112, 166n19
Horack, Frank E., 107
Houston, William C., 155n20
Hubbard, Clifford C., 123
Huber, John D., 96
Hull, N. E. H., 99, 165n1
Huntington, Samuel P., 7, 160n27
Hyneman, Charles S., 131, 142, 152

Idaho state legislature, changing membership size, 46; member pension plan in, 74–75
Illinois state legislature, bipartisan coalition in, 103; change in committee gatekeeping powers, 108; change in membership size in 1983, 46; change in number of committee assignments over time, 165n9; committees unimportant in, 108; discharge petitions in, 125, 126; effects of multi-member districts in, 59; farmers in, 132; first African American elected to, 138; lawyers in, 132; membership turnover in, 141; membership qualifications, 50; residency requirements, 53; rise of standing committees in, 107, 151; session lengths and per diem limits, 162n7; source of original rules and procedures in, 116; terms of office, 62, 63
impeachment process, in Alaska, 99; in colonial legislatures, 99, 165n1; lack of in Oregon, 99; in Missouri, 99; in New York, 99

informational theories, 78–79
Indiana state legislature, farmers in, 132; lawyers in, 132; membership turnover in, 141; rise of standing committees in, 107, 151; session length limits, 69; source of original rules and procedures in, 116
In re: Advisory Opinion to the Governor, 158n5
institutionalization. *See* legislative institutionalization
Iowa state legislature, farmers in, 132; lawyers in, 132; majoritarian rules in, 120; membership turnover in, 141; session length limits, 69, 162n7; standing committees established, 107, 151; terms of office, 62

Jacklin, Michele, 103
Jackson, John S. III., 142, 152
Jacobson, Gary C., 161n31
Jameson, J. Franklin, 12, 106, 151
Jay, John, 39, 48, 159n17
Jefferson City News Tribune, 51
Jefferson, Thomas, 19
Jenifer, Daniel of St. Thomas, 155n20
Jenkins, Jeffrey A., 105, 106, 107, 166n16
Jennings, W. Ivor, 157n39
Jewell, Malcolm E., 42, 49, 53, 58, 78, 103, 123, 131, 132, 145, 161n35, 164n21
Jewett, Aubrey, 100
Jillson, Calvin, 12, 106
Johnson, Alvin W., 10, 43, 44
Johnson, Richard R., 116
Johnson, William Samuel, 155n20
Jones, Charles C., Jr., 7
Jones, Harry W., 76
Jordan, David W., 9–10, 13, 14
Judge, David, 144

Kammen, Michael, 6, 7, 8, 9, 10, 153n1, 153n5, 154n8
Kanengiser, Andy, 166n25
Ka, Sangjoon, 96
Kansas state legislature, discharge petitions in, 125, 126; supermajoritarian rules in, 120

INDEX

Karnig, Albert K., 165n32
Katsky, David L., 44, 153n5
Kawato, Sadafumi, 70, 140
Kazee, Thomas A., 106
Kearney, Richard C., 79
Keefe, William J., 68, 126
Kellams, Laura, 162n7
Keller, Clair W., 55
Kellough, J. E., 96
Kennedy, John J., 61
Kentucky state legislature, daily wage in, 74; discharge petitions in, 125, 126, 166n24, 167n26; farmers in, 132; lawyers in, 132; membership turnover in, 140; membership qualifications, 156n32; switch to annual sessions, 162n3
Kenyon, Cecelia M., 156n23
Kernell, Samuel, 64, 144
Kersh, Rogan, 39, 40
Kettleborough, Charles, 158n4
Key, V. O., Jr., 131
Kid's Caucus, 53
Kiewiet, D. Roderick, 153n3
Kile, Charles, 158n7
King, David C., 42
King, James D., 79, 81, 86
King, Julia A., 167n11
King, Rufus, 155n20
Kinsey, John, 154n12
Kirby, John B., 27
Kirkley v. Maryland, 156n33
Klain, Maurice, 58
Klock, Francis S., 136
Kogan, Bruce I., 158n5
Kolp, John G., 17
Krasno, Jonathon S., 55, 60
Krehbiel, Keith, 78, 79, 104, 105, 106, 108, 114, 118, 124, 144, 147, 149
Kromkowski, Charles A., 159n15
Kromkowski, John A., 159n15
Kukla, Jon, 6, 7, 13, 14, 153n4
Kurtz, Karl, T., 80, 164n22

Lange, Howard B., Jr., 131
Langdon, John, 155n20
Lansing, John Jr., 155n20

Lapp, John A., 76
Lawrence, Eric D., 104, 105, 111, 122
leadership. *See* legislative leadership; speakers
Lee, Richard Henry, 19
legislative careers, direction of career movements in other systems, 130; evolution of career hierarchy, 129–30; full-time legislators, 134–35; and legislative organization, 135, 144–45. *See also* legislators, occupations of
legislative committees, assignments, 14–15, 111–13, 165n9; conference committees, 12–13, 113–15, 166n13, 166n14; importance as decision-making loci, 108–10; importance in U.S. Congress, 105–6; joint 44, 108, 158n10; and jurisdictions, 110; party ratios on, 111; rise of standing committees in colonial assemblies, 12–13; rise of standing committees in state legislatures, 106–7, 151; rise of standing committees in U.S. Congress, 106, 165n7; size of membership, 15; subcommittees, 12, 113. *See also* legislative rules and procedures; seniority system
legislative districts, constituency size 55–58; geographic size, 60, 161n31; single-member; multi-member, 58–59;
legislative institutionalization, and changing issue agenda, 147–48; in colonial assemblies, 12–18; and member careers, 144–45; and membership size, 148–49, 150; and membership turnover, 149, 150, 151–52; and organizational inertia, 151–52; and path dependency, 149–51; regression of, 151–52; relationship with time at which legislature is established, 151; and workload, 147–48, 150
legislative journals, 14
legislative leadership, and campaign committees, 104; early constitutional provisions on, 30–31; importance as decision-making loci, 108–10; increasing tenures in, 101; problems studying, 100; term limits effects on, 101; varia-

200

INDEX

tions in power of, 101–3; variation in size of, 101; women and, 137–38. *See also* speakers

legislative parties, bipartisan coalitions between in state legislatures, 103–4; and campaign committees, 104; and caucuses, 104; effects of on member behavior, 104–5; importance as decision-making loci, 108–10; one-party legislatures, 104

legislative pay, constitutional limits on, 162n10; 163n11; comparisons between U.S. Congress and state legislatures, 72–73, 82–85; effect on legislative careers, 75; per diems in, 74, 163n17; relationship with turnover, 70; in state legislatures, 71–74; *See also* legislative pensions

legislative pensions, 74–75, 163n18, 164n19. *See also* legislative pay

legislative professionalization, 67, 164n22, 164n24; consequences of, 95–97; measures of, 79–81; professionalization revolution, 67, 81–82; relationship with state population, 86, 97–98; relationship with state wealth, 86–95, 97–98; rise of, 81–85; Squire's measure of, 79–80; in state legislatures, 79; in U.S. Congress, 67, 81

Legislative Reorganization Act of 1946, 74, 75

legislative rules and procedures, 157n38; bill reference procedures, 120; change in over time, 100; in colonial assemblies, 13–14; difficulties in doing comparative research on, 121; early constitutional provisions on, 30–31; endogenous generation of, 38–39; exogenous generation of, 38–39, 158n2, 158n3, 158n4; floor calendars, 122; on germaneness, 122; and membership size 45; original source of, 116, 151, 166n16. *See also* discharge petitions; filibusters; majoritarian and supermajoritarian rules

legislative sessions, annual, 68; biennial, 67, 162n3; comparison of state legislatures and U.S. Congress on over time, 85–86; effects of length, 69–70; joint, 44; limitations on, 68–70; in New York Assembly, 12; quadrennial, 67, 162n2; split (or bifurcated), 69, 162n8; in U.S. Congress, 81; in Virginia House of Burgesses, 12

legislative staff, casework and, 78; in colonial assemblies, 14; differences in how legislators use, 78–79; establishment and growth of, 75–76; legislative reference bureaus, 76; in state legislatures, 77–78; in U.S. Congress, 75

legislative supremacy, advisory opinions and, 158n5; in original state legislatures, 39–40; in Rhode Island, 39–40, 158n5

legislative turnover, and legislative institutionalization, 149, 150, 151; over time in colonial assemblies, 14, 140, 149; over time in state legislatures, 140–43, 168n13; over time in U.S. Congress, 140; relationship with pay, 70; and springboard bodies, 142, 143; and term limits, 143–44

legislators, membership qualifications of, 21–28, 49–54; age 27, 50–51; felon disqualification and, 54; for Congress, 50; differences between houses, 26–27; occupation, 27, 55; religious, 26, 27–28, 156n29, 156n31, 156n32; residency, 53–54, 160n26; wealth, 26–27, 54

legislators, occupations of, farmers, 131–34, 135; full-time legislators, 134–35; lawyers, 131–34, 135; in twentieth century, 134–35, 167n4. *See also* legislative careers

legislatures, state, African Americans in, 138–39; changing names of chambers, 21, 26; effects of constituency size, 55–58; effects of membership size, 49; Hispanics in, 139; occupations in, 132–35; membership sizes, 21, 26, 44–49, 159n12, 159n13, 159n14; membership turnover in, 140–43; reasons to study, 1–3; relationship between population and membership size, 48; term

201

limits in, 28, 63–65, 168n15; terms of office, 28, 60–63; women in, 136–37; work productivity in, 116–18. *See also* specific state legislatures.
Leibowitz, Arleen, 42
LeLoup, Lance T., 165n32
Leonard, Cynthia Miller, 23, 25
Leonard, Sister Joan de Lourdes, 11, 12, 14, 17, 18, 140, 149
Levine, Peter D., 107, 140
Lexington Herald-Leader, 166n24
Little, Thomas H., 137
Livingston, William, 19, 155n20
Loewenberg, Gerhard, 10, 50, 153n3
Loftus, Tom, 167n26
Logan, Rayford W., 138
Lokken, Roy N., 10
Longley, Lawrence D., 44, 114
Longmore, Paul K., 12
Louisiana state legislatures, discharge petitions in, 125, 126; election calendar, 161n33; few leadership posts in, 101; membership qualifications in, 156n32; as one-party body, 104; term of office, 161n33
Lounsbury, Carl R., 17
Luce, Robert, 10, 14, 20, 26, 28, 45, 50, 53, 54, 61, 64, 68, 71, 140, 141, 153n6, 156n24, 156n25, 156n28, 156n34, 157n35, 158n10, 159n14, 161n32, 161n33
Luttbeg, Norman R., 95
Lutz, Donald S., 5, 18, 21, 23, 25, 27, 148, 150, 155n22

Macartney, John, 76
Mackey, Scott, 111
Madison, James, 19, 28, 29, 39, 48, 155n20, 156n34, 159n17
Maestas, Cherie, 80, 95, 142
Maine state legislature, bill reference procedures in, 120; election calendar, 161n33; Kid's Caucus, 53; joint committees in, 44, 108; session length limits, 69; term of office, 161n32
Main, Jackson Turner, 7, 10, 14, 18, 20, 21, 25, 26, 27, 43, 132, 148

majoritarian and supermajoritarian rules, 118–20; range of in state legislatures, 119–20; in U.S. Congress, 119–20
Malbin, Michael J., 75, 77, 85, 117, 135, 164n23, 164n26
Maltzman, Forrest, 104, 105
Mann, Thomas E., 75, 77, 85, 117, 135, 164n23, 164n26
Martin, Alexander, 155n20
Martorano, Nancy, 104, 106, 110, 111, 112, 121, 122
Maryland Assembly, 6, 7, 11, 13, 14, 16, 18; lawyers in, 131; membership qualifications, 26, 28, 156n29; membership size, 148; planters in, 131; possible African American member of, 167n11; woman fails to join, 136
Maryland state legislature, electoral college in, 157n37; filibuster in, 123; membership qualifications, 27, 156n33; as one-party body, 104; rise of standing committees in, 106; rules governing filibuster, 166n20; term of office, 28, 61, 161n33
Mason, George, 29, 155n20
Mason, John Brown, 135
Massachusetts (Bay) Assembly, 6, 7, 11, 14, 15, 18, 116; meeting places, 17; membership size, 148
Massachusetts state legislature, bipartisan coalition in, 103; changing membership size in nineteenth century, 46, 159n16; election of upper house, 26; exogenous generation of rules and procedures, 158n4; farmers in, 132–33; first African American in, 138; full-time legislators in, 167n4; Harvard faculty disqualification, 54; joint committees in, 44, 108; lawyers in, 132–33; linkage between member pay and household income, 70; member pay, 163n12; original membership size, 26; as professionalizing body, 81; rise of standing committees in, 106; session length limits, 69; term of office, 61, 161n32
Massachusetts state library, 76
Matsusaka, John G., 49

INDEX

Mayhew, David R., 164n29
McAllister, Bill, 60
McBeath, Gerald A., 44, 99, 162n6
McCarthy, Charles, 76
McCarty, Nolan, 104–5
McConachie, Lauros G., 116
McCormick, Richard P., 23, 25
McCormick, Robert E., 71
McCubbins, Mathew D., 106, 112
McDaniel v. Paty, 156n33
McGinness, Louis J., 142, 168n14
McGranahan, Leslie Moscow, 122
McHenry, Dean E., 131
McKibben, Carroll R., 130, 133
McKinley, James C., Jr., 114
Medina, J. Michael, 42, 158n6
Mercer, John Francis, 155n20
Merl, Jean, 78
Mettler, Suzanne B., 39, 40
Michigan state legislature, first African American elected to, 138; full-time legislators underreported in, 134; membership turnover in, 141, 168n14; as professionalized body, 81; seniority used in, 112; supermajoritarian rules in, 120; term of office, 161n32
Mifflin, Thomas, 155n20
Miller, Elmer I., 7, 13, 31, 71, 154n13
Miller, Gary J., 158n7
Miller, Michael B., 157n38
Minnesota state legislature, changing use of conference committees in, 114; discharge petitions in, 125, 126; first African American elected to, 138; full-time legislators in, 134; and nonpartisanship, 103; membership size, 45
Minzner, Max, 120
Mississippi state legislature, discharge petitions in, 166n25; election calendar, 161n33; few leadership posts in, 101; large number of standing committees, 107, 108; membership qualifications in, 156n32; membership turnover in, 141; as one-party body, 104; residency requirement, 53; seniority used in, 112; term of office, 161n33
Missouri state legislature, discharge petitions in, 124; impeachment procedure in, 99; membership qualifications, 50–51, 156n32
Mitchell, Charles L., 138
Moncrief, Gary F., 53, 79, 106, 128, 142, 143, 145, 152, 164n22
Money, Jeannette, 43, 113, 114, 115
Monroe, J. P., 78
Montana state legislature, daily wage in, 74; first women minority leader in, 137; membership size of, 159n13; referenda on legislative sessions, 68; terms of office, 62
Mooney, Christopher Z., 80, 81, 86
Moore, William V., 166n10
Moran, Thomas Francis, 7, 153n3,n5, 9, 10, 21, 44
Morehouse, Sarah McCally, 58, 79
Morehouse, Thomas A., 44, 99, 162n6
Morey, William C., 153n5, 8, 9, 10, 21, 23, 25, 150, 155n19, 155n21
Morgan, David R., 88
Morris, Gouverneur, 19, 155n20
Morris, Robert, 155n20
Moschos, Demitrios M., 44, 153n5
Munroe, John A., 7
Myerson, Roger B., 42, 43

National Association of Latino Elected and Appointed Officials Educational Fund, 139
National Association of Social Workers v. Harwood, 157n38
National Association of State Budget Officers, 43
Nebraska state legislature, and nonpartisanship, 103; rules governing filibusters in, 123, 166n20; and unicameralism, 43
Neustadt, Richard E., 39
Nevada state legislature, change in membership size, 46, 159n18; conference committees in, 166n15; residency requirement, 53; session length changes, 162n4; terms of office, 61
Nevin, Allan, 19, 20
New Hampshire Assembly, 7, 11, 18;

203

INDEX

membership size, 148
New Hampshire state legislature, annual salary in, 74; constituency size, 55; constitutional limit on pay, 70, 83–84, 162n10; election of upper house, 26; low professionalization level, 81; membership qualifications, 50; membership size, 45, 148, 159n12, 161n29; name change, 156n28; professionalization trends, 84; name changes, 21, 26; residency requirement, 53; session length limits, 69; term of office, 161n32
New Jersey (East and West) Assembly, 7, 11, 14, 15, 16, 18, 153n3; lawyers in, 131–32; member pay in, 71; membership size, 148; membership turnover in, 149; multi-member districts, 58; planters in, 131–32
New Jersey state legislature, committees unimportant in, 108; effects of professionalization in, 96–97; election calendar, 161n33; membership turnover in, 140; name changes, 26; as professionalizing body, 81; rise of standing committees in, 106, 107; split (or bifurcated) session in, 162n8; term of office, 61, 62, 63, 161n32
New Mexico state legislature, bipartisan coalition in, 103; Hispanic legislators in, 139; as one-party body, 104; party caucus importance in, 104; low professionalization level, 81; per diem in, 74; split (or bifurcated) session in, 69
New York Assembly, 7, 11, 12, 16, 18, membership size, 148
New York state legislature, change in membership size, 46–48, 160n21; conference committees in, 114, 166n13; continuity with colonial assembly, 150; election of upper house, 26; full-time legislators in, 167n4; impeachment procedure in, 99; member pay over time in, 74, 163n16; membership qualifications, 27; membership turnover in, 140; pay in 1910, 82; as professionalized body, 81; relationship of pay and turnover in, 70; rise of standing committees in, 106;

and speaker tenure in nineteenth century, 150; staff in nineteenth century in, 76; term of office, 28, 61, 161n32
New York state library, 76
North Carolina Assembly, 7, 11, 16; meeting places, 154n17; membership size, 148
North Carolina state legislature, bipartisan coalition in, 103; farmers in, 134; membership turnover in, 140; membership qualifications, 27; name changes 21, 27, 156n25; as one-party body, 104
North Dakota state legislature, change in membership size in 2003, 46, 160n20; farmers in, 134; lawyers in, 134; first woman speaker, 137; low professionalization level of, 81; term of office, 161n33
Niemi, Richard G., 79, 142, 143, 152

Official Manual of Kentucky, 72, 82, 83, 164n25
Ogul, Morris S., 68
O'Halloran, Sharyn, 70, 140
Ohio state legislature, 18 year old representative in, 51; first African American elected to, 138; as professionalizing body, 81
Oklahoma state legislature, first African American elected to, 138; as one-party body, 104; party caucus importance in, 104; supermajoritarian rules in, 120
Oleszek, Walter J., 44, 49, 61, 100, 110, 111, 121, 122, 124, 143, 145, 165n3
Olson, Alison G., 11, 12, 13, 14, 17, 18, 147, 148
Olson, David M., 44
Oregon Family Council, 160n25
Oregonian, The, 160n25
Oregon state legislature, attempt to change age qualification, 51; lack of impeachment procedure in, 99
Ornstein, Norman J., 75, 77, 85, 117, 135, 164n23,n26
Orth, Samuel P., 131
Ostrogorski, M., 37
Otis, James, 19

204

INDEX

Overby, L. Marvin, 106
Owings, Stephanie, 96

Pacheco, Romualdo, 139
Packenham, Robert A., 117
Paine, Thomas, 20, 156n23
Parents Education Association Political Action Committee, 160n25
Pargellis, S. M., 12, 13, 14, 15, 17, 116, 154n13
Parker, Glenn R., 49, 70
Parliament (of Great Britain), 11; bicameralism in, 10; impeachment procedure in, 99; multi-member districts in, 58; relationship to colonial assemblies, 7–8; residency requirements, 160n27; as source of rules and procedures, 116; taxation powers, 30–31, 157n39
Patterson, Samuel C., 42, 49, 50, 103, 123, 131, 132
Patterson, William, 155n20
Patzelt, Werner J., 128
Peabody, Robert L., 100
Pelosi, Nancy, 137
Penn, Ivan, 166n20
Pennsylvania Assembly, 7, 8, 11, 14, 16, 18; meeting places 17–18, 154n15; member pay in, 71; membership qualifications, 26; membership size, 148; membership turnover in, 140, 149
Pennsylvania state legislature, discharge petitions in, 124, 125, 126; farmers in, 167n3; full-time legislators in, 134, 167n4; lawyers in, 167n3; member pay in, 71; as professionalizing body, 81; rise of standing committees in, 106; term limits in, 28, 63–64; term of office, 61, 62, 161n32
Perez-Pena, Richard, 160n21
Perkins, John A., 76
Peters, Ronald M., 101
petitions, 154n10; in colonial assemblies, 11–12; increase in number of, 147–48
Phillips, Hubert, 26
Pierce, William Leigh, 155n20
Pierson, Paul, 151
Pinckney, Charles Cotesworth, 155n20

Pindyck, Robert S., 88
Pinney, Neil, 78
Pole, J. R., 10, 11, 153n5
political culture, 87–88
political parties. *See* legislative parties
Polsby, Nelson W., 2, 6, 12, 75, 101, 129, 140, 144, 147, 149
Poole, Keith T., 105
Powell, Alden J., 37, 162n2, 162n8
Powell, Lynda W., 79, 143, 152
Powell, Richard J., 143
Price, Charles M., 142
Price, H. Douglas, 1, 75, 98, 144, 164n24
Price, Polly J., 160n23
Prince, David W., 106
professionalization. *See* legislative professionalization
Purvis, Thomas L., 11, 14, 15, 16, 71, 132, 147

qualifications for office. *See* legislators, membership qualifications of

Rainbolt, John C., 11
Ray, David, 142, 152
Read, George, 155n20
Redfield, Kent D., 108
Reed, Brian C., 140, 143
Reeher, Grant D., 39, 40
Reingold, Beth, 138
Reinsch, Paul S., 68, 158n3, 165n9, 166n14
Reynolds v. Sims (1964), 46, 55, 161n28
Rhode Island Assembly, 7, 8; member pay in, 71; membership size, 148
Rhode Island state legislature, change in membership size in 2003, 46, 160n19; constitutional limit on pay, 70, 163n11; end of pension plan in, 74, 164n19; filibuster in, 123; first African American elected to, 138; legislative supremacy in, 39–40, 158n5; name change, 156n28; small districts and representation in, 60; term of office, 28, 61, 161n32; wealth qualifications abolished, 54
Rich, Andrew, 124

205

Richardson, Lilliard E., Jr., 78
Riker, William H., 29, 40, 129
Risjord, Norman K., 106
Ritter, Charles F., 132
Ritt, Leonard G., 165n32
Rivers, Douglas, 70, 140
Robertson, Cheryl L., 158n5
Roeder, Phillip W., 165n32
Rogers, James R., 42, 44
Rogers, Lindsay, 75
Rohde, David W., 140
Rosenthal, Alan, 30, 38, 49, 67, 68, 70, 78, 79, 80, 96–97, 101, 103, 104, 135, 142, 144, 150, 165n4
Rosenthal, Cindy Simon, 96, 138
Rosenthal, Howard, 105
Rossiter, Clinton, 12
rotation, in state legislatures, 64; in U.S Congress, 64; in West Virginia constitution (1863), 64. *See also* rotation agreements; term limits
rotation agreements, 161n35. *See also* rotation; term limits
Rothstein, Paul, 140
Rubinfeld, Daniel L., 88
rules and procedures. *See* legislative rules and procedures
Rundquist, Barry, 115, 144
Rutledge, John, 19, 155n20
Ryerson, Richard Alan, 12, 15, 154n12

salaries. *See* legislative pay; legislative pensions
Salisbury, Robert H., 76
Scalia, Laura J., 44
Schaffner, Brian F., 105
Scharf, J. Thomas, 23, 25
Schickler Eric, 124, 144
Schlesinger, Joseph A., 135
Schneiderman, Stuart, 79, 95, 145
Schumacker, Waldo, 82, 83, 164n25
Seale, William, 17, 154n14, 154n15, 154n17
Seeberger, Edward D., 78, 114
Selden, S. C., 96
Selsam, J. Paul, 20, 21
seniority system, in colonial assemblies, 15–16, 154n12; in Georgia, 112; in Michigan, 112; in Mississippi, 112; in South Carolina, 112, 166n10; in state legislatures, 111–12; in Texas, 112
separation of powers, 39–40
Serra, George, 78
sessions. *See* legislative sessions
Shepsle, Kenneth A., 35, 76, 106, 124
Sherman, Roger, 155n20
Shields, Johanna Nicol, 48
Shin, Kwang S., 142, 152
Shipan, Charles R., 96
Shull, Charles W., 142, 168n14
Sigelman, Lee, 165n32
Silbur, Kenneth, 114
Sims v. Amos, 159n13
Sirmans, M. Eugene, 10, 154n7
Sisson, Richard, 144
Skladony, Thomas W., 106
Skocpol, Theda, 151
Slonim, Shlomo, 157n37
Smith, C. Lysle, 124, 165n9
Smith, Steven S., 45, 111, 113, 114, 122
Snyder, Steven B., 54
Solis, Hilda, 78
Sousa, Mathias de, 167n11
South Carolina Assembly, 7, 11, 116, 154n7; meeting places, 154n16; member pay in, 71; membership size, 148; standing committees in, 12, 15, 16, 17
South Carolina state legislature, African Americans in during Reconstruction, 138; election of upper house, 26; membership size, 21; membership qualifications, 27; name changes, 21; as one-party body, 104; rise of standing committees in, 106; rules governing filibusters in, 123, 166n19; seniority used in, 112, 166n10; session length limits, 69; term of office, 28
South Dakota state legislature, low professionalization level, 81
Spaight, Richard Dobbs, Sr., 155n20
Spangenberg, Bradford, 156n31
Spaw, Patsy McDonald, 107, 151
speakers, changing tenures of in nineteenth century, 150; in colonial assemblies,

INDEX

14–15; comparison of powers of in state legislatures and U.S. Congress, 101–3; first woman speaker, 137; occupations of in nineteenth century, 132; women holding position, 138, 167n10. *See also* legislative leadership
Spence, David B., 70
Sprague, John D., 135
Squire, Peverill, 53, 58, 70, 75, 79, 80, 81, 83, 95, 96, 101, 106; 118, 137; 142, 145, 149, 153n3, 164n22
staff. *See* legislative staff
Stark, Jack, 158n2
state constitutions. *See* constitutions, state
State Government, 136
state legislatures. *See* legislatures, state
state partisanship, 87
State of Rhode Island and Providence Plantations, 60
Steiner, Gilbert Y., 115
Stewart, Charles, III, 30, 105, 106, 110, 113, 118, 121
Stigler, George J., 49, 86, 159n12
Stiles v. Blunt, 160n24
Stokes, Anson Phelps, 28
Stolz, Klaus, 130
Stonecash, Jeffrey M., 39, 40, 70
Story, Tim, 161n34
Stourzh, Gerald, 21
Straayer, John A., 38, 114
Strom, Gerald S., 115
Strong, Caleb, 155n20
Sullivan's diversity index, 88
Swain, Carol M., 139
Swain, John W., 140, 143
Swem, E. G., 27, 156n32
Swift, Elaine K., 106, 145

Taswell-Langmead, Thomas Pitt, 10, 31
Teaford, Jon C., 81
Teicher, Stacy A., 53
Tennessee state legislature, bipartisan coalition in, 103; membership qualifications, 28, 156n32, 156n33; as one-party body, 104; session length limits, 69
term limits, 63–65, 161n39; abolished in Idaho and Utah, 64, 161n36, 168n13; in Congress under the Articles of Confederation, 28; and membership turnover, 143–44; in Pennsylvania, 28, 63, 64; in Pennsylvania Council, 157n35; and springboard bodies, 143; state courts and, 168n15; in state legislatures, 28; U.S. Supreme Court and, 64. *See also* rotation; rotation agreements
Teske, Paul, 96
Texas state legislature, African Americans in during Reconstruction, 138; constitutional limit on pay, 70, 162n10; filibuster in, 123, 166n17; member pension plan in, 75; membership qualifications in, 156n32; role of lt. governor in state senate, 101; as one-party body, 104; rules governing filibusters in, 123, 166n18; seniority used in, 112; standing committees established, 107, 151; terms of office, 61, 62
Thomas, Sue, 138
Thompson, Joel A., 96
Thoughts on Government (Adams), 20
Tocqueville, Alexis de, 61
Tolbert, Caroline J., 88
Toll, Henry W., 161n33
Tollison, Robert D., 42, 49, 71
Topf, Mel A., 158n5
Traugott, Santa A., 130, 133
Trevett v. Weeden (1786), 40
Tsebelis, George, 43, 113, 114, 115
Tullock, Gordon, 35
Tully, Alan, 11–12, 14, 27, 147, 149
turnover. *See* legislative turnover
Twilight, Alexander L., 138

Underwood, Joseph, 160n22
unicameralism, 42, 156n23; consequences of, 43; in Bermuda, 154n8; in Delaware, 10; in Georgia, 21, 43, 153n6, 156n24; in Guam, 158n8; in Pennsylvania, 10, 21, 43, 153n6; in U.S. Virgin Islands, 158n8; in Vermont, 21, 43–44, 153n6, 158n9. *See also* bicameralism

207

Unruh, Jesse, 67, 87, 98
Updyke, Frank A., 76
U.S. Congress. *See* Congress, U.S.
U.S. Term Limits, Inc. v. Thornton, 161n37
Utah state legislature, first woman elected to, 136

VanderMeer, Philip R., 64, 132, 142
Van Der Slik, Jack R., 108
Vermont state legislature, bipartisan coalition in, 103; first African American in, 138; joint committees in, 158n10; term of office, 161n32; weekly salary in, 74
veto power, adopted in North Carolina, 43; adopted in Ohio, 43; adopted in Rhode Island, 43; evolution of in the states, 43; in Illinois, 157n40; in New York, 157n40; in original state constitutions, 32–34; in U.S. Constitution, 32–34; in Vermont, 157n40
Victor, Jennifer Nicoll, 158n7
Virginia House of Burgesses, 6, 7, 11, 12, 14, 15, 16, 18, 153n4, 154n13; Committee on Propositions and Grievances, 15; Committee on Religion, 12; member pay in, 71; rules and procedures in, 13–14; membership size, 148, 154n18; meeting places, 17; standing committees in, 12–13; vestrymen in, 156n31
Virginia state legislature, bank officer disqualification, 54; bill reference procedures in, 120; continuity with House of Burgesses, 150; election calendar, 161n33; election of upper house, 26; membership turnover in, 140; membership qualifications, 27, 50; name changes, 26; as one-party body, 104; rise of standing committees in, 106; term of office, 28
Vogel, David J., 115
Vogel, Ed, 157n38
Volden, Craig, 118

Wahlke, John C., 165n8
Wakelyn, John L., 132
Walker, Edward G., 138
Walsh, Justin E., 107, 116, 151

Walthoe, N., 7
Ward, Daniel S., 67, 82, 150
Washington, George, 55, 155n20
Washington state legislature, bipartisan coalition in, 103; free conference committee process in, 114; staff in 1950s, 77–78; women as majority of majority party in, 137, 167n9
Waterhouse, Richard, 140
Watts, Irma A., 43
Watts, Meredith W., Jr., 76
Weber, Ronald E., 95
Webster, William Clarence, 21, 27, 28
Weingast, Barry R., 35, 106, 124
Weir, Robert M., 10, 140, 154n7, 156n30
Wells, Donald T., 107, 108
Wendel, Thomas, 14, 15, 30
West, Victor J., 69
West Virginia state legislature, lawyers in, 134; railroad officer disqualification, 54; split (or bifurcated) session in, 69
Whaley, Sean, 157n38
Wheare, K. C., 48
Whistler, Donald E., 137
White, Howard, 69
Wilkerson, John D., 70
Williamson, Hugh, 155n20
Wilson, James, 155n20
Wilson, Laura Ann, 88
Wilson, Rick K., 12, 106
Wilson, Woodrow, 45, 105
Winsky, Laura R., 142
Winslow, C. I., 124, 166n14, 166n15
Winston, Michael R., 138
Wisconsin Legislative Reference Bureau, 76
Wisconsin state legislature, farmers in, 132; full-time legislators in, 167n4; lawyers in, 132; legislative reference bureau in, 76; membership size of, 159n13; membership turnover in, 141; as professionalizing body, 81; session lengths and per diem limits, 162n7; split (or bifurcated) session in, 162n8; staff in nineteenth century in, 76; term of office, 161n32
Wissel, Peter, 140

INDEX

Witmer, T. Richard, 70
women in legislatures: in state legislatures, 136–38; in U.S. Congress, 136
Wood, Gordon S., 27, 40
Wood, Margaret K., 156n33
Wooster, Ralph A., 64, 140, 142, 150, 167n2
Wright, Benjamin F., Jr., 20, 39, 153n5, 155n19
Wright, Gerald C., 105
Wyoming state legislature, change in membership size, 46; lack of facilities in, 78; large districts and representation, 60; low professionalization level, 81
Wythe, George, 155n20

Young, C. C., 101
Young, Chester Raymond, 8, 26, 71

Zagarii, Rosemarie, 21
Zeller, Belle, 44, 68, 69, 74, 76, 78, 131, 162n1, 162n8
Zemsky, Robert M., 13, 14, 15, 17
Zimmerman, Joseph F., 161n32, 163n16

PARLIAMENTS AND LEGISLATURES
Janet M. Box-Steffensmeier and David T. Canon, Series Editors

Authorizing Policy
THAD HALL

Congress Responds to the Twentieth Century
EDITED BY SUNIL AHUJA AND ROBERT E. DEWHIRST

Committees in Post-Communist Democratic Parliaments: Comparative Institutionalization
EDITED BY DAVID M. OLSON AND WILLIAM E. CROWTHER

U.S. Senate Exceptionalism
EDITED BY BRUCE I. OPPENHEIMER

Political Consultants in U.S. Congressional Elections
STEPHEN K. MEDVIC

Hitching a Ride: Omnibus Legislating in the U.S. Congress
GLEN S. KRUTZ

Reforming Parliamentary Committees: Israel in Comparative Perspective
REUVEN Y. HAZAN

Comparing Post-Soviet Legislatures: A Theory of Institutional Design and Political Conflict
JOEL M. OSTROW

Beyond Westminster and Congress: The Nordic Experience
EDITED BY PETER ESAIASSON AND KNUT HEIDAR

Parliamentary Representation: The Case of the Norwegian Storting
DONALD R. MATTHEWS AND HENRY VALEN

Party Discipline and Parliamentary Government
EDITED BY SHAUN BOWLER, DAVID M. FARRELL, AND RICHARD S. KATZ

Senates: Bicameralism in the Contemporary World
EDITED BY SAMUEL C. PATTERSON AND ANTHONY MUGHAN

Citizens as Legislators: Direct Democracy in the United States
EDITED BY SHAUN BOWLER, TODD DONOVAN, AND CAROLINE J. TOLBERT

Coalition Government, Subnational Style: Multiparty Politics in Europe's Regional Parliaments
WILLIAM M. DOWNS

Creating Parliamentary Government: The Transition to Democracy in Bulgaria
ALBERT P. MELONE

Politics, Parties, and Parliaments: Political Change in Norway
WILLIAM R. SHAFFER

Cheap Seats: The Democratic Party's Advantage in U.S. House Elections
JAMES E. CAMPBELL

CPSIA information can be obtained
at www.ICGtesting.com
Printed in the USA
LVHW111337281222
735820LV00001B/19